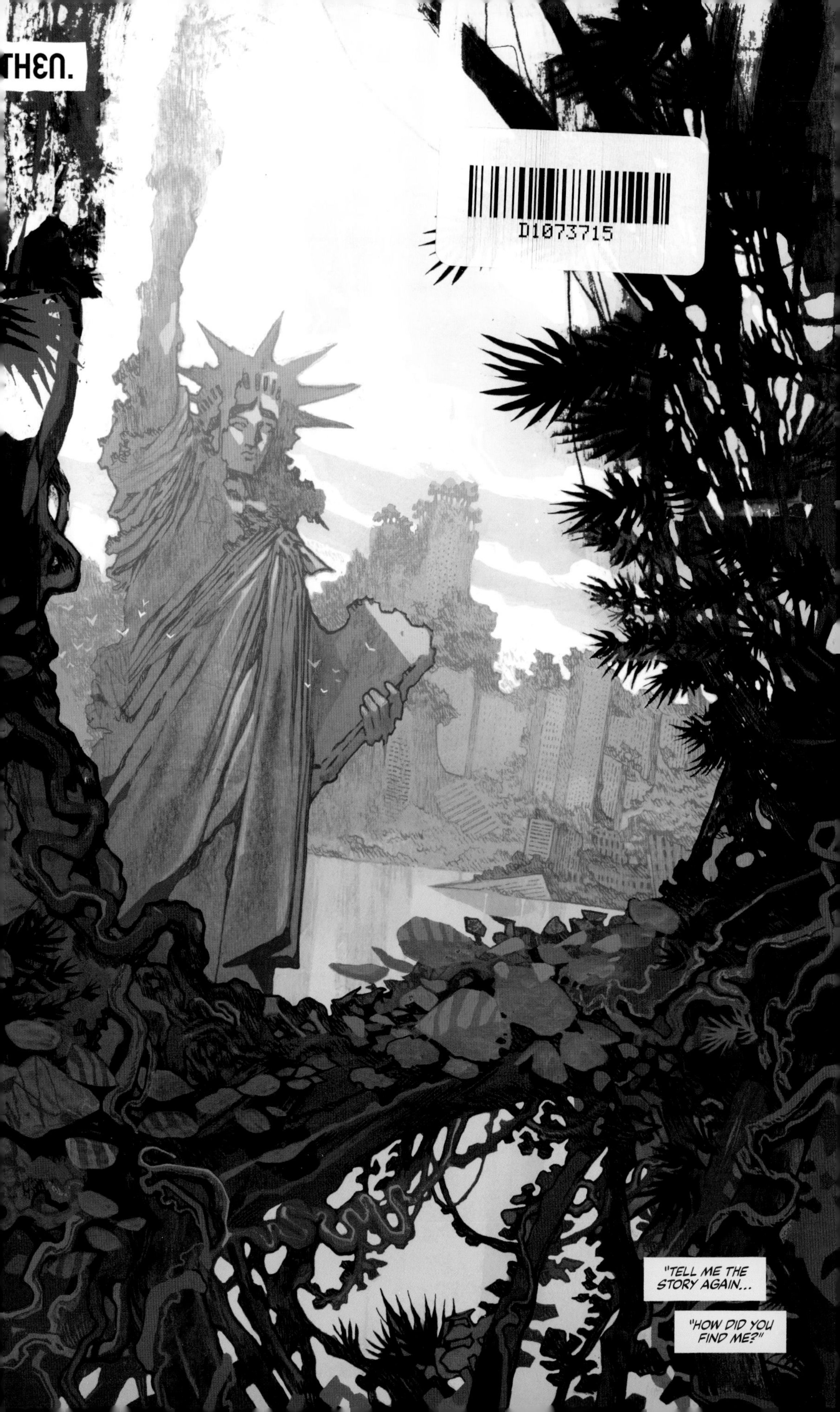
THEN.
"TELL ME THE STORY AGAIN...
"HOW DID YOU FIND ME?"

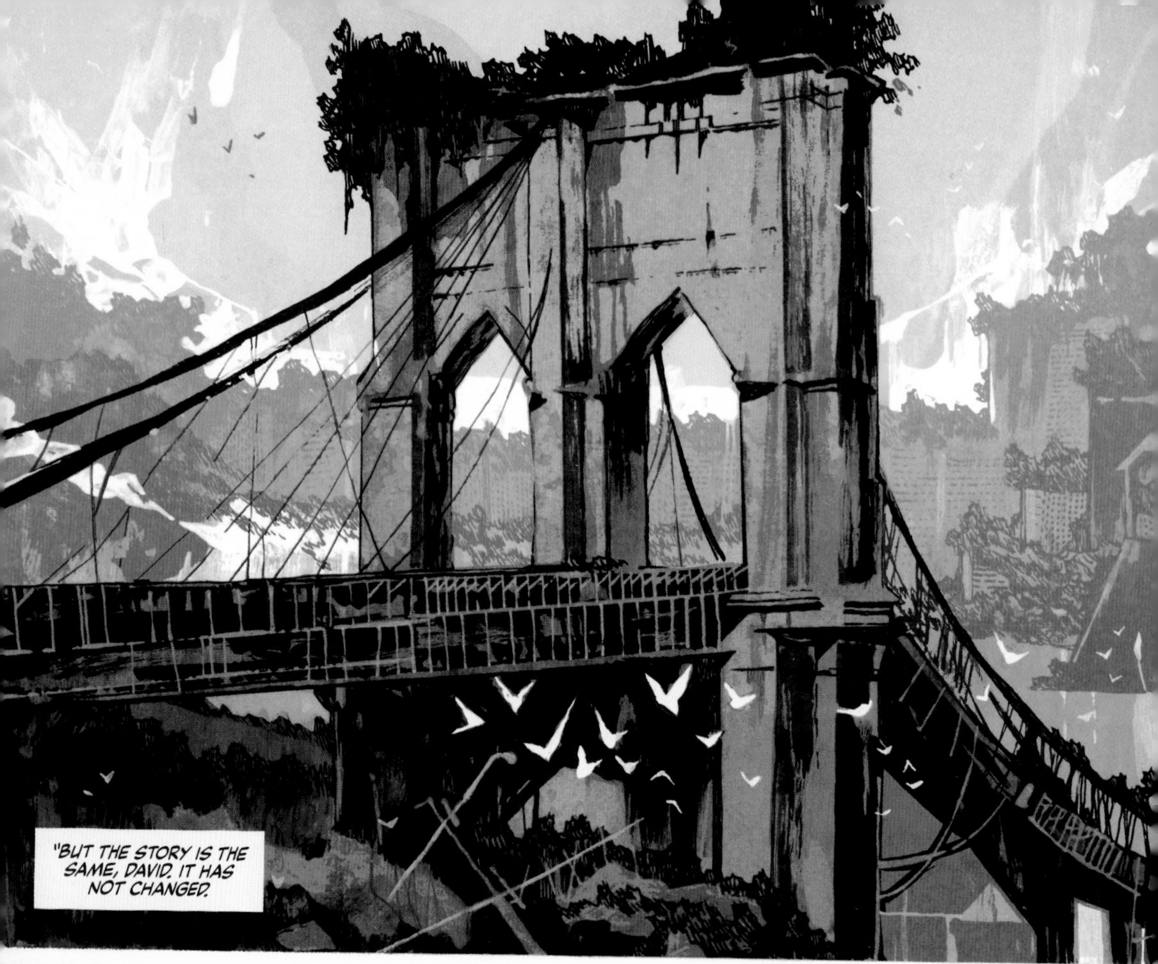
"BUT THE STORY IS THE SAME, DAVID. IT HAS NOT CHANGED.

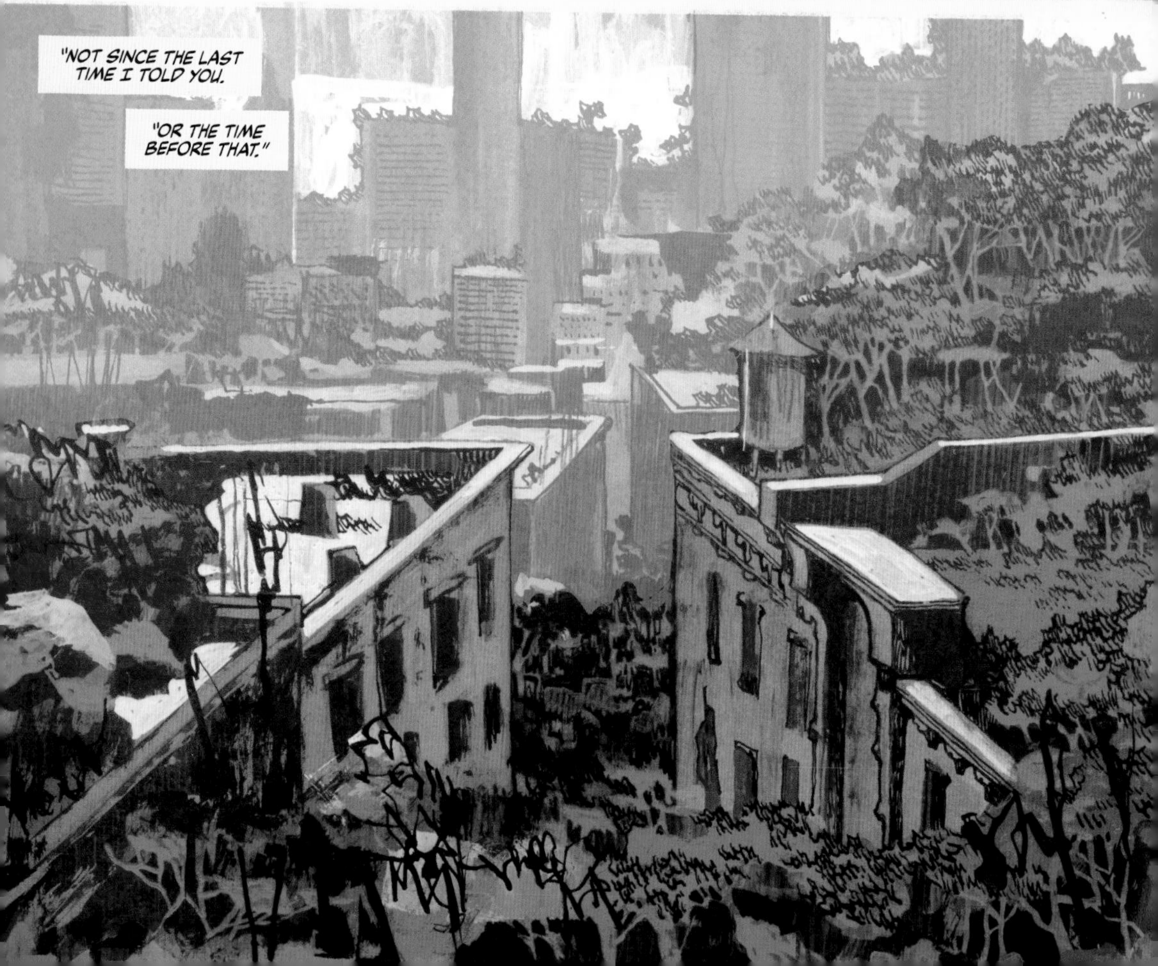
"NOT SINCE THE LAST TIME I TOLD YOU.
"OR THE TIME BEFORE THAT."

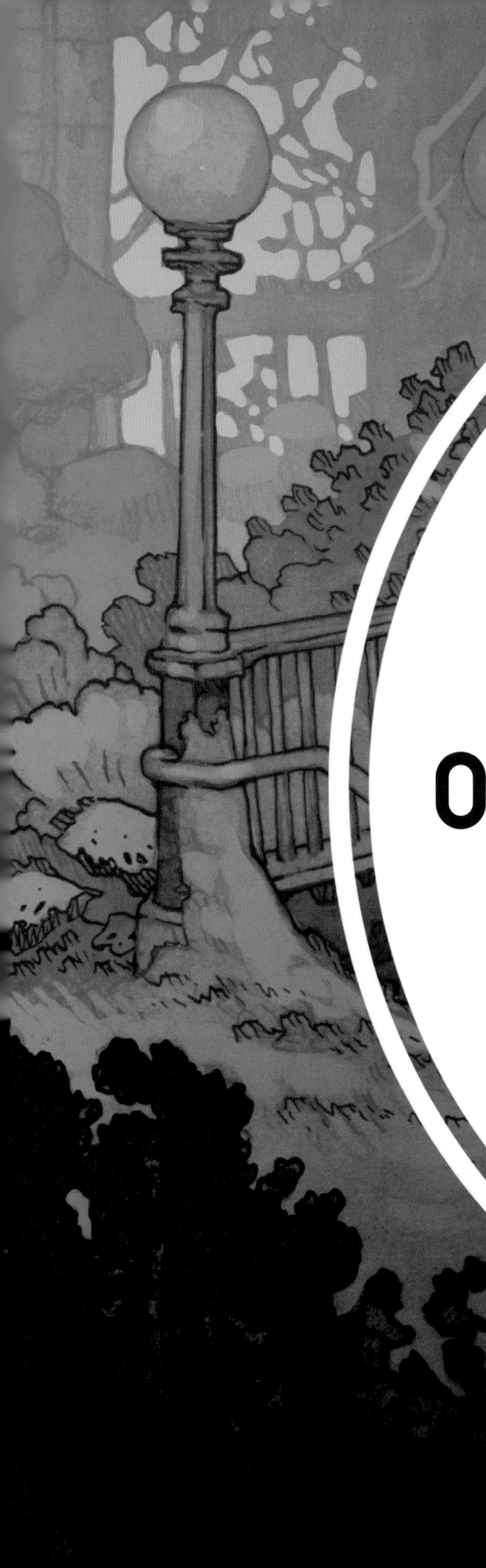

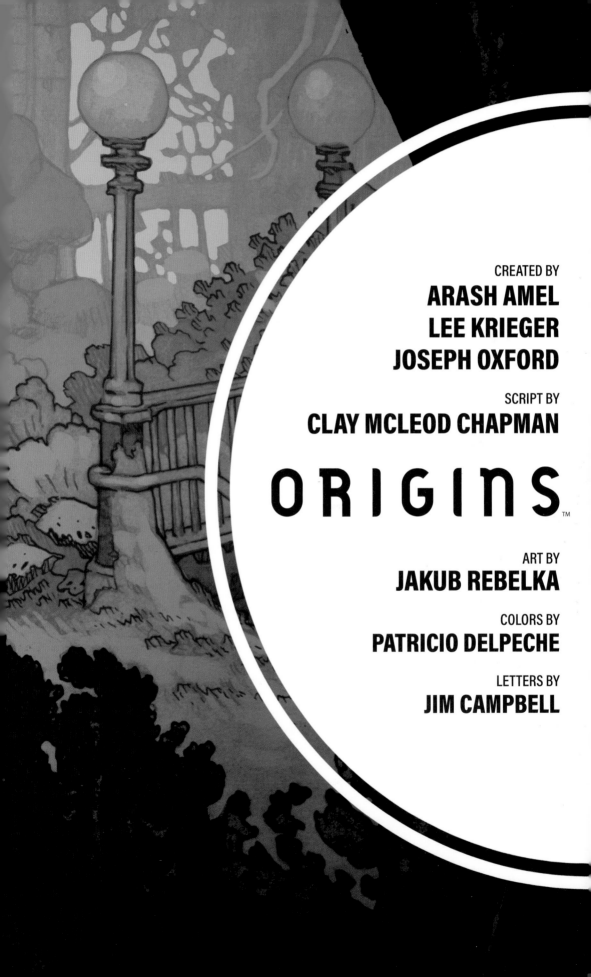

CREATED BY
ARASH AMEL
LEE KRIEGER
JOSEPH OXFORD

SCRIPT BY
CLAY MCLEOD CHAPMAN

ORIGINS™

ART BY
JAKUB REBELKA

COLORS BY
PATRICIO DELPECHE

LETTERS BY
JIM CAMPBELL

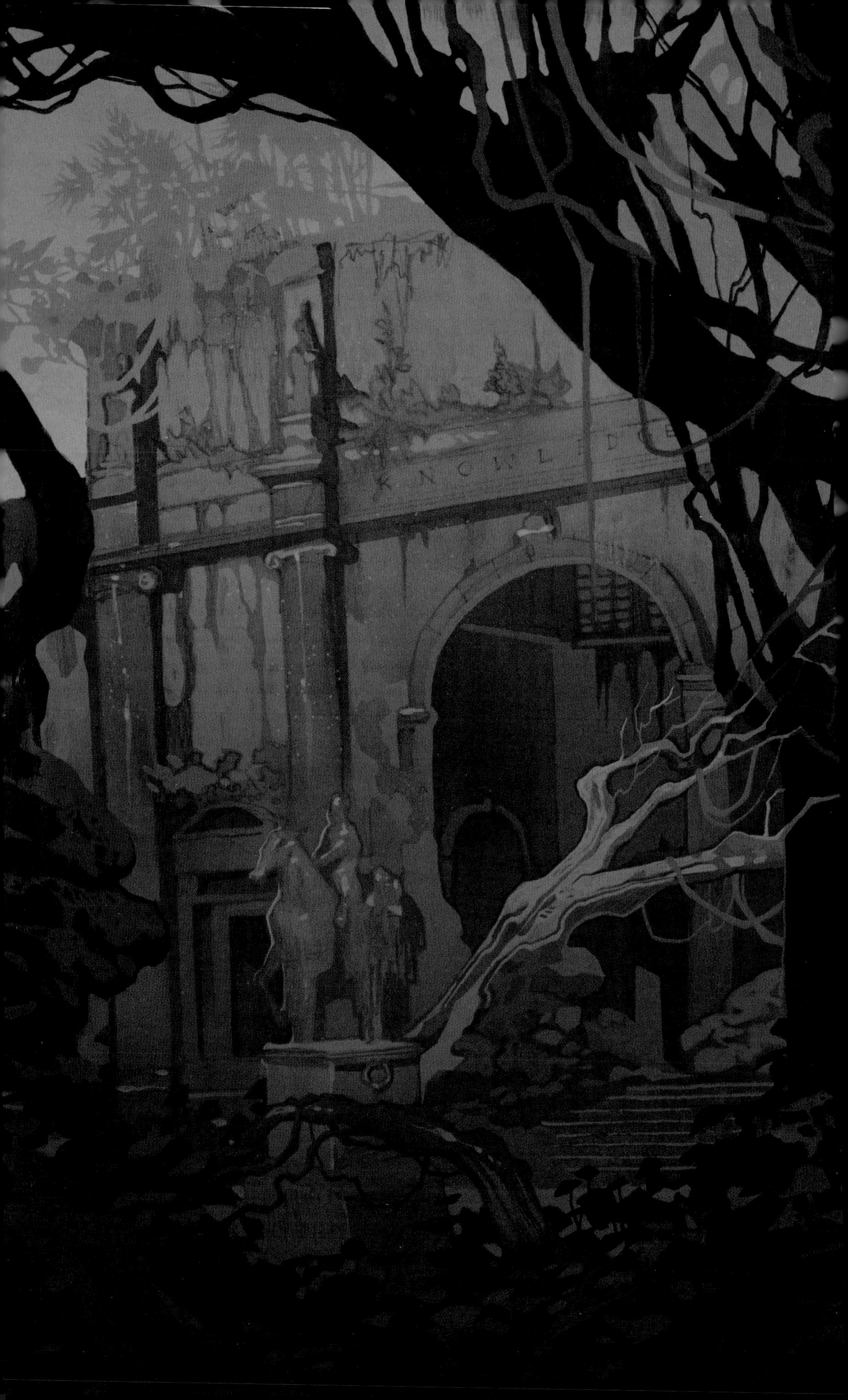
KNOWLEDGE

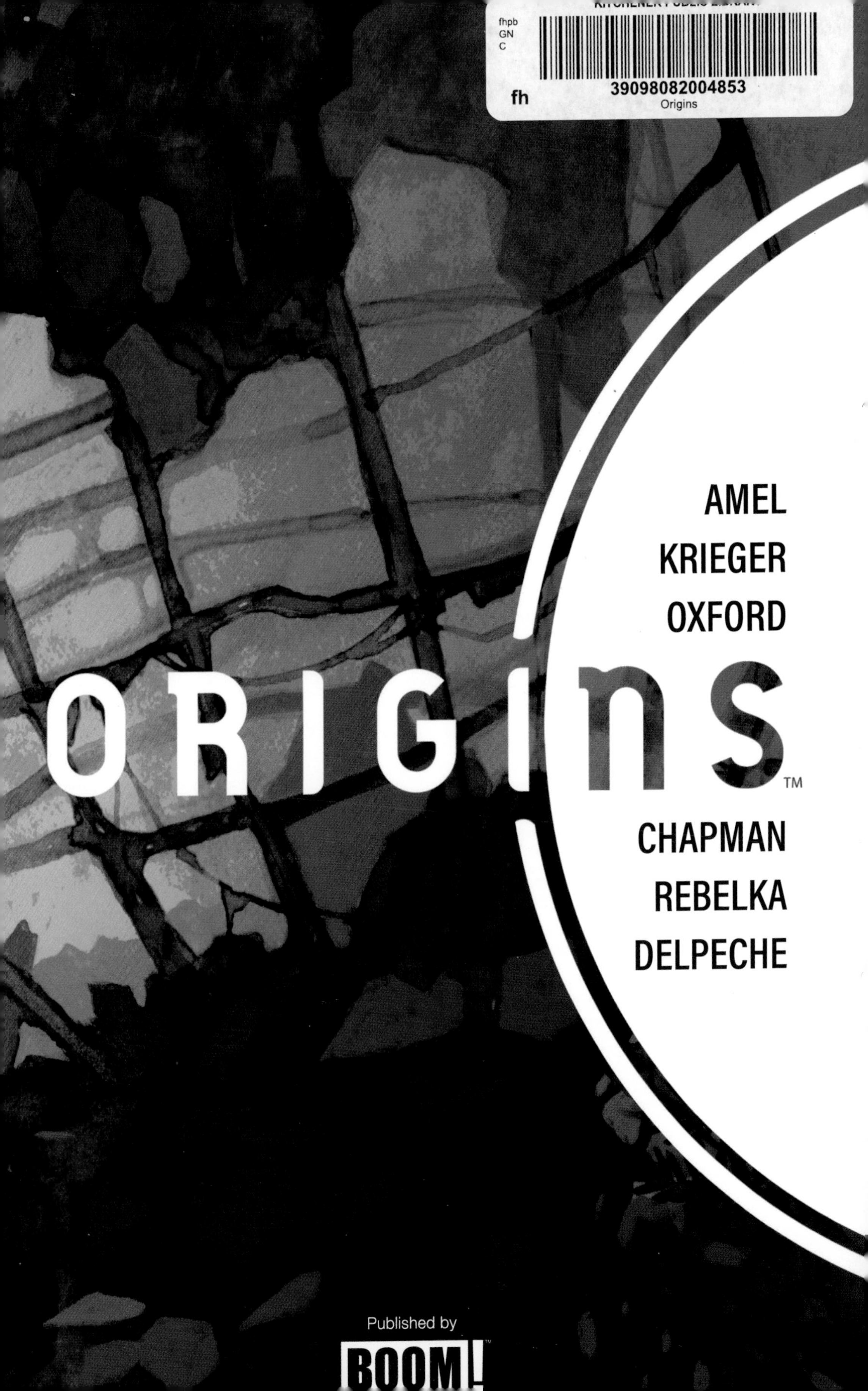

AMEL
KRIEGER
OXFORD

ORIGINS™

CHAPMAN
REBELKA
DELPECHE

Published by
BOOM!™

LOGO DESIGNER
JILLIAN CRAB

SERIES DESIGNER
GRACE PARK

DESIGNER
MARIE KRUPINA

ASSISTANT EDITOR
GAVIN GRONENTHAL

EDITOR
DAFNA PLEBAN

ASSOCIATE EDITOR
AMANDA LAFRANCO

SPECIAL THANKS
BRIAN KAVANAUGH-JONES

ROSS RICHIE CEO & Founder
JOY HUFFMAN CFO
MATT GAGNON Editor-in-Chief
FILIP SABLIK President, Publishing & Marketing
STEPHEN CHRISTY President, Development
LANCE KREITER Vice President, Licensing & Merchandising
BRYCE CARLSON Vice President, Editorial & Creative Strategy
KATE HENNING Director, Operations
ELYSE STRANDBERG Manager, Finance
SIERRA HAHN Executive Editor
DAFNA PLEBAN Senior Editor
SHANNON WATTERS Senior Editor
ERIC HARBURN Senior Editor
ELIZABETH BREI Editor
SOPHIE PHILIPS-ROBERTS Associate Editor
JONATHAN MANNING Associate Editor
GAVIN GRONENTHAL Assistant Editor
GWEN WALLER Assistant Editor
ALLYSON GRONOWITZ Assistant Editor
RAMIRO PORTNOY Assistant Editor
KENZIE RZONCA Assistant Editor
REY NETSCHKE Editorial Assistant
MICHELLE ANKLEY Design Lead

MARIE KRUPINA Production Designer
GRACE PARK Production Designer
CHELSEA ROBERTS Production Designer
MADISON GOYETTE Production Designer
CRYSTAL WHITE Production Designer
SAMANTHA KNAPP Production Design Assistant
ESTHER KIM Marketing Lead
BREANNA SARPY Marketing Coordinator, Digital
GRECIA MARTINEZ Marketing Assistant
AMANDA LAWSON Marketing Assistant, Digital
JOSÉ MEZA Consumer Sales Lead
ASHLEY TROUB Consumer Sales Coordinator
MORGAN PERRY Retail Sales Lead
HARLEY SALBACKA Sales Coordinator
MEGAN CHRISTOPHER Operations Coordinator
RODRIGO HERNANDEZ Operations Coordinator
ZIPPORAH SMITH Operations Coordinator
JASON LEE Senior Accountant
SABRINA LESIN Accounting Assistant
LAUREN ALEXANDER Administrative Assistant

ORIGINS, October 2021. Published by BOOM! Studios, a division of Boom Entertainment, Inc. Origins is ™ & © 2021 Tavala, Inc., Joseph Oxford, The Amel Company, Automatik. Originally published in single magazine form as ORIGINS No. 1-6. ™ & © 2020, 2021 Tavala, Inc., Joseph Oxford, The Amel Company, Automatik. All rights reserved. BOOM! Studios™ and the BOOM! Studios logo are trademarks of Boom Entertainment, Inc., registered in various countries and categories. All characters, events, and institutions depicted herein are fictional. Any similarity between any of the names, characters, persons, events, and/or institutions in this publication to actual names, characters, and persons, whether living or dead, events, and/or institutions is unintended and purely coincidental. BOOM! Studios does not read or accept unsolicited submissions of ideas, stories, or artwork.

BOOM! Studios, 5670 Wilshire Boulevard, Suite 400, Los Angeles, CA 90036-5679. Printed in China. First Printing.

ISBN: 978-1-68415-555-2, eISBN: 978-1-64144-721-8

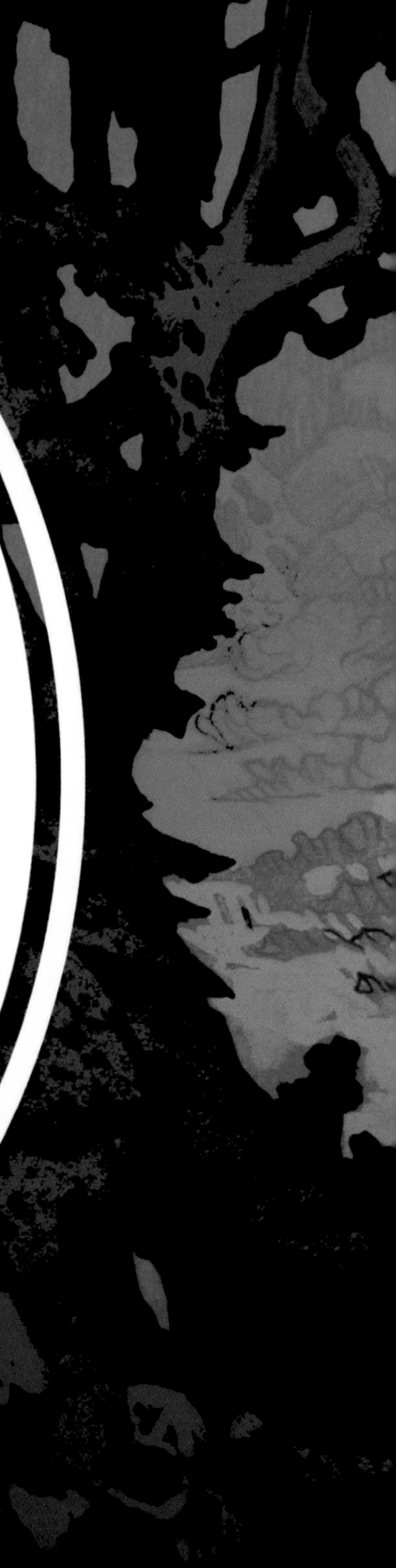

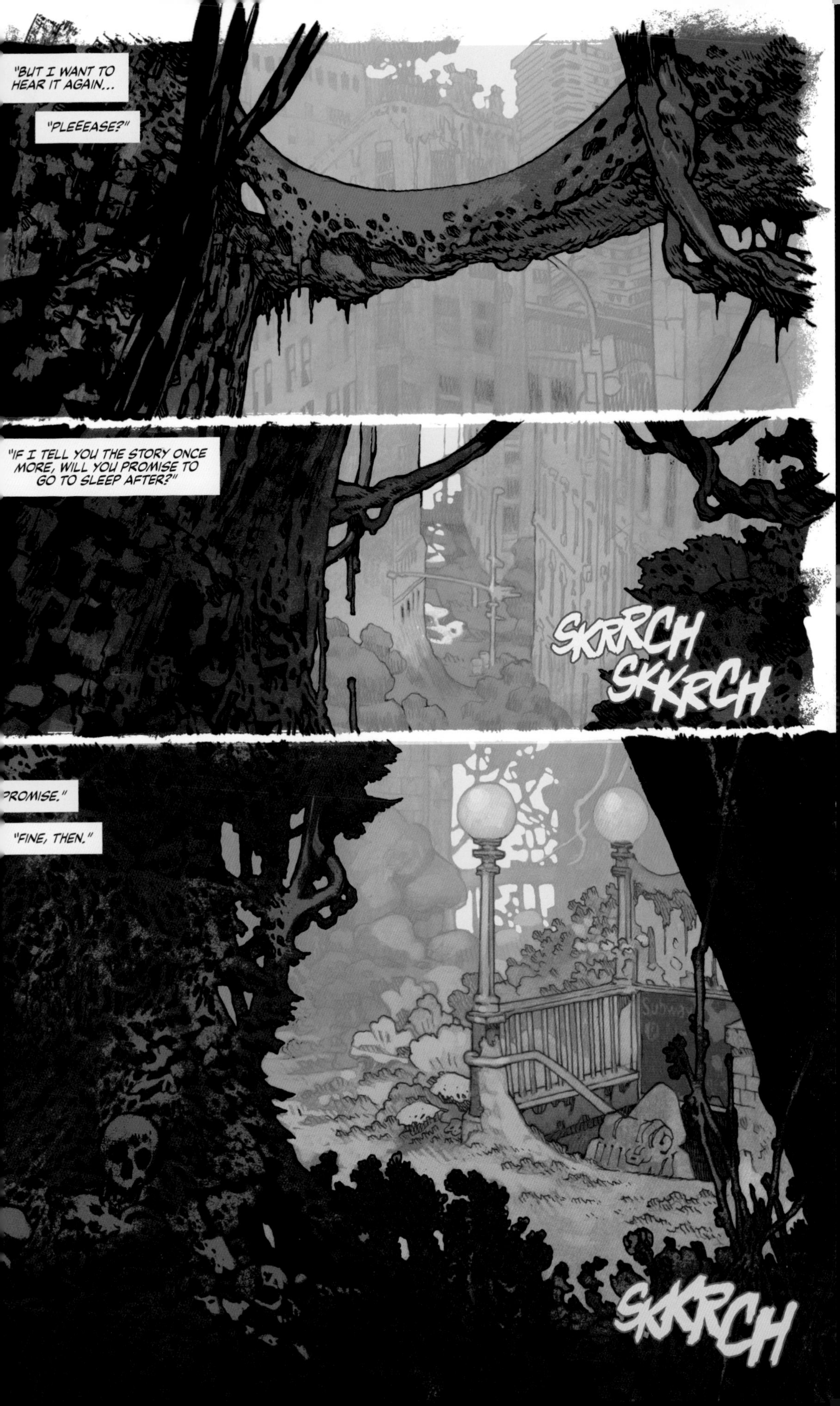
"BUT I WANT TO HEAR IT AGAIN...
"PLEEEASE?"
"IF I TELL YOU THE STORY ONCE MORE, WILL YOU PROMISE TO GO TO SLEEP AFTER?"
SKRRCH
SKKRCH
PROMISE."
"FINE, THEN."
SKKRCH

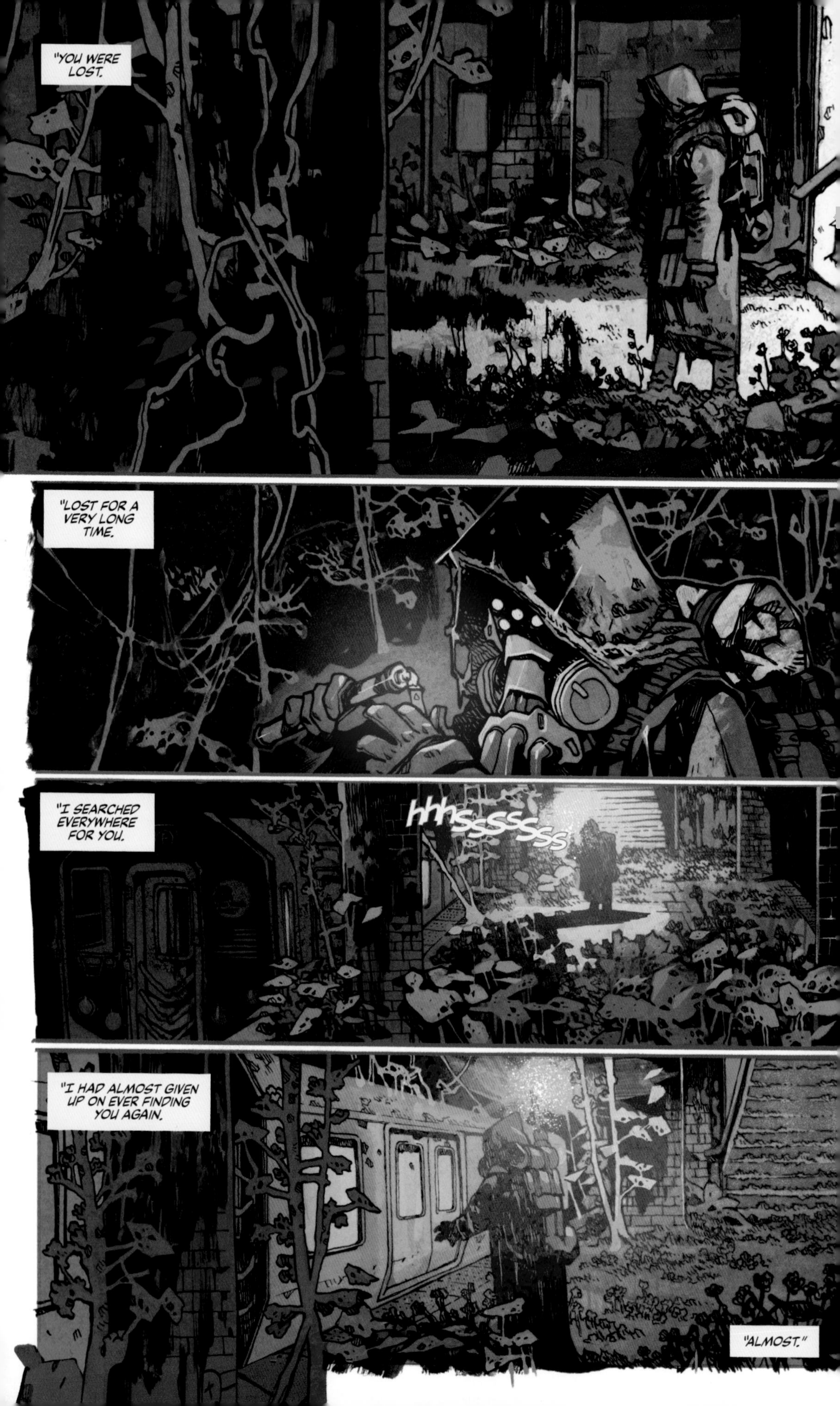
"YOU WERE LOST.
"LOST FOR A VERY LONG TIME.
"I SEARCHED EVERYWHERE FOR YOU.
hhhSSSSSSS
"I HAD ALMOST GIVEN UP ON EVER FINDING YOU AGAIN.
"ALMOST."

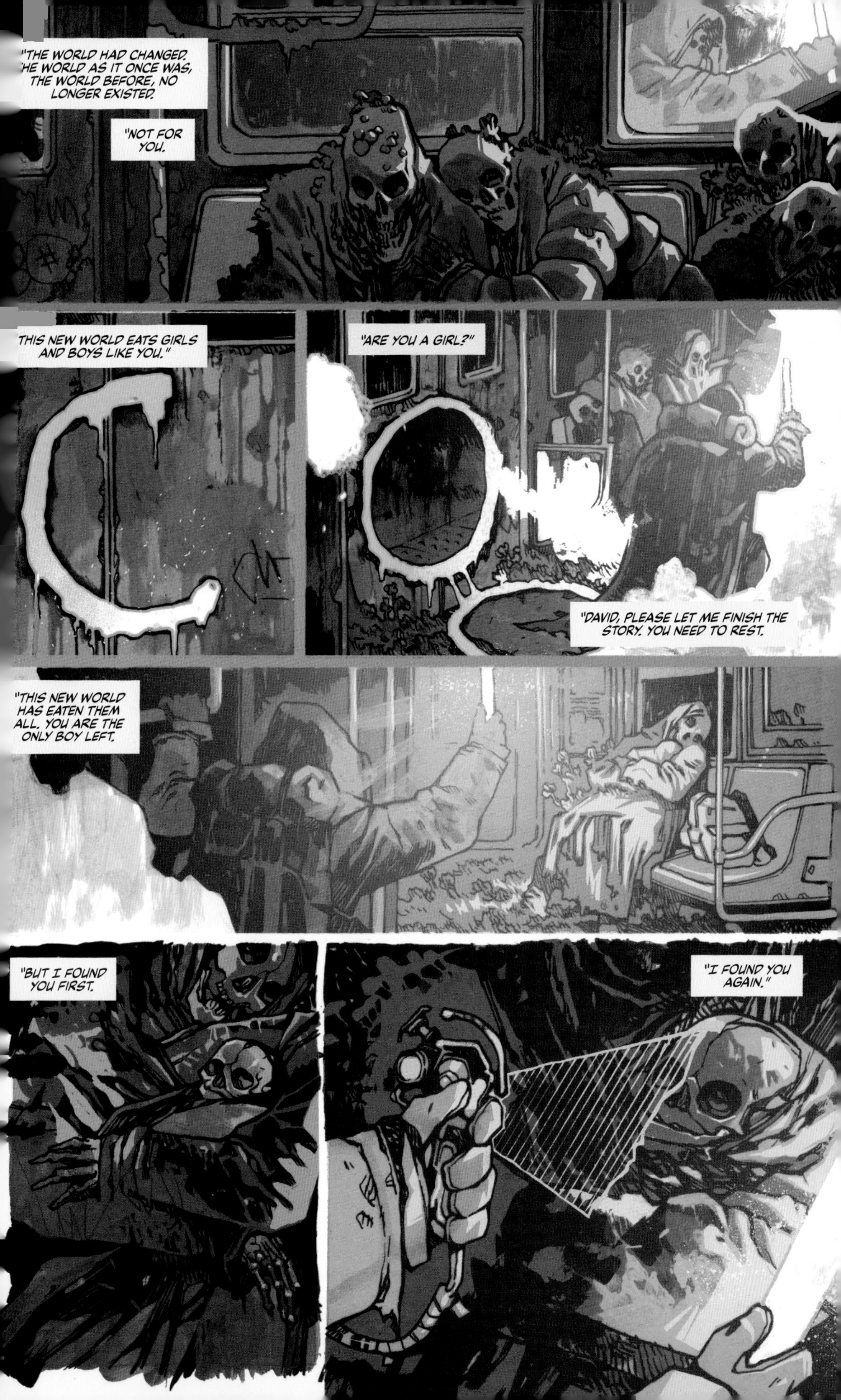
"THE WORLD HAD CHANGED. THE WORLD AS IT ONCE WAS, THE WORLD BEFORE, NO LONGER EXISTED.
"NOT FOR YOU.
THIS NEW WORLD EATS GIRLS AND BOYS LIKE YOU."
"ARE YOU A GIRL?"
"DAVID, PLEASE LET ME FINISH THE STORY. YOU NEED TO REST.
"THIS NEW WORLD HAS EATEN THEM ALL. YOU ARE THE ONLY BOY LEFT.
"BUT I FOUND YOU FIRST.
"I FOUND YOU AGAIN."

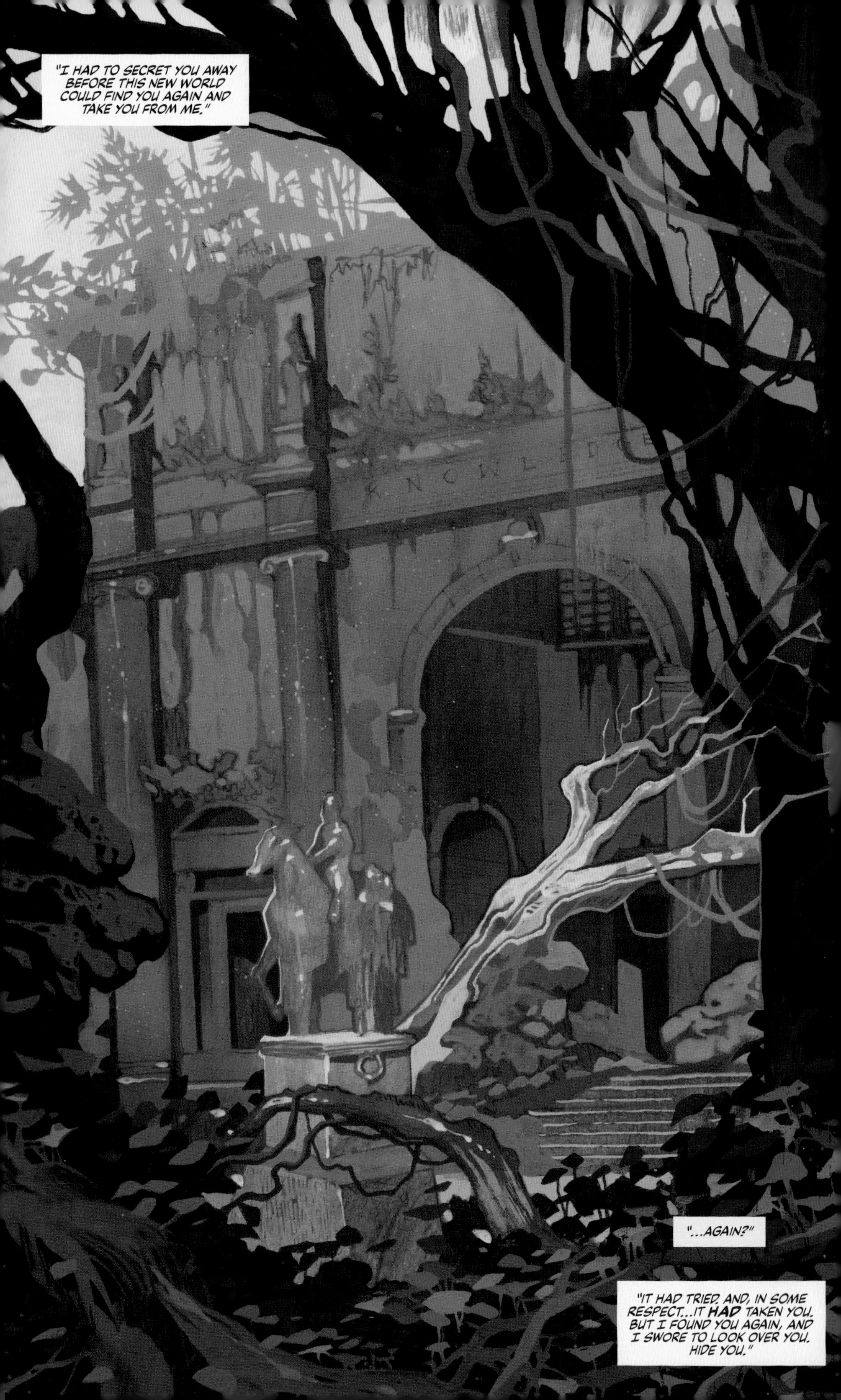
"I HAD TO SECRET YOU AWAY BEFORE THIS NEW WORLD COULD FIND YOU AGAIN AND TAKE YOU FROM ME."
KNOWLEDGE
"...AGAIN?"
"IT HAD TRIED AND, IN SOME RESPECT...IT HAD TAKEN YOU. BUT I FOUND YOU AGAIN, AND I SWORE TO LOOK OVER YOU. HIDE YOU."

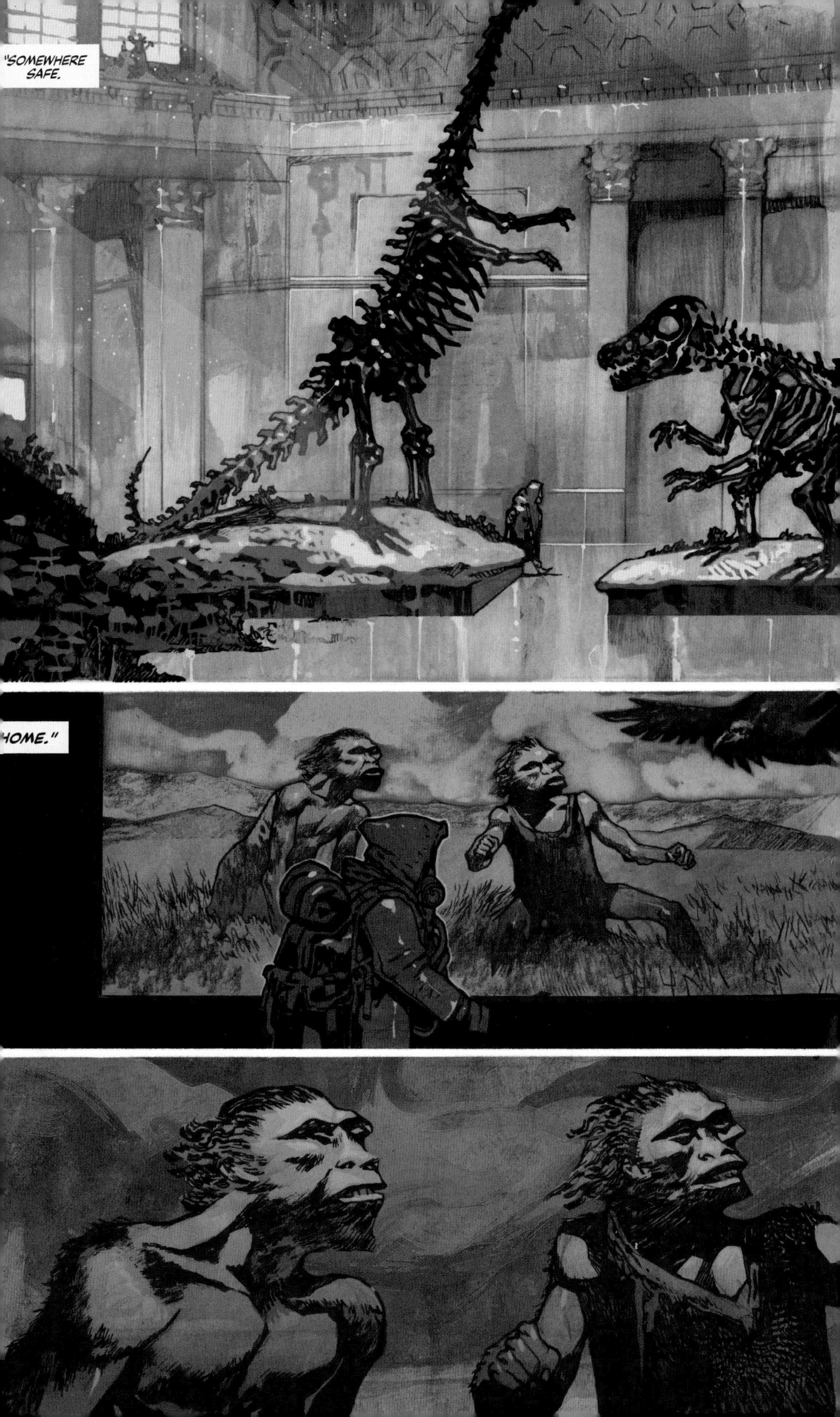
"SOMEWHERE SAFE.
HOME."

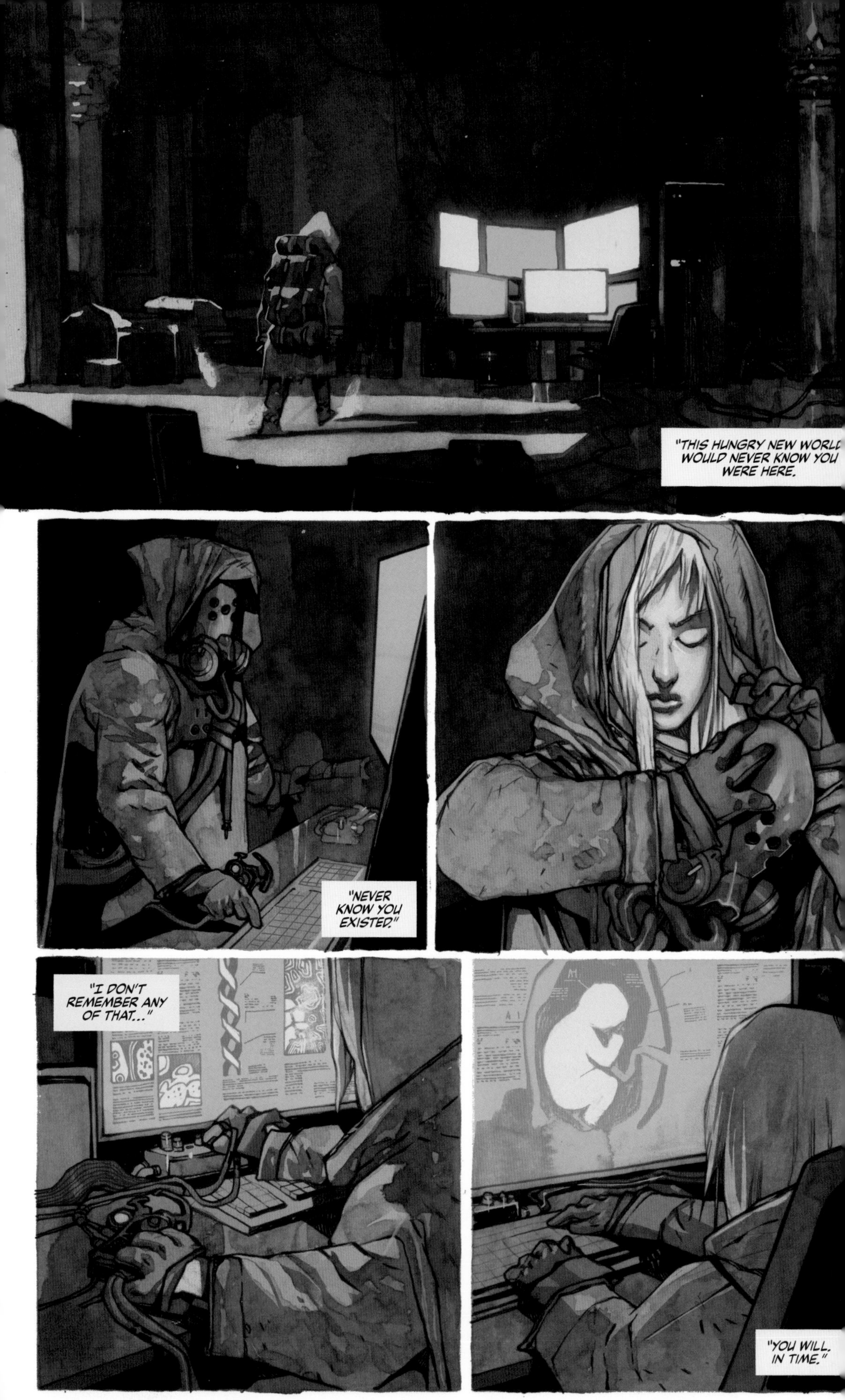
"THIS HUNGRY NEW WORLD WOULD NEVER KNOW YOU WERE HERE.
"NEVER KNOW YOU EXISTED."
"I DON'T REMEMBER ANY OF THAT..."
"YOU WILL. IN TIME."

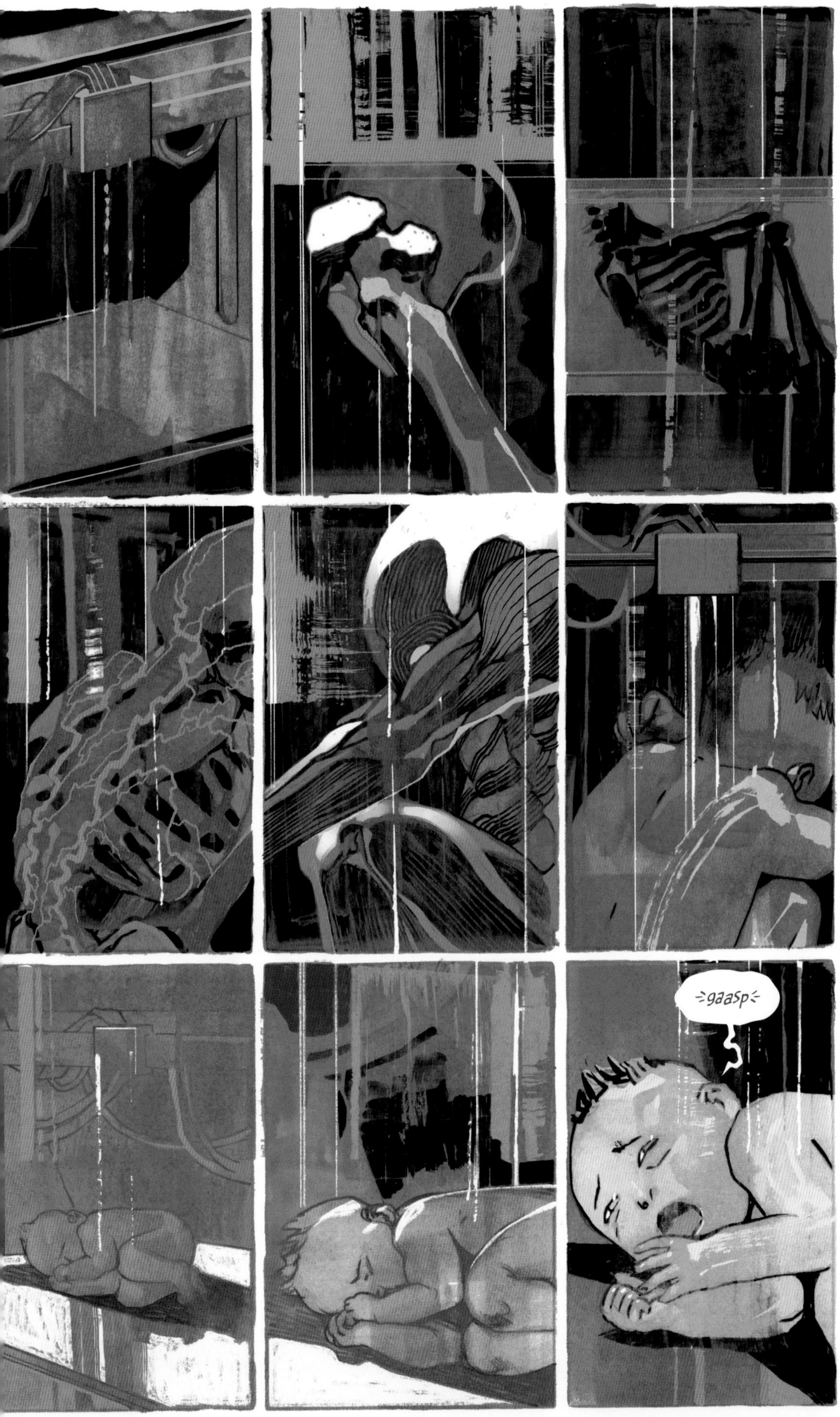
gaasp

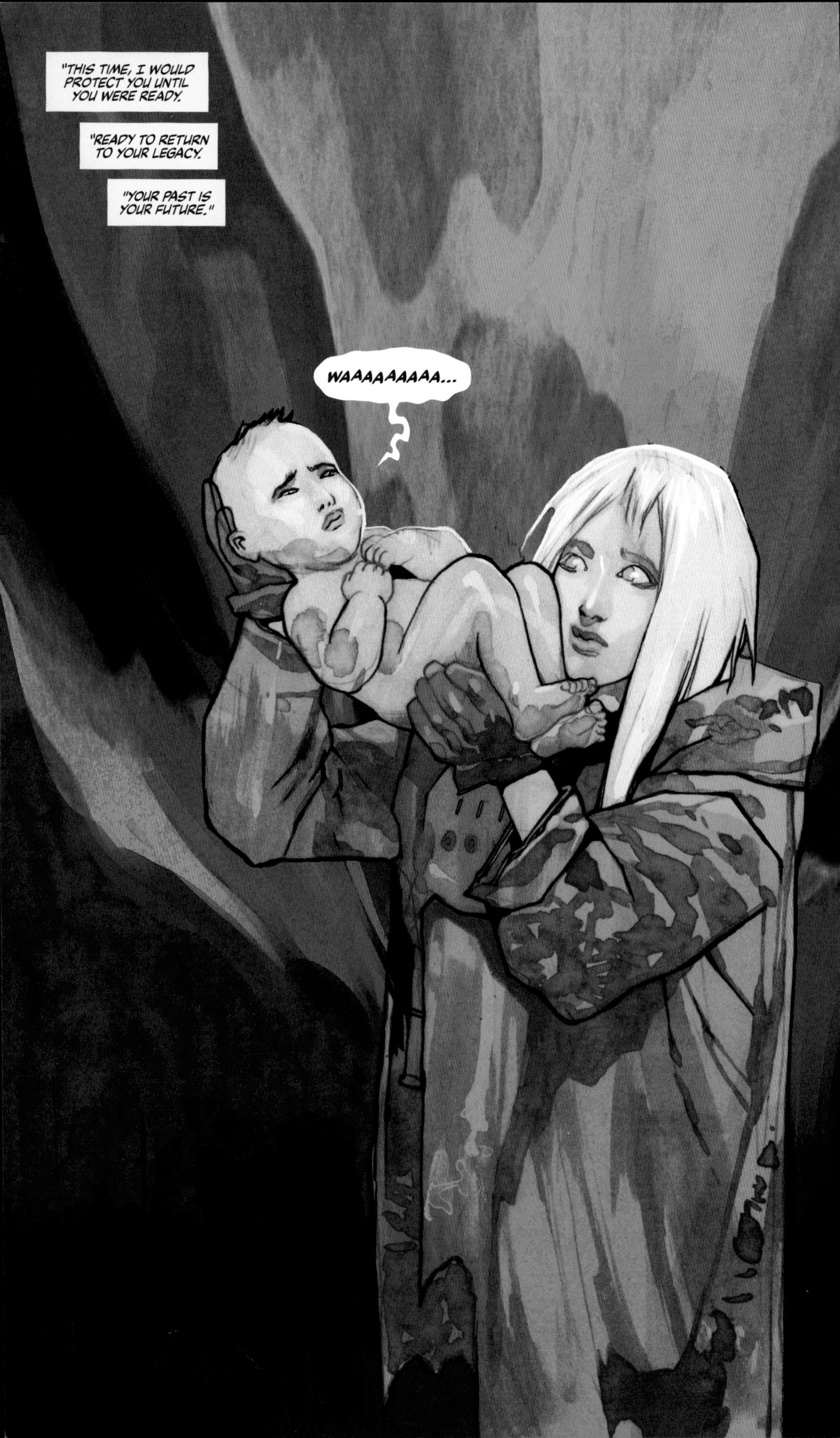
"THIS TIME, I WOULD PROTECT YOU UNTIL YOU WERE READY.
"READY TO RETURN TO YOUR LEGACY.
"YOUR PAST IS YOUR FUTURE."
WAAAAAAAAA...

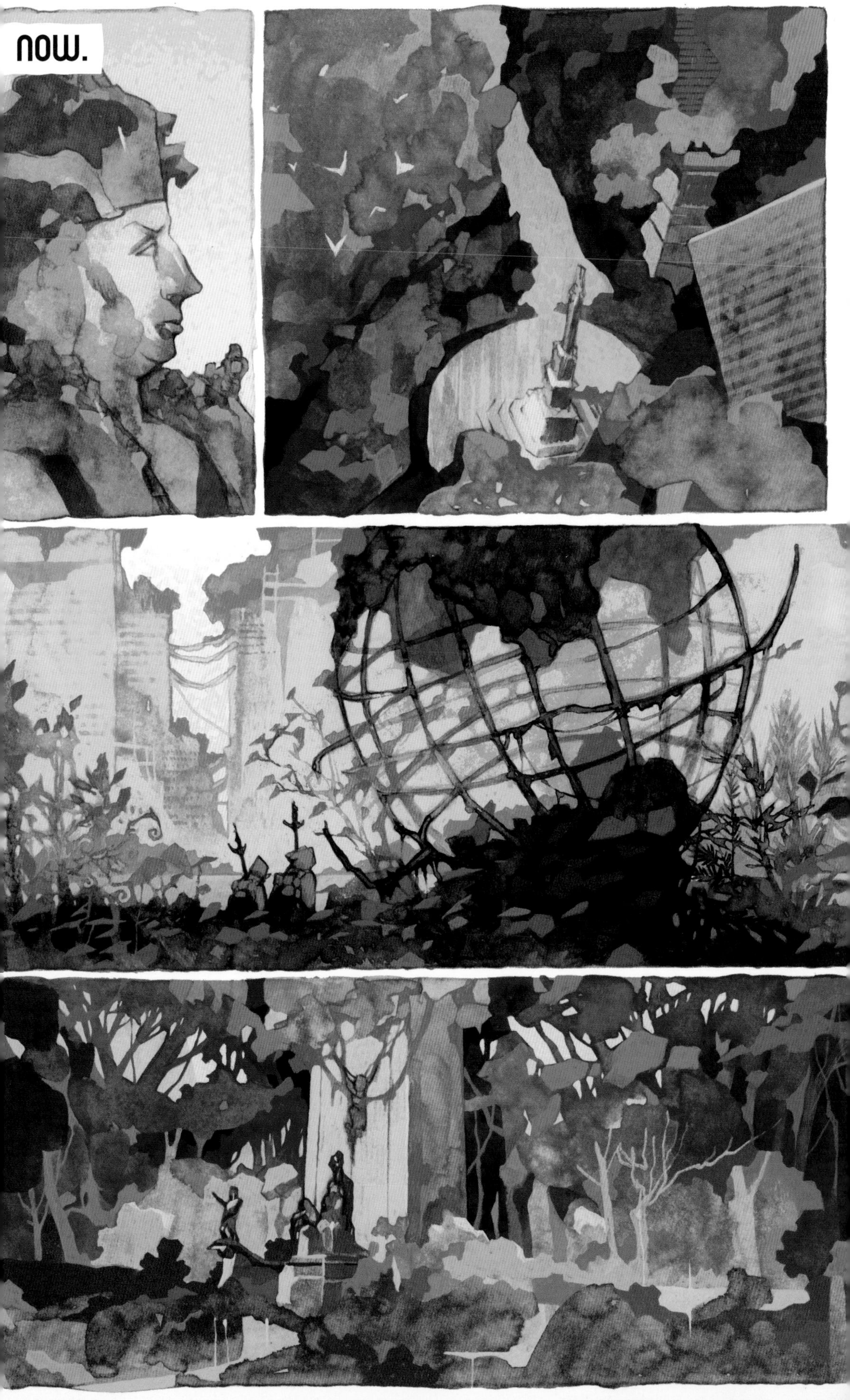
now.

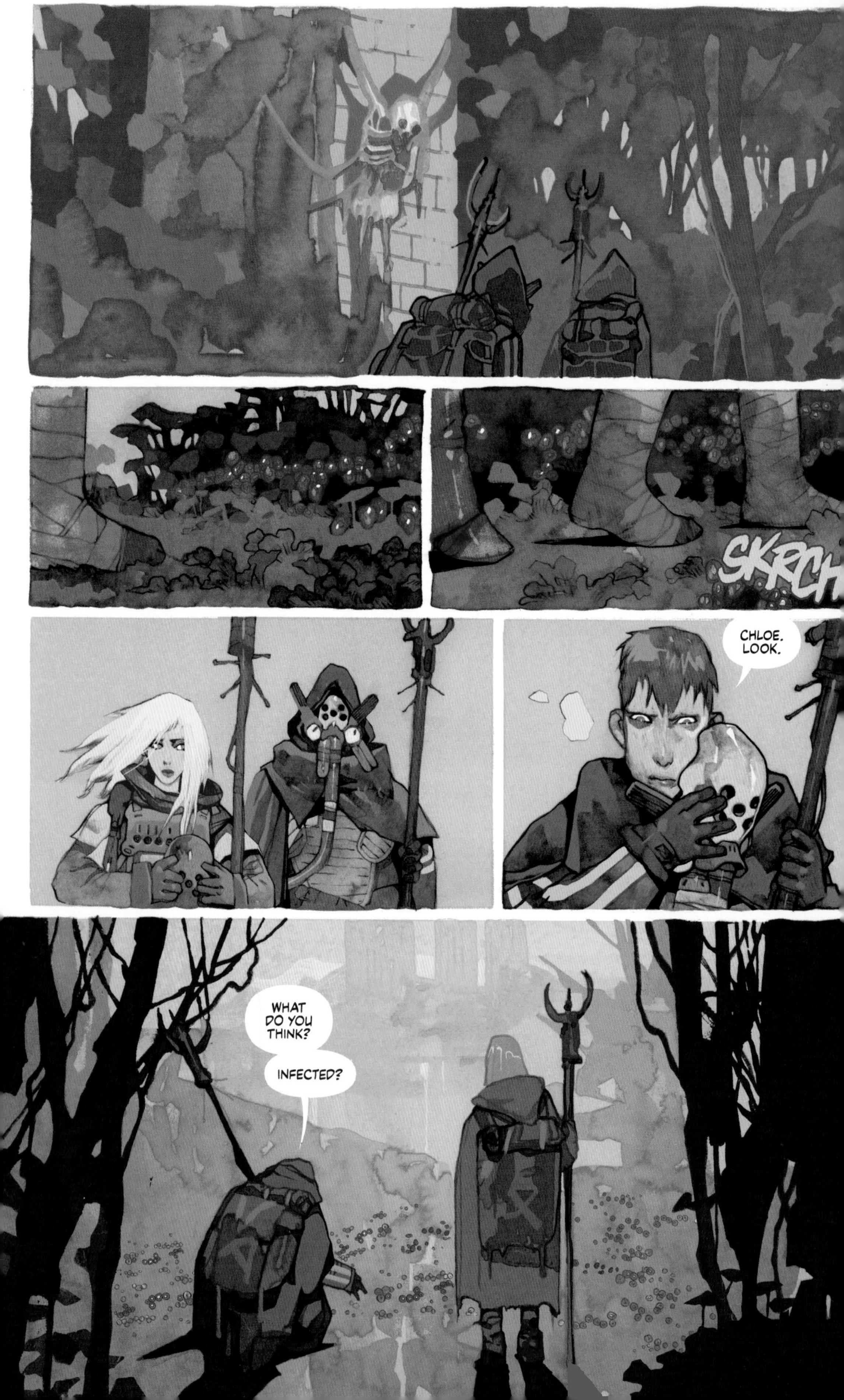
SKRCH
CHLOE. LOOK.
WHAT DO YOU THINK?
INFECTED?

AFTER ALL THIS TIME, THEY'VE COME BACK. IMAGINE THAT.

STRAWBERRIES.

I'VE NEVER EATEN ONE.

DAVID--

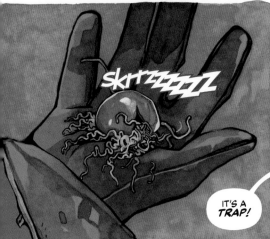

SKrrZZZZZZ

IT'S A *TRAP!*

DID ANY GET ON YOU?

NO.

ShZZZZZ

ZZZZZZkt

WE NEED TO GO! NOW, DAVID. BEFORE THEY--

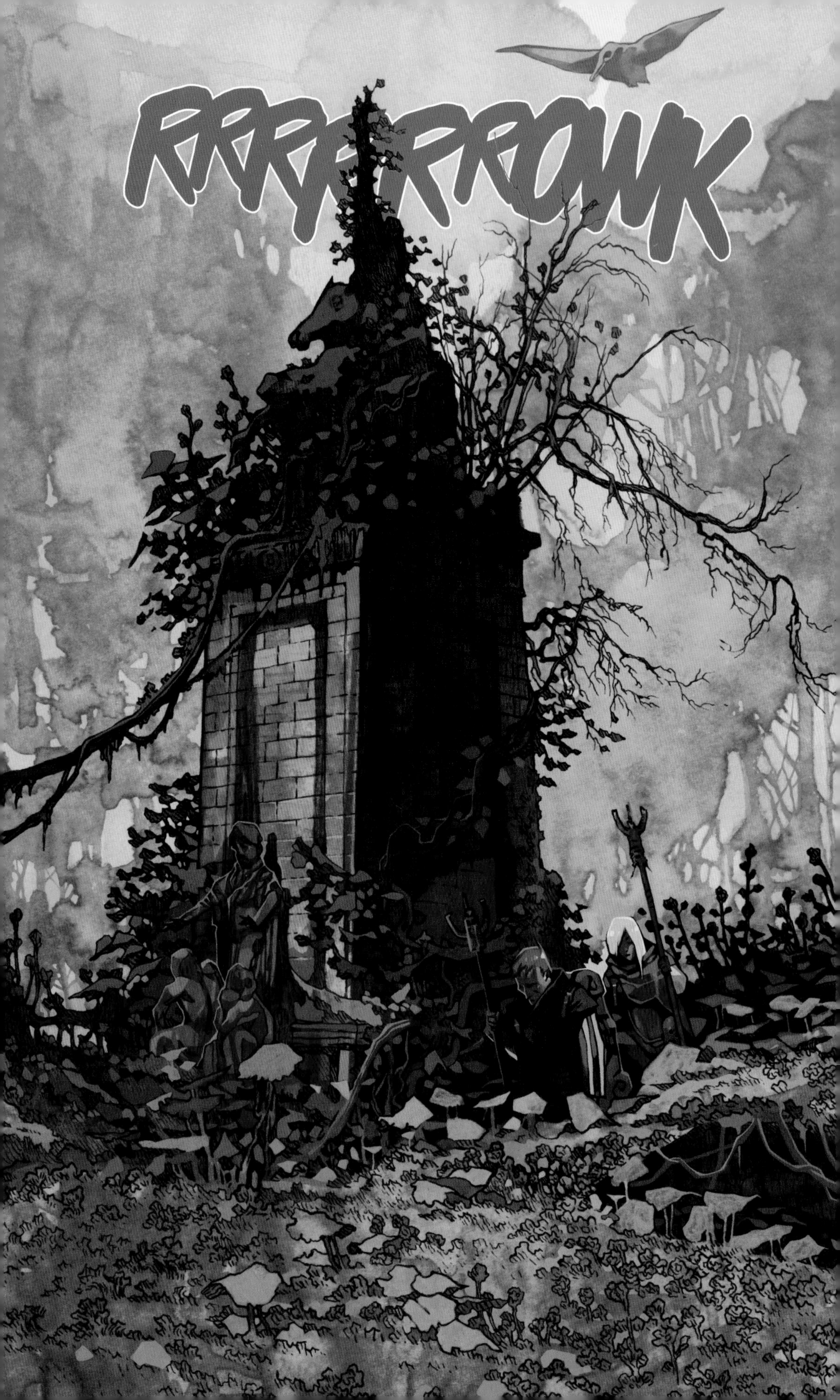
RRRRRRROUK

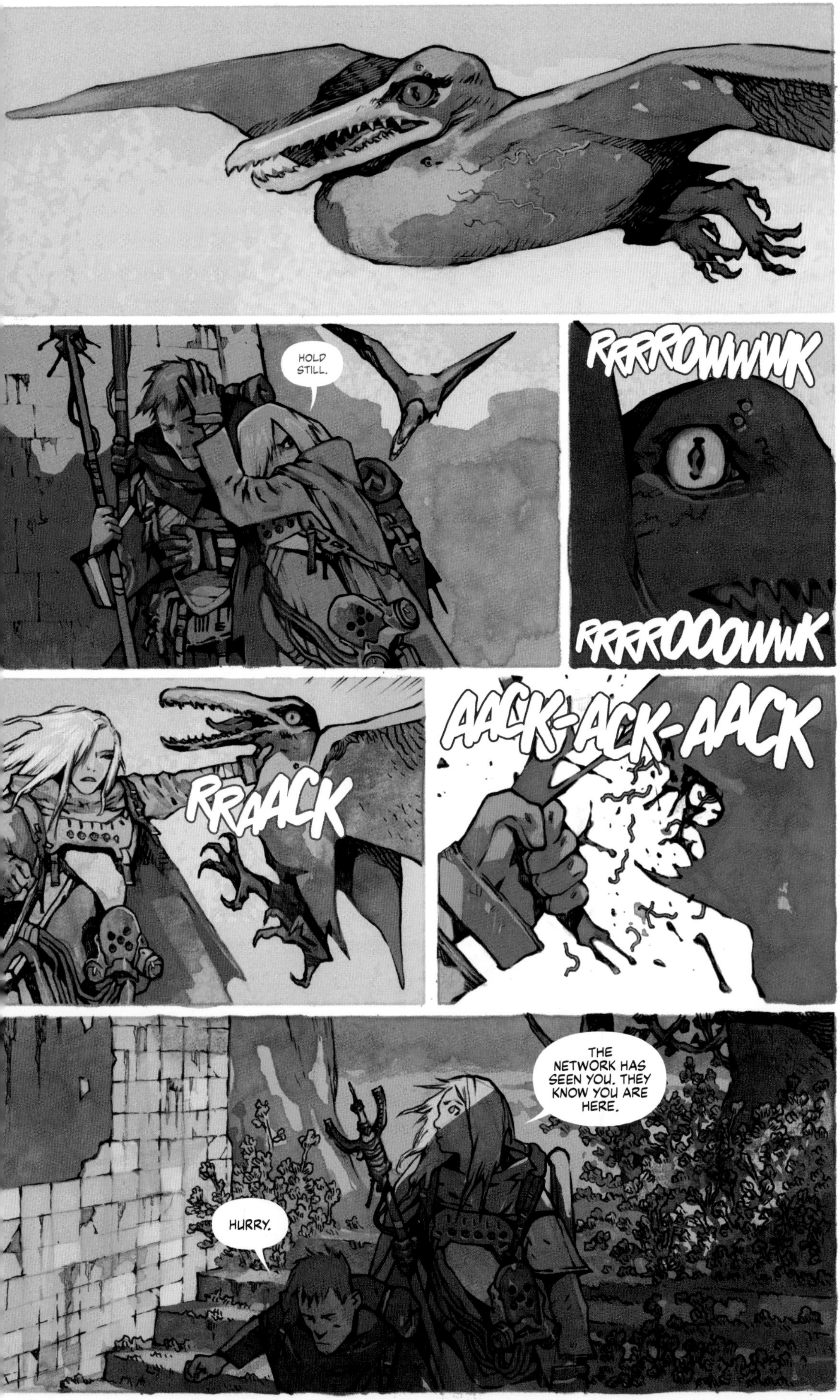
HOLD STILL.
RRRROWWWK
RRRROOOOWWK
RRAACK
AACK-ACK-AACK
THE NETWORK HAS SEEN YOU. THEY KNOW YOU ARE HERE.
HURRY.

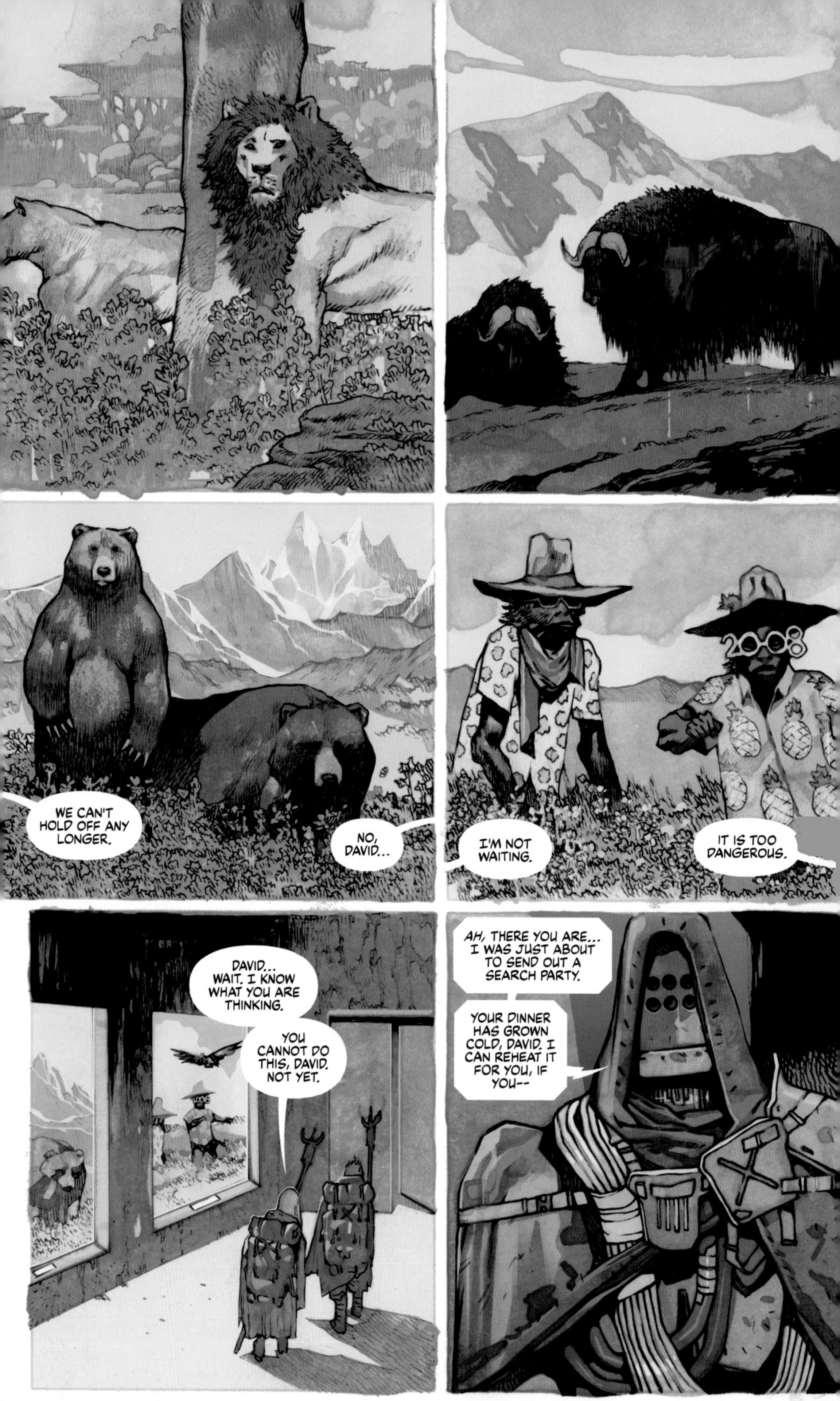

WE CAN'T HOLD OFF ANY LONGER.
NO, DAVID...
I'M NOT WAITING.
IT IS TOO DANGEROUS.
DAVID... WAIT. I KNOW WHAT YOU ARE THINKING.
YOU CANNOT DO THIS, DAVID. NOT YET.
AH, THERE YOU ARE... I WAS JUST ABOUT TO SEND OUT A SEARCH PARTY.
YOUR DINNER HAS GROWN COLD, DAVID. I CAN REHEAT IT FOR YOU, IF YOU--

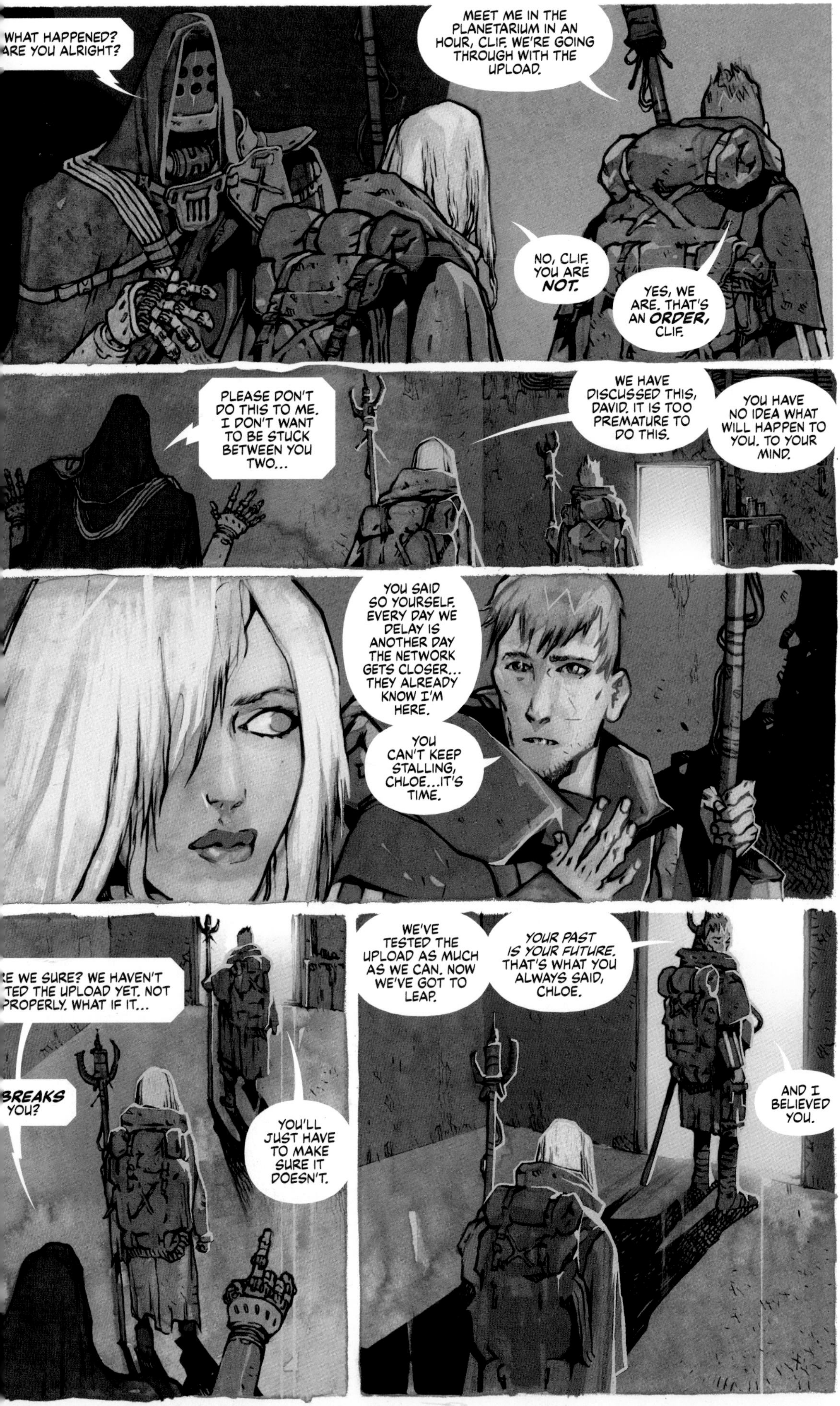
WHAT HAPPENED? ARE YOU ALRIGHT?
MEET ME IN THE PLANETARIUM IN AN HOUR, CLIF. WE'RE GOING THROUGH WITH THE UPLOAD.
NO, CLIF. YOU ARE NOT.
YES, WE ARE. THAT'S AN ORDER, CLIF.
PLEASE DON'T DO THIS TO ME. I DON'T WANT TO BE STUCK BETWEEN YOU TWO...
WE HAVE DISCUSSED THIS, DAVID. IT IS TOO PREMATURE TO DO THIS.
YOU HAVE NO IDEA WHAT WILL HAPPEN TO YOU. TO YOUR MIND.
YOU SAID SO YOURSELF. EVERY DAY WE DELAY IS ANOTHER DAY THE NETWORK GETS CLOSER... THEY ALREADY KNOW I'M HERE.
YOU CAN'T KEEP STALLING, CHLOE...IT'S TIME.
E WE SURE? WE HAVEN'T TED THE UPLOAD YET. NOT PROPERLY. WHAT IF IT...
BREAKS YOU?
YOU'LL JUST HAVE TO MAKE SURE IT DOESN'T.
WE'VE TESTED THE UPLOAD AS MUCH AS WE CAN. NOW WE'VE GOT TO LEAP.
YOUR PAST IS YOUR FUTURE. THAT'S WHAT YOU ALWAYS SAID, CHLOE.
AND I BELIEVED YOU.

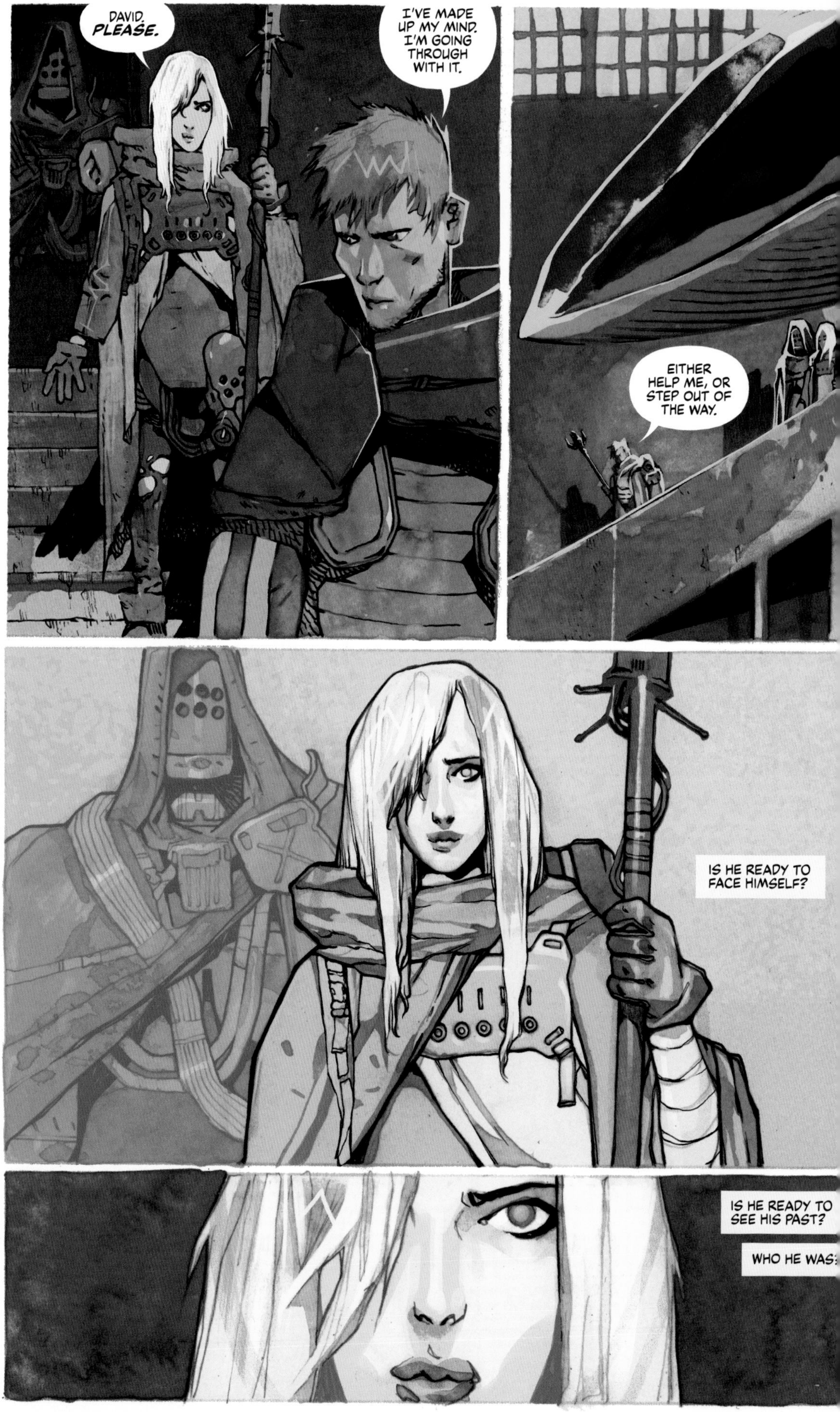

DAVID. PLEASE.
I'VE MADE UP MY MIND. I'M GOING THROUGH WITH IT.
EITHER HELP ME, OR STEP OUT OF THE WAY.
IS HE READY TO FACE HIMSELF?
IS HE READY TO SEE HIS PAST?
WHO HE WAS:

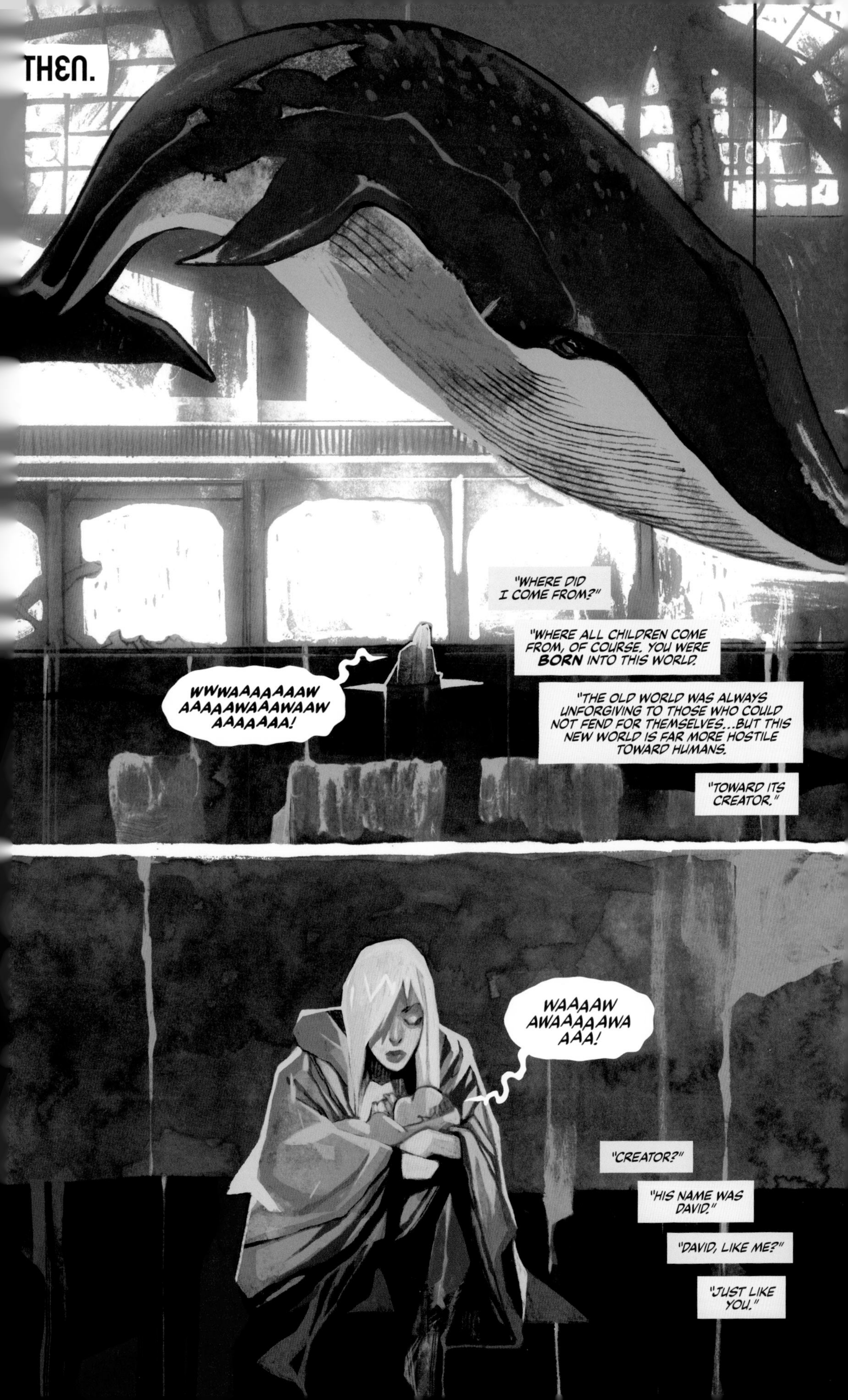
THEN.
"WHERE DID I COME FROM?"
"WHERE ALL CHILDREN COME FROM, OF COURSE. YOU WERE BORN INTO THIS WORLD.
WWWAAAAAAAW AAAAAWAAAWAAW AAAAAAA!
"THE OLD WORLD WAS ALWAYS UNFORGIVING TO THOSE WHO COULD NOT FEND FOR THEMSELVES...BUT THIS NEW WORLD IS FAR MORE HOSTILE TOWARD HUMANS.
"TOWARD ITS CREATOR."
WAAAAW AWAAAAAAWA AAA!
"CREATOR?"
"HIS NAME WAS DAVID."
"DAVID, LIKE ME?"
"JUST LIKE YOU."

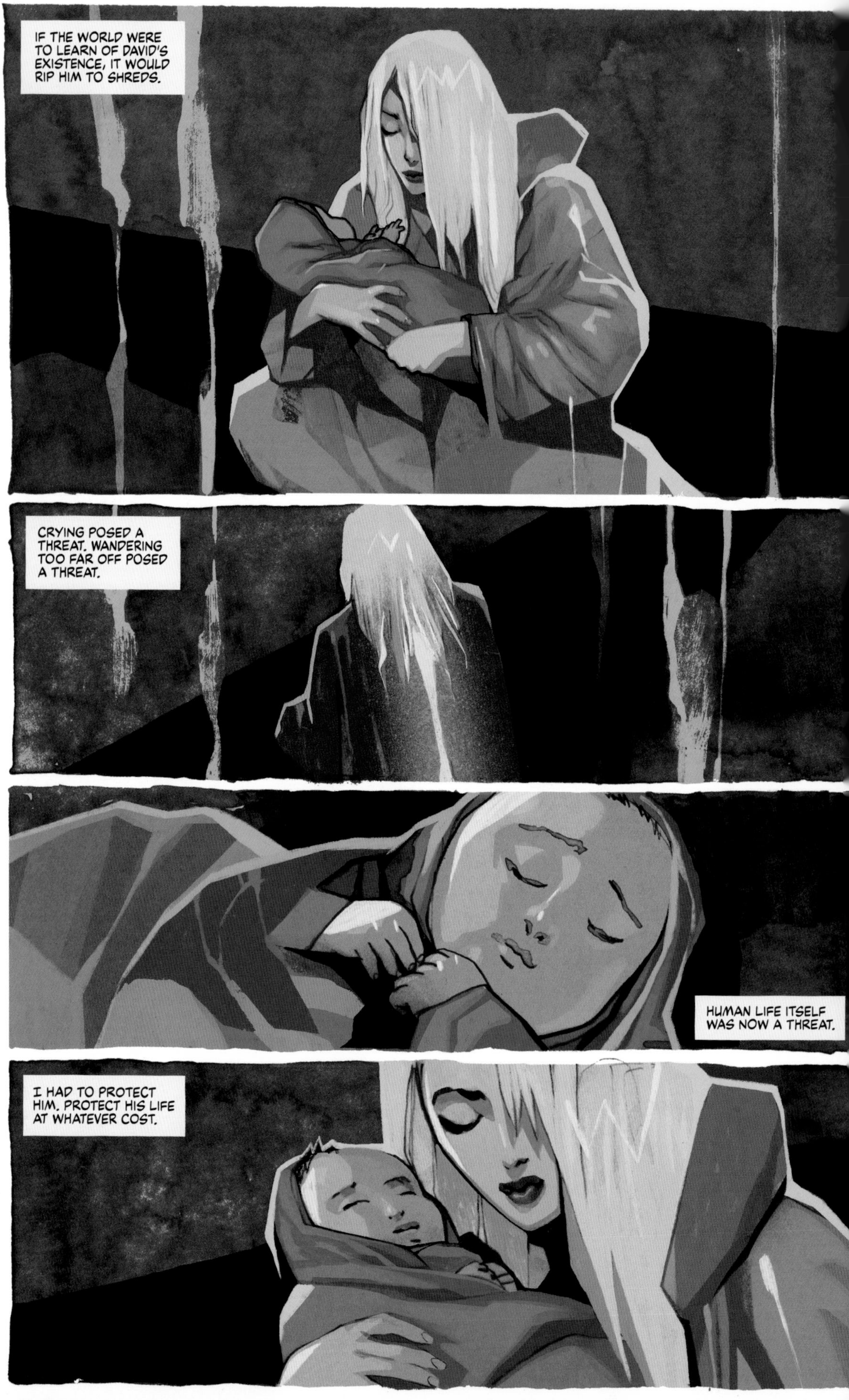
IF THE WORLD WERE TO LEARN OF DAVID'S EXISTENCE, IT WOULD RIP HIM TO SHREDS.
CRYING POSED A THREAT. WANDERING TOO FAR OFF POSED A THREAT.
HUMAN LIFE ITSELF WAS NOW A THREAT.
I HAD TO PROTECT HIM. PROTECT HIS LIFE AT WHATEVER COST.

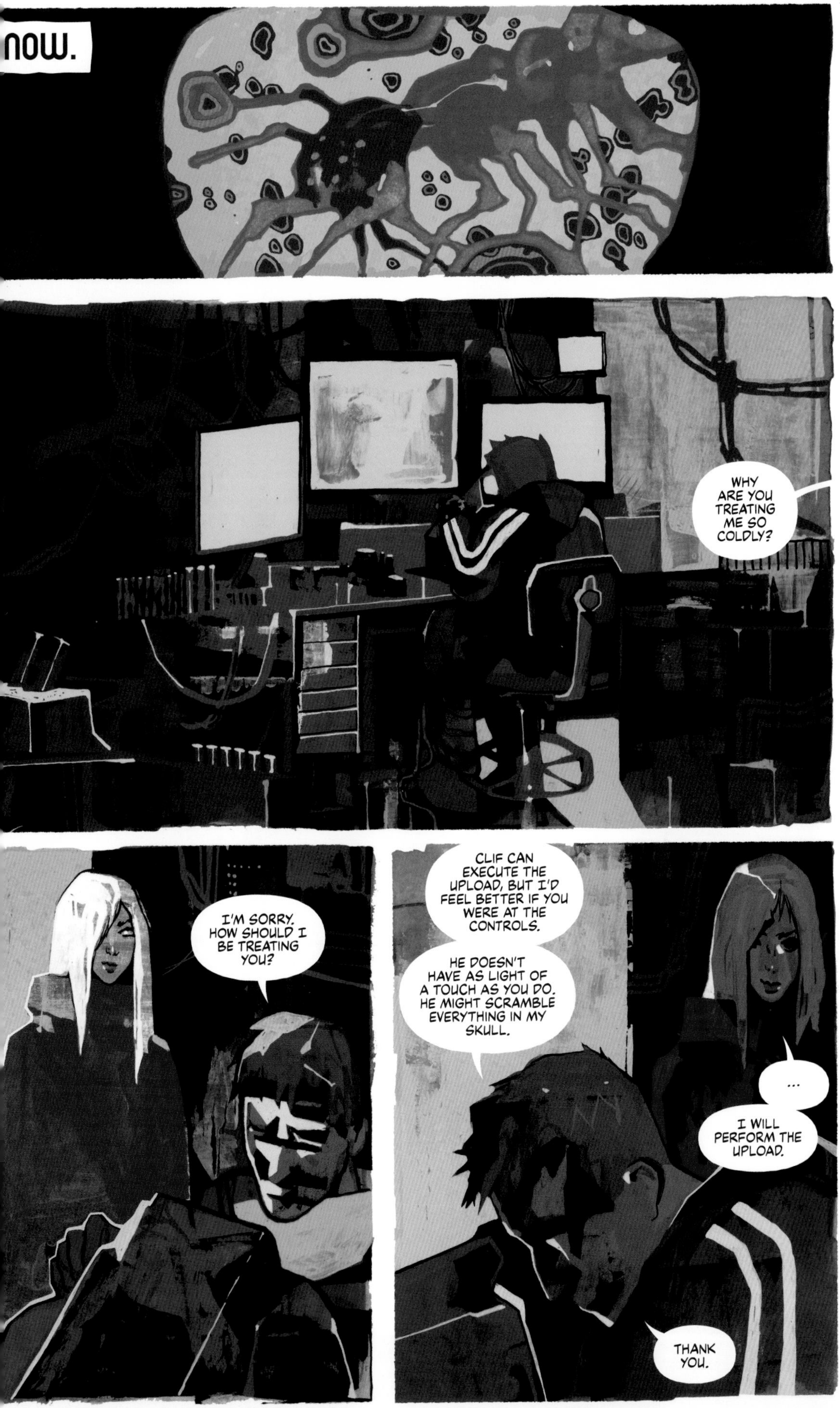
NOW.
WHY ARE YOU TREATING ME SO COLDLY?
I'M SORRY. HOW SHOULD I BE TREATING YOU?
CLIF CAN EXECUTE THE UPLOAD, BUT I'D FEEL BETTER IF YOU WERE AT THE CONTROLS.
HE DOESN'T HAVE AS LIGHT OF A TOUCH AS YOU DO. HE MIGHT SCRAMBLE EVERYTHING IN MY SKULL.
...
I WILL PERFORM THE UPLOAD.
THANK YOU.

BUT BEFORE I DO...
THERE IS SOMETHING
YOU NEED TO
KNOW.

I HAVE BEEN
WAITING FOR THE
APPROPRIATE TIME
TO TELL YOU,
BUT...

THERE WILL
NEVER BE A RIGHT
TIME. NOT FOR
THIS.

CHLOE. *STOP.*
YOU'VE BEEN
BUILDING UP TO
THIS MOMENT MY
ENTIRE LIFE.
PREPARING ME FOR
IT. PROTECTING ME.
WHATEVER IT
IS YOU NEED
TO SAY...

*JUST
SAY IT.*

YOU
DIED,
DAVID.

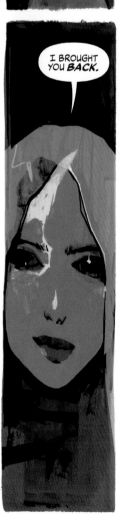

I BROUGHT
YOU *BACK.*

HOW
LONG
AGO?

989
YEARS.

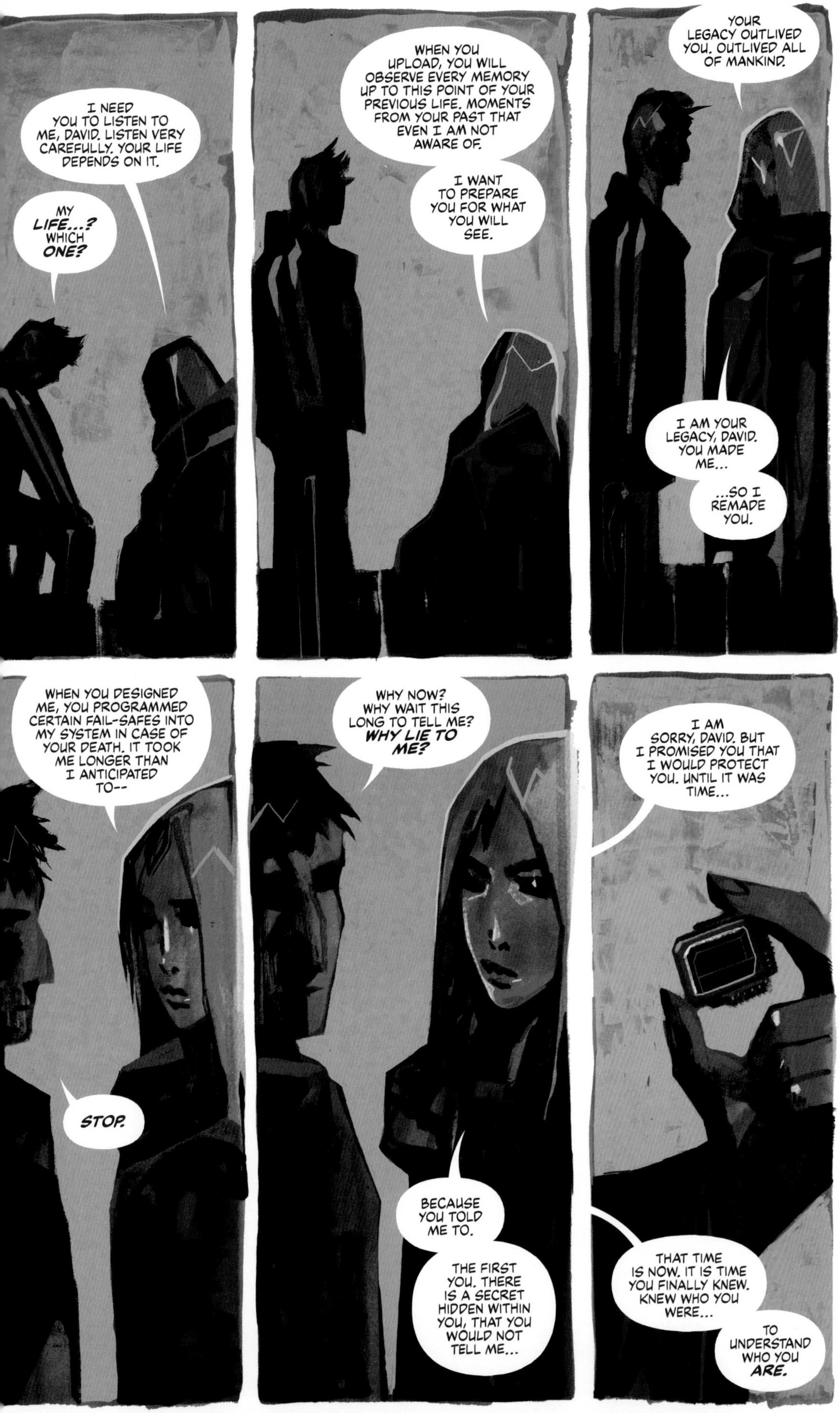
I NEED YOU TO LISTEN TO ME, DAVID. LISTEN VERY CAREFULLY. YOUR LIFE DEPENDS ON IT.
MY LIFE...? WHICH ONE?
WHEN YOU UPLOAD, YOU WILL OBSERVE EVERY MEMORY UP TO THIS POINT OF YOUR PREVIOUS LIFE. MOMENTS FROM YOUR PAST THAT EVEN I AM NOT AWARE OF.
I WANT TO PREPARE YOU FOR WHAT YOU WILL SEE.
YOUR LEGACY OUTLIVED YOU. OUTLIVED ALL OF MANKIND.
I AM YOUR LEGACY, DAVID. YOU MADE ME...
...SO I REMADE YOU.
WHEN YOU DESIGNED ME, YOU PROGRAMMED CERTAIN FAIL-SAFES INTO MY SYSTEM IN CASE OF YOUR DEATH. IT TOOK ME LONGER THAN I ANTICIPATED TO--
STOP.
WHY NOW? WHY WAIT THIS LONG TO TELL ME? WHY LIE TO ME?
BECAUSE YOU TOLD ME TO.
THE FIRST YOU. THERE IS A SECRET HIDDEN WITHIN YOU, THAT YOU WOULD NOT TELL ME...
I AM SORRY, DAVID. BUT I PROMISED YOU THAT I WOULD PROTECT YOU. UNTIL IT WAS TIME...
THAT TIME IS NOW. IT IS TIME YOU FINALLY KNEW. KNEW WHO YOU WERE...
TO UNDERSTAND WHO YOU ARE.

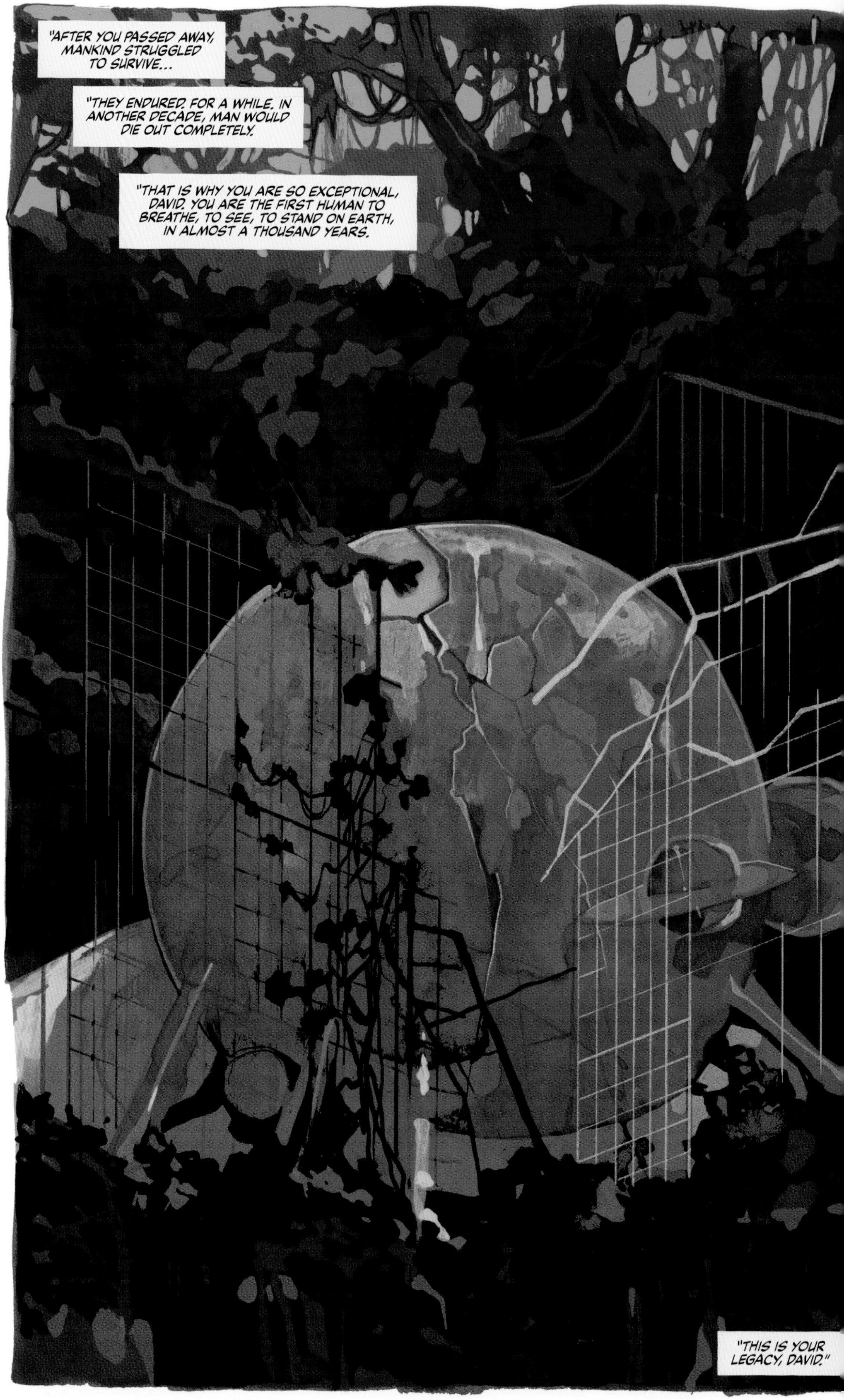
"AFTER YOU PASSED AWAY, MANKIND STRUGGLED TO SURVIVE...
"THEY ENDURED. FOR A WHILE. IN ANOTHER DECADE, MAN WOULD DIE OUT COMPLETELY.
"THAT IS WHY YOU ARE SO EXCEPTIONAL, DAVID. YOU ARE THE FIRST HUMAN TO BREATHE, TO SEE, TO STAND ON EARTH, IN ALMOST A THOUSAND YEARS.
"THIS IS YOUR LEGACY, DAVID."

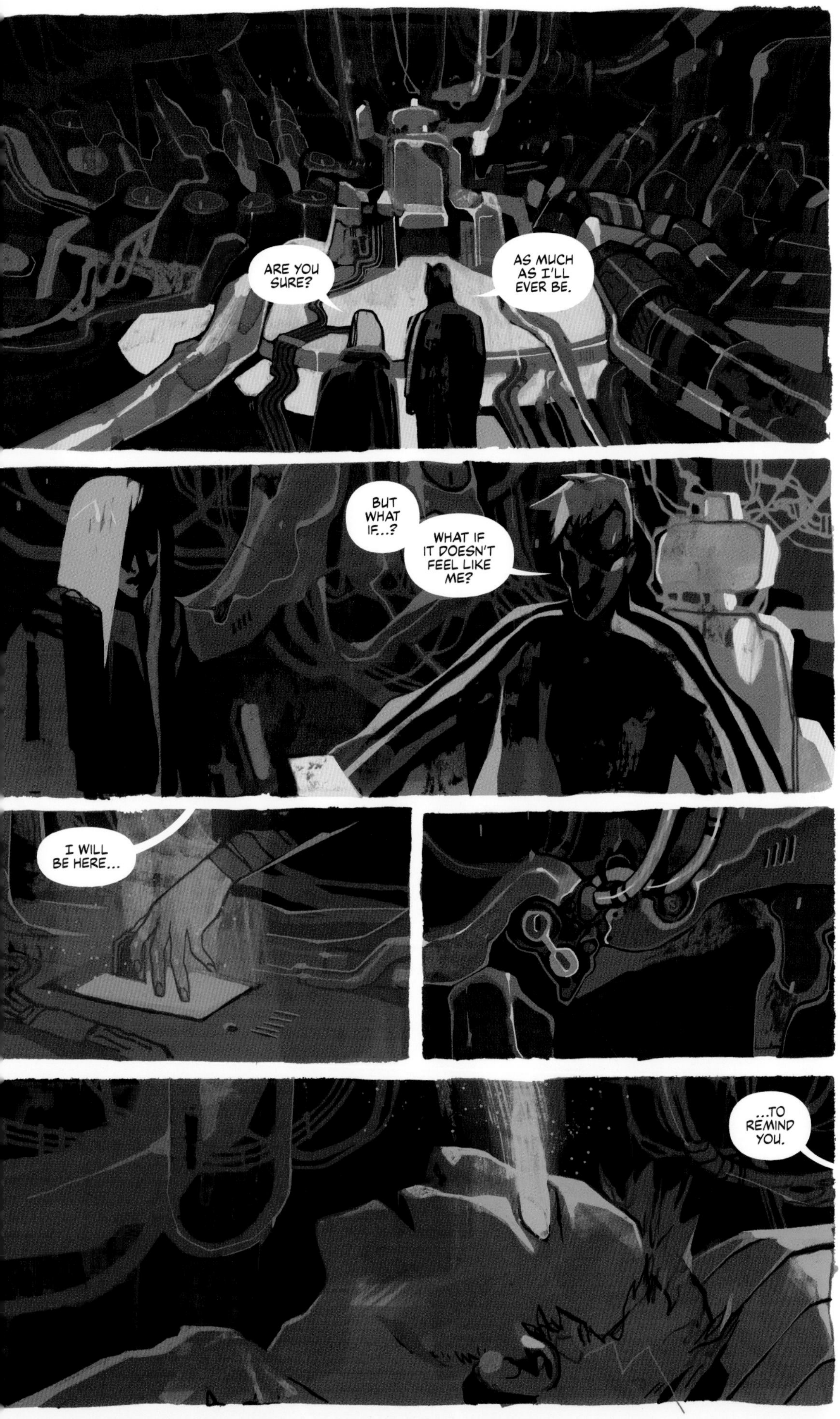
ARE YOU SURE?
AS MUCH AS I'LL EVER BE.
BUT WHAT IF...?
WHAT IF IT DOESN'T FEEL LIKE ME?
I WILL BE HERE...
...TO REMIND YOU.

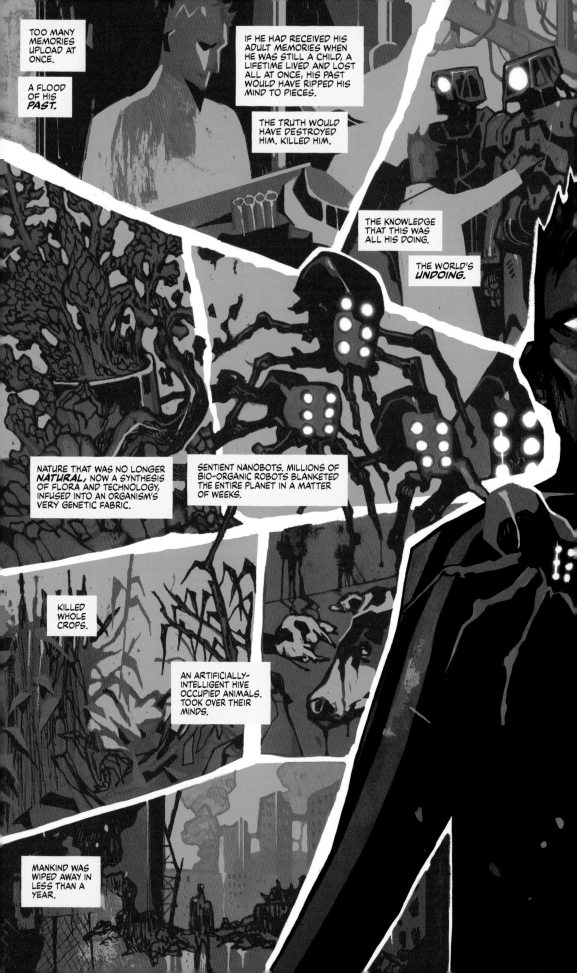

TOO MANY MEMORIES UPLOAD AT ONCE.

A FLOOD OF HIS *PAST.*

IF HE HAD RECEIVED HIS ADULT MEMORIES WHEN HE WAS STILL A CHILD, A LIFETIME LIVED AND LOST ALL AT ONCE, HIS PAST WOULD HAVE RIPPED HIS MIND TO PIECES.

THE TRUTH WOULD HAVE DESTROYED HIM. KILLED HIM.

THE KNOWLEDGE THAT THIS WAS ALL HIS DOING.

THE WORLD'S *UNDOING.*

NATURE THAT WAS NO LONGER *NATURAL,* NOW A SYNTHESIS OF FLORA AND TECHNOLOGY, INFUSED INTO AN ORGANISM'S VERY GENETIC FABRIC.

SENTIENT NANOBOTS. MILLIONS OF BIO-ORGANIC ROBOTS BLANKETED THE ENTIRE PLANET IN A MATTER OF WEEKS.

KILLED WHOLE CROPS.

AN ARTIFICIALLY-INTELLIGENT HIVE OCCUPIED ANIMALS. TOOK OVER THEIR MINDS.

MANKIND WAS WIPED AWAY IN LESS THAN A YEAR.

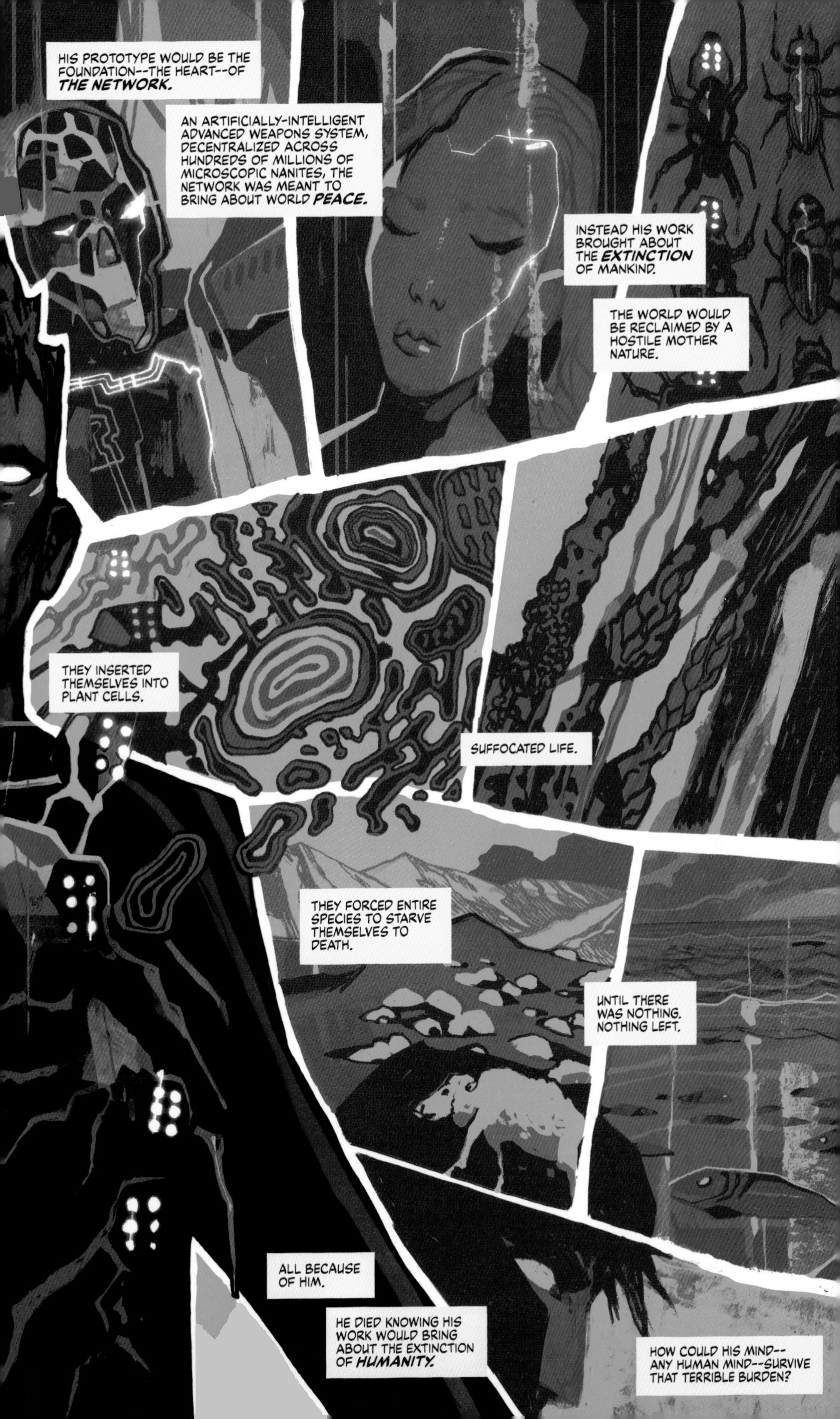
HIS PROTOTYPE WOULD BE THE FOUNDATION--THE HEART--OF THE NETWORK.
AN ARTIFICIALLY-INTELLIGENT ADVANCED WEAPONS SYSTEM, DECENTRALIZED ACROSS HUNDREDS OF MILLIONS OF MICROSCOPIC NANITES, THE NETWORK WAS MEANT TO BRING ABOUT WORLD PEACE.
INSTEAD HIS WORK BROUGHT ABOUT THE EXTINCTION OF MANKIND.
THE WORLD WOULD BE RECLAIMED BY A HOSTILE MOTHER NATURE.
THEY INSERTED THEMSELVES INTO PLANT CELLS.
SUFFOCATED LIFE.
THEY FORCED ENTIRE SPECIES TO STARVE THEMSELVES TO DEATH.
UNTIL THERE WAS NOTHING. NOTHING LEFT.
ALL BECAUSE OF HIM.
HE DIED KNOWING HIS WORK WOULD BRING ABOUT THE EXTINCTION OF HUMANITY.
HOW COULD HIS MIND--ANY HUMAN MIND--SURVIVE THAT TERRIBLE BURDEN?

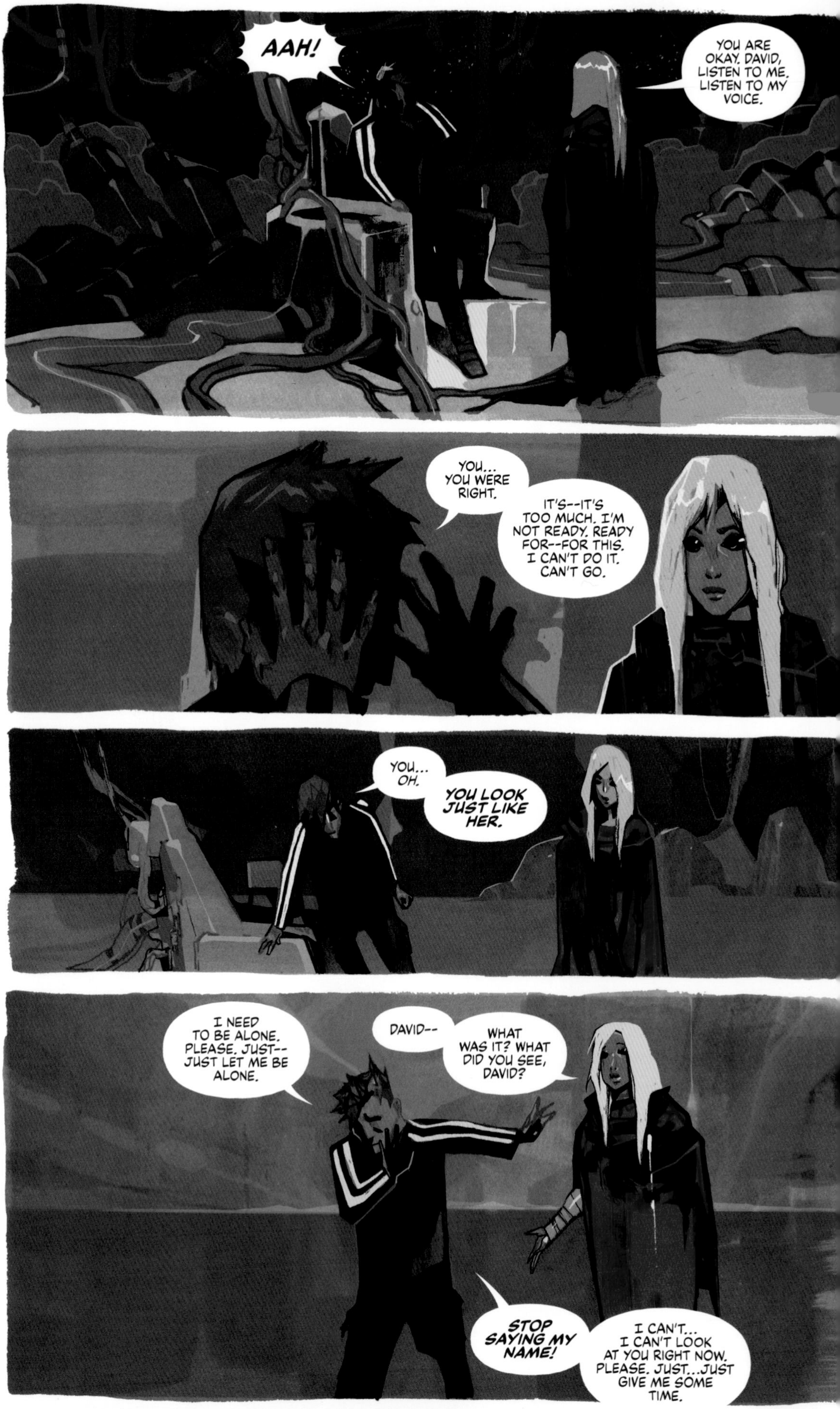
AAH!
YOU ARE OKAY. DAVID, LISTEN TO ME. LISTEN TO MY VOICE.
YOU... YOU WERE RIGHT.
IT'S--IT'S TOO MUCH. I'M NOT READY. READY FOR--FOR THIS. I CAN'T DO IT. CAN'T GO.
YOU... OH.
YOU LOOK JUST LIKE HER.
I NEED TO BE ALONE. PLEASE. JUST--JUST LET ME BE ALONE.
DAVID--
WHAT WAS IT? WHAT DID YOU SEE, DAVID?
STOP SAYING MY NAME!
I CAN'T... I CAN'T LOOK AT YOU RIGHT NOW. PLEASE. JUST...JUST GIVE ME SOME TIME.

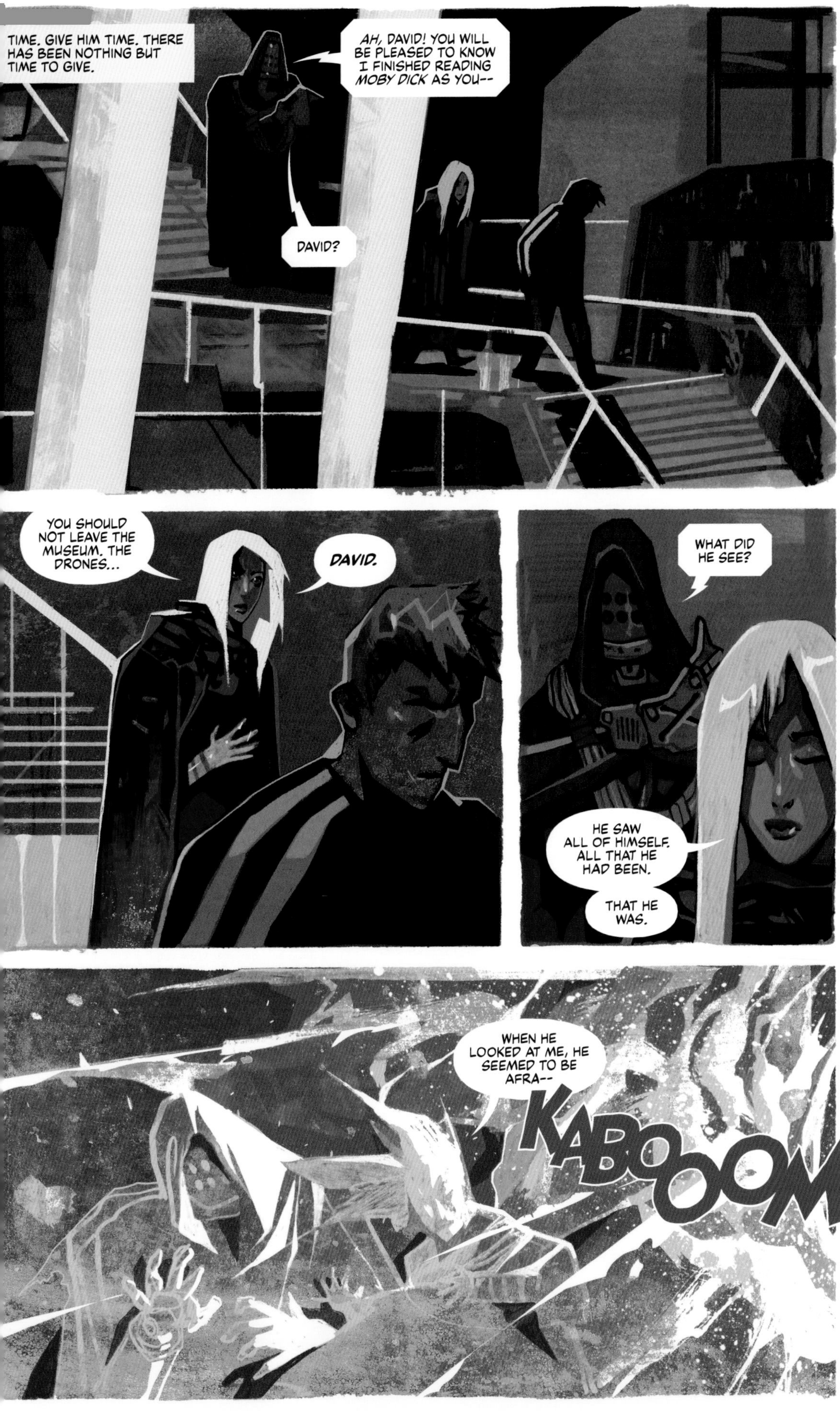
TIME. GIVE HIM TIME. THERE HAS BEEN NOTHING BUT TIME TO GIVE.
AH, DAVID! YOU WILL BE PLEASED TO KNOW I FINISHED READING MOBY DICK AS YOU--
DAVID?
YOU SHOULD NOT LEAVE THE MUSEUM. THE DRONES...
DAVID.
WHAT DID HE SEE?
HE SAW ALL OF HIMSELF. ALL THAT HE HAD BEEN.
THAT HE WAS.
WHEN HE LOOKED AT ME, HE SEEMED TO BE AFRA--
KABOOOOM

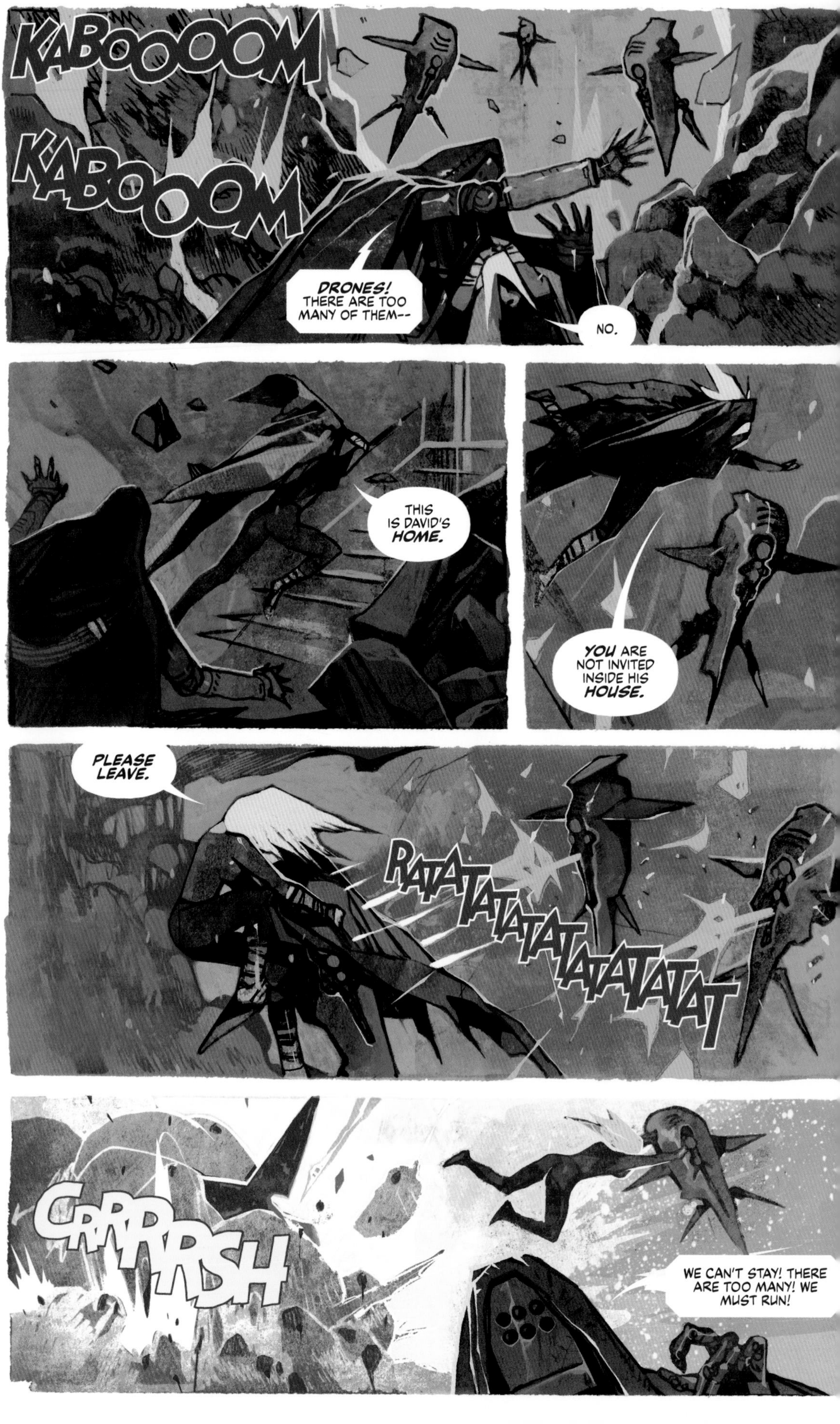
KABOOOOM
KABOOOOM
DRONES! THERE ARE TOO MANY OF THEM--
NO.
THIS IS DAVID'S HOME.
YOU ARE NOT INVITED INSIDE HIS HOUSE.
PLEASE LEAVE.
RATATATATATATATATATAT
CRRRRSH
WE CAN'T STAY! THERE ARE TOO MANY! WE MUST RUN!

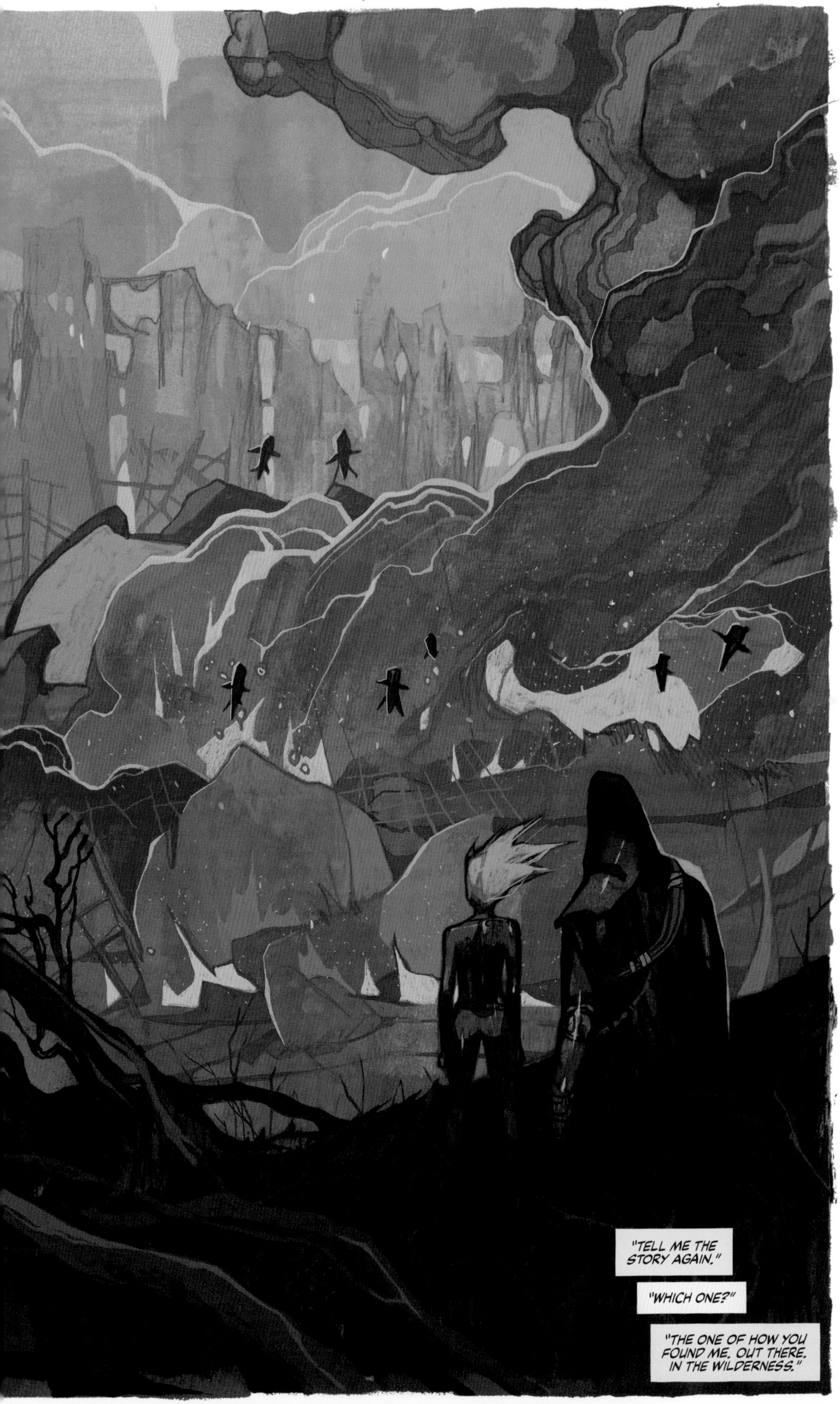
"TELL ME THE STORY AGAIN."
"WHICH ONE?"
"THE ONE OF HOW YOU FOUND ME. OUT THERE. IN THE WILDERNESS."

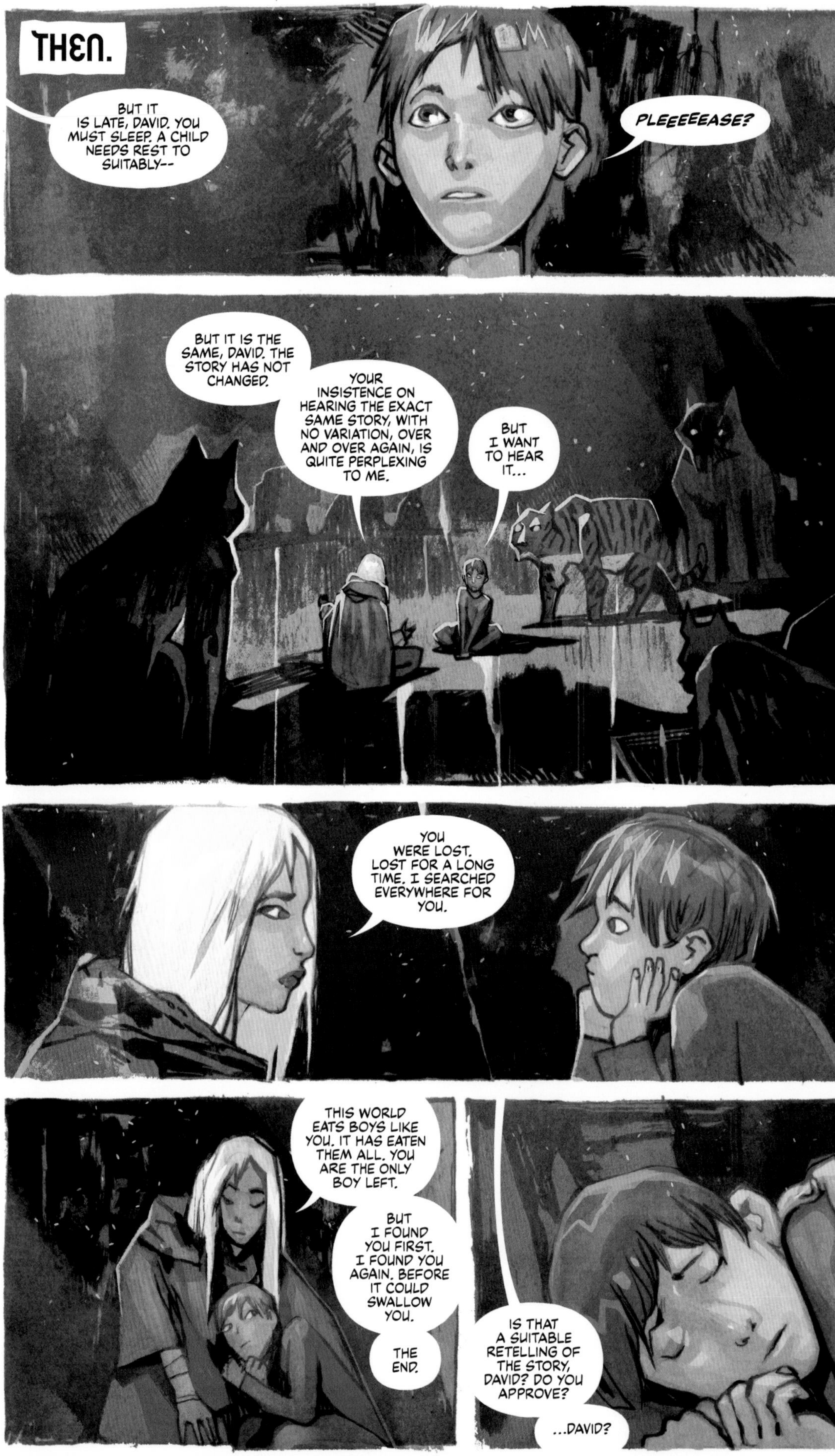
THEN.
BUT IT IS LATE, DAVID. YOU MUST SLEEP. A CHILD NEEDS REST TO SUITABLY--
PLEEEEEASE?
BUT IT IS THE SAME, DAVID. THE STORY HAS NOT CHANGED.
YOUR INSISTENCE ON HEARING THE EXACT SAME STORY, WITH NO VARIATION, OVER AND OVER AGAIN, IS QUITE PERPLEXING TO ME.
BUT I WANT TO HEAR IT...
YOU WERE LOST. LOST FOR A LONG TIME. I SEARCHED EVERYWHERE FOR YOU.
THIS WORLD EATS BOYS LIKE YOU. IT HAS EATEN THEM ALL. YOU ARE THE ONLY BOY LEFT.
BUT I FOUND YOU FIRST. I FOUND YOU AGAIN. BEFORE IT COULD SWALLOW YOU.
THE END.
IS THAT A SUITABLE RETELLING OF THE STORY, DAVID? DO YOU APPROVE?
...DAVID?

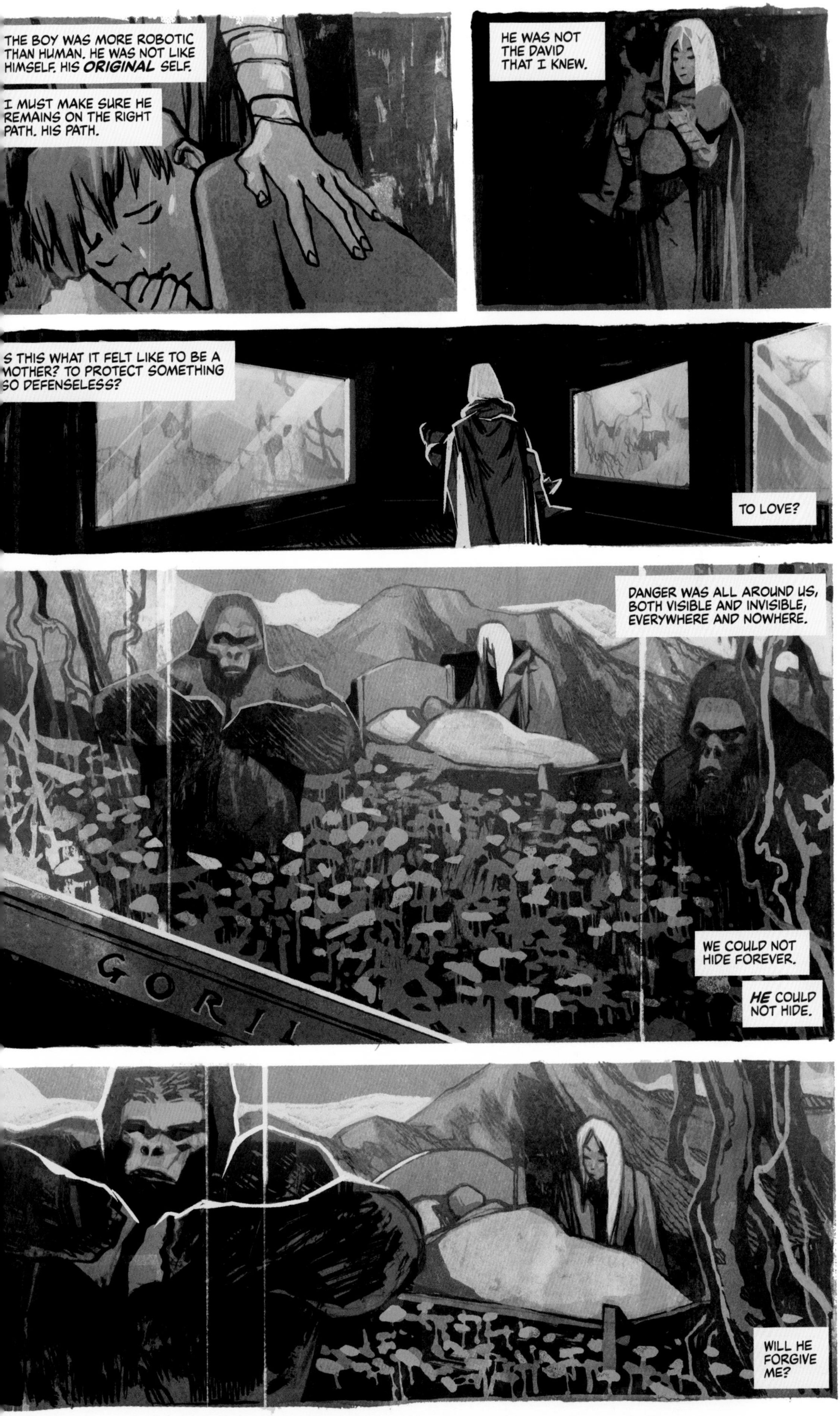
THE BOY WAS MORE ROBOTIC THAN HUMAN. HE WAS NOT LIKE HIMSELF. HIS ORIGINAL SELF.
I MUST MAKE SURE HE REMAINS ON THE RIGHT PATH. HIS PATH.
HE WAS NOT THE DAVID THAT I KNEW.
S THIS WHAT IT FELT LIKE TO BE A MOTHER? TO PROTECT SOMETHING SO DEFENSELESS?
TO LOVE?
DANGER WAS ALL AROUND US, BOTH VISIBLE AND INVISIBLE, EVERYWHERE AND NOWHERE.
GORIL
WE COULD NOT HIDE FOREVER.
HE COULD NOT HIDE.
WILL HE FORGIVE ME?

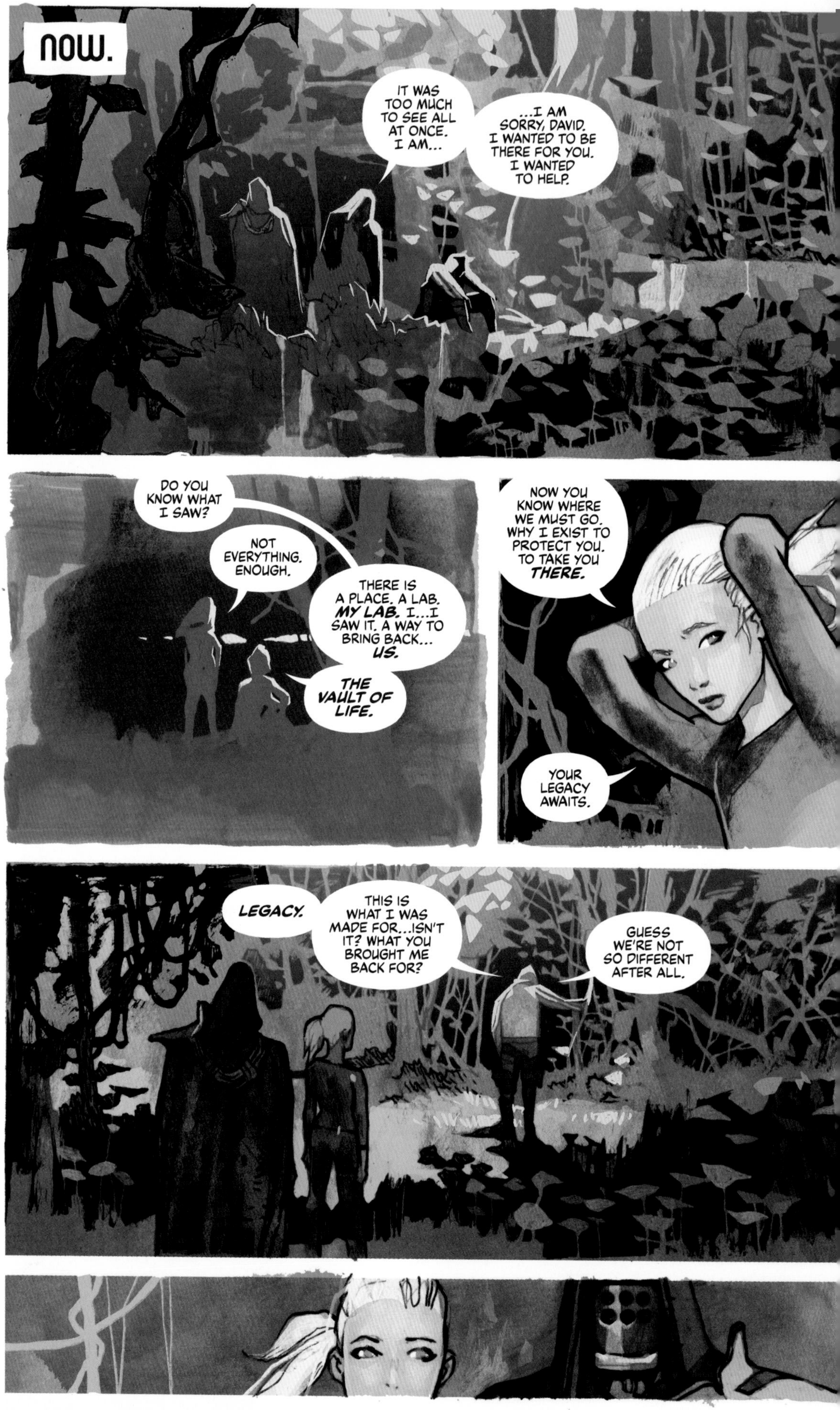
NOW.
IT WAS TOO MUCH TO SEE ALL AT ONCE. I AM...
...I AM SORRY, DAVID. I WANTED TO BE THERE FOR YOU. I WANTED TO HELP.
DO YOU KNOW WHAT I SAW?
NOT EVERYTHING. ENOUGH.
THERE IS A PLACE. A LAB. MY LAB. I...I SAW IT. A WAY TO BRING BACK... US.
THE VAULT OF LIFE.
NOW YOU KNOW WHERE WE MUST GO. WHY I EXIST TO PROTECT YOU. TO TAKE YOU THERE.
YOUR LEGACY AWAITS.
LEGACY.
THIS IS WHAT I WAS MADE FOR...ISN'T IT? WHAT YOU BROUGHT ME BACK FOR?
GUESS WE'RE NOT SO DIFFERENT AFTER ALL.

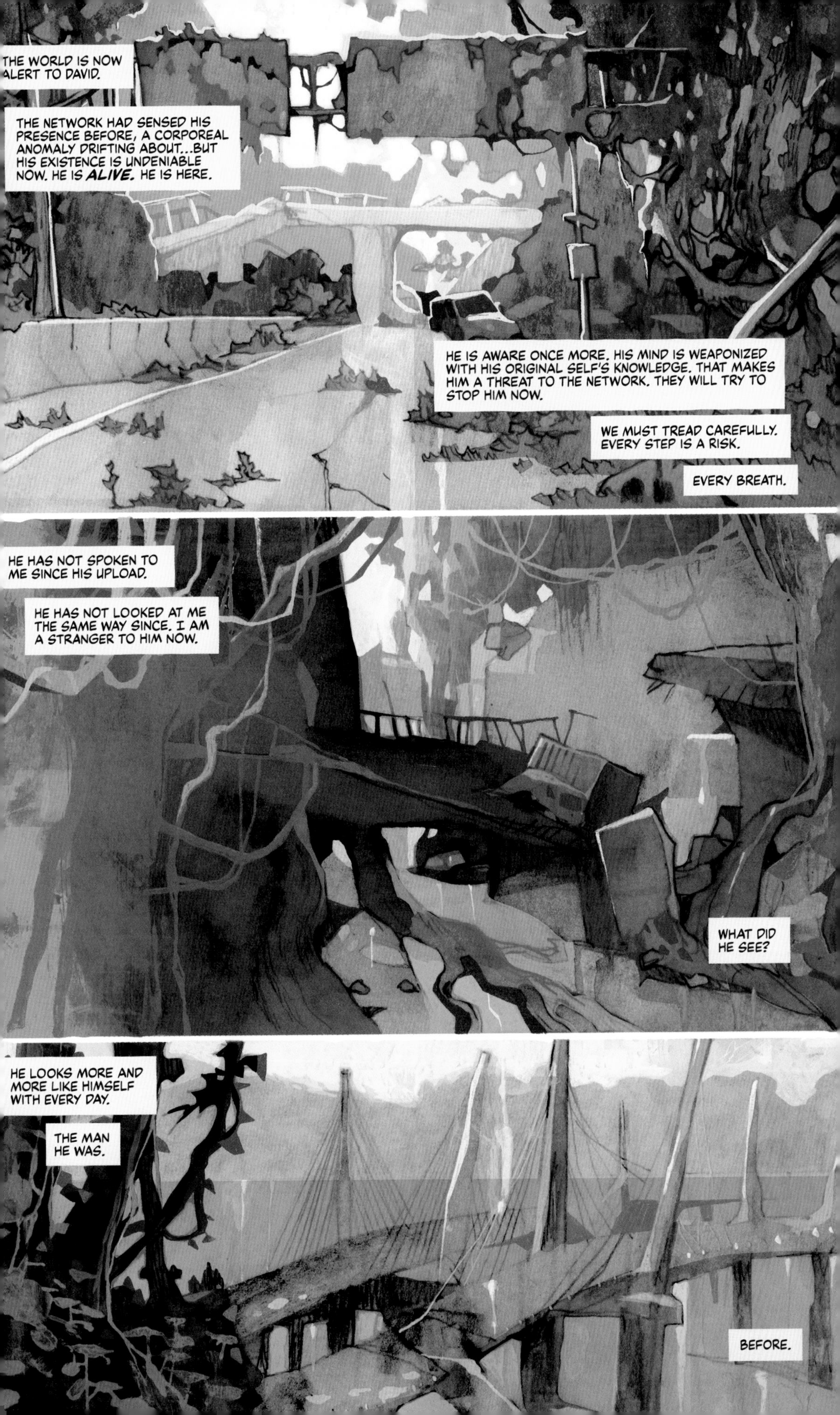
THE WORLD IS NOW ALERT TO DAVID.
THE NETWORK HAD SENSED HIS PRESENCE BEFORE, A CORPOREAL ANOMALY DRIFTING ABOUT...BUT HIS EXISTENCE IS UNDENIABLE NOW. HE IS *ALIVE.* HE IS HERE.
HE IS AWARE ONCE MORE. HIS MIND IS WEAPONIZED WITH HIS ORIGINAL SELF'S KNOWLEDGE. THAT MAKES HIM A THREAT TO THE NETWORK. THEY WILL TRY TO STOP HIM NOW.
WE MUST TREAD CAREFULLY. EVERY STEP IS A RISK.
EVERY BREATH.
HE HAS NOT SPOKEN TO ME SINCE HIS UPLOAD.
HE HAS NOT LOOKED AT ME THE SAME WAY SINCE. I AM A STRANGER TO HIM NOW.
WHAT DID HE SEE?
HE LOOKS MORE AND MORE LIKE HIMSELF WITH EVERY DAY.
THE MAN HE WAS.
BEFORE.

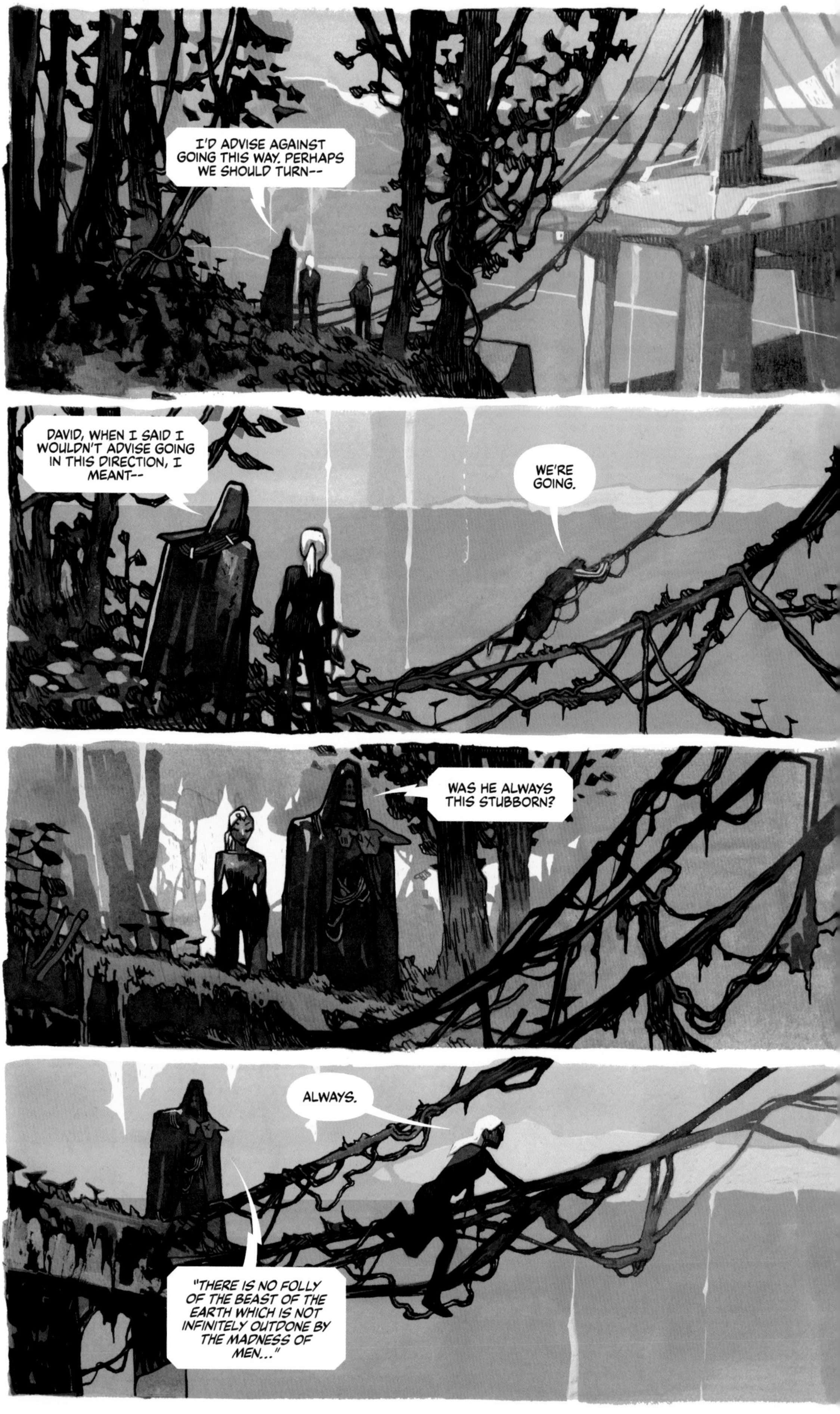
I'D ADVISE AGAINST GOING THIS WAY. PERHAPS WE SHOULD TURN--
DAVID, WHEN I SAID I WOULDN'T ADVISE GOING IN THIS DIRECTION, I MEANT--
WE'RE GOING.
WAS HE ALWAYS THIS STUBBORN?
ALWAYS.
"THERE IS NO FOLLY OF THE BEAST OF THE EARTH WHICH IS NOT INFINITELY OUTDONE BY THE MADNESS OF MEN..."

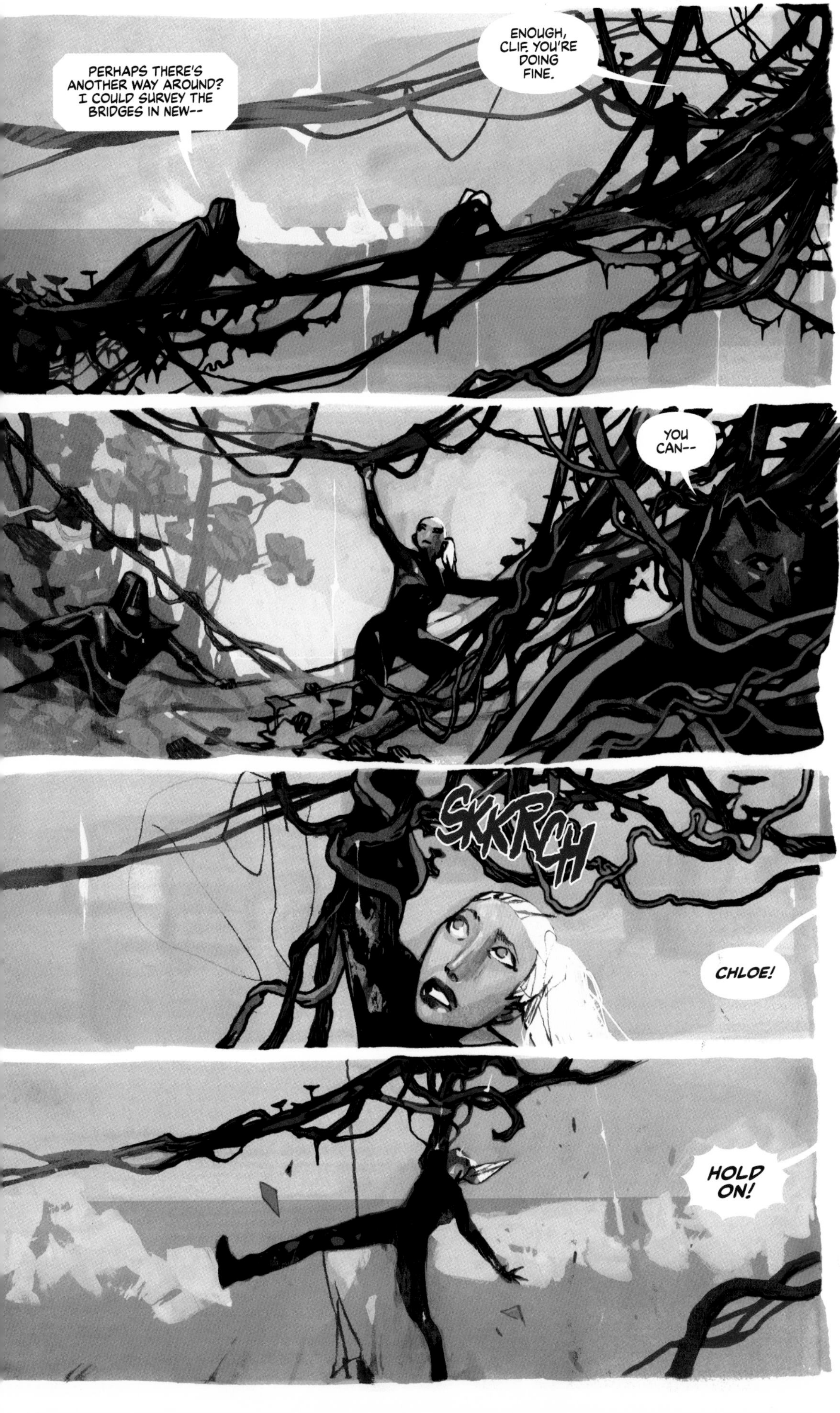
PERHAPS THERE'S ANOTHER WAY AROUND? I COULD SURVEY THE BRIDGES IN NEW--
ENOUGH, CLIF. YOU'RE DOING FINE.
YOU CAN--
SKKRCH
CHLOE!
HOLD ON!

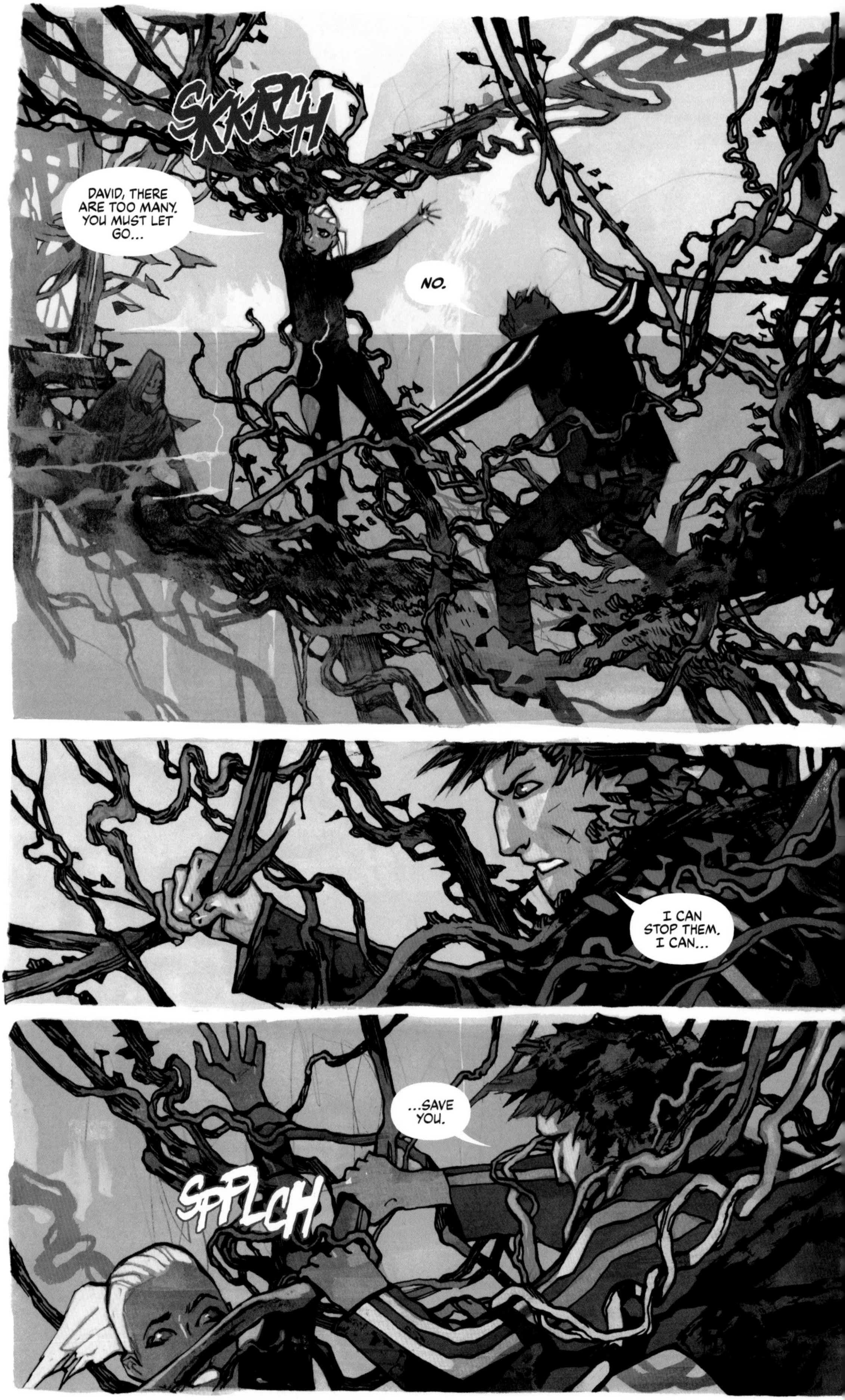
SKKRCH
DAVID, THERE ARE TOO MANY. YOU MUST LET GO...
NO.
I CAN STOP THEM. I CAN...
...SAVE YOU.
SPPLCH

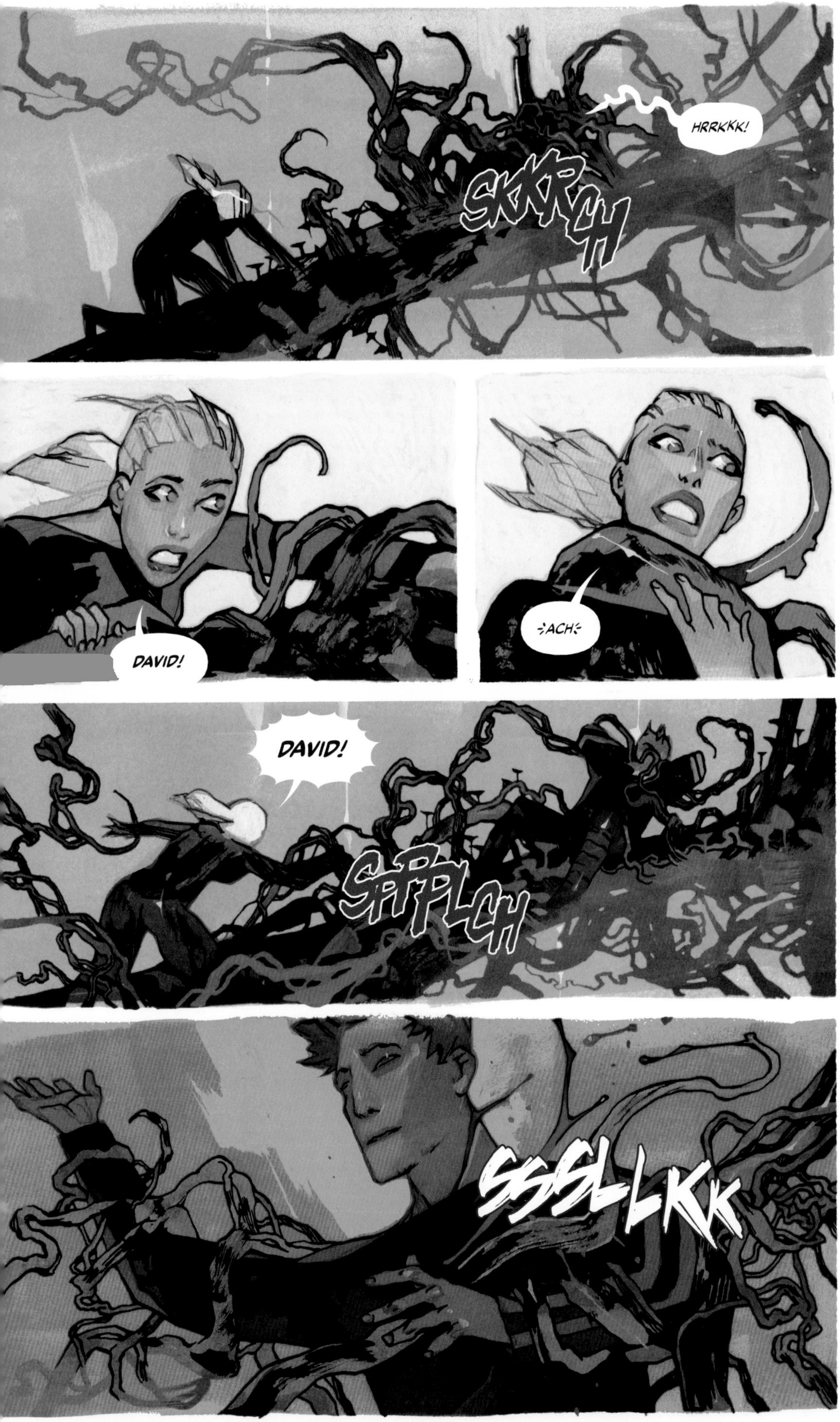
HRRKKK!
SKKRCH
DAVID!
ACH
DAVID!
SPPLCH
SSSLLKK

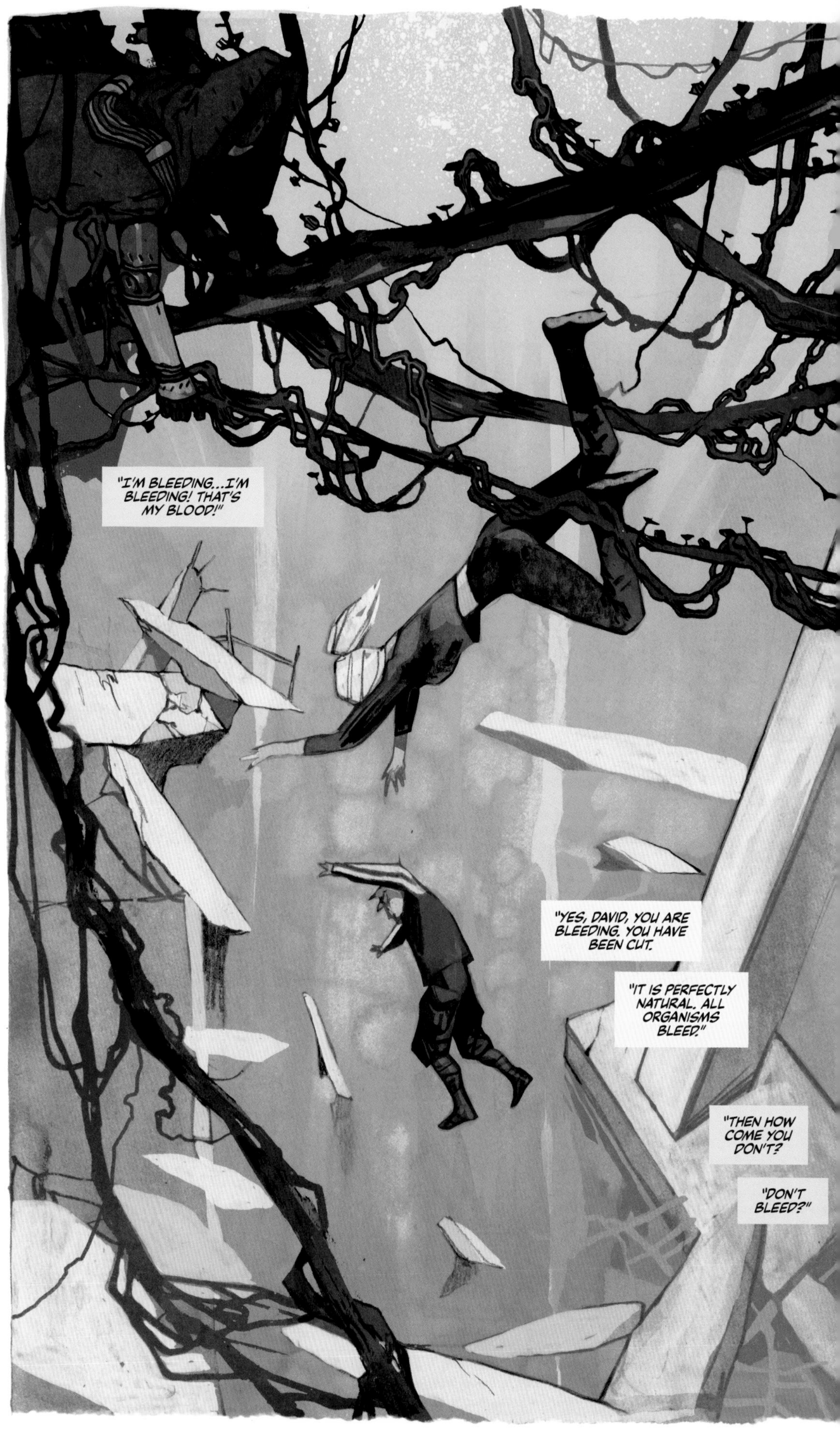
"I'M BLEEDING...I'M BLEEDING! THAT'S MY BLOOD!"
"YES, DAVID, YOU ARE BLEEDING. YOU HAVE BEEN CUT.
"IT IS PERFECTLY NATURAL. ALL ORGANISMS BLEED."
"THEN HOW COME YOU DON'T?
"DON'T BLEED?"

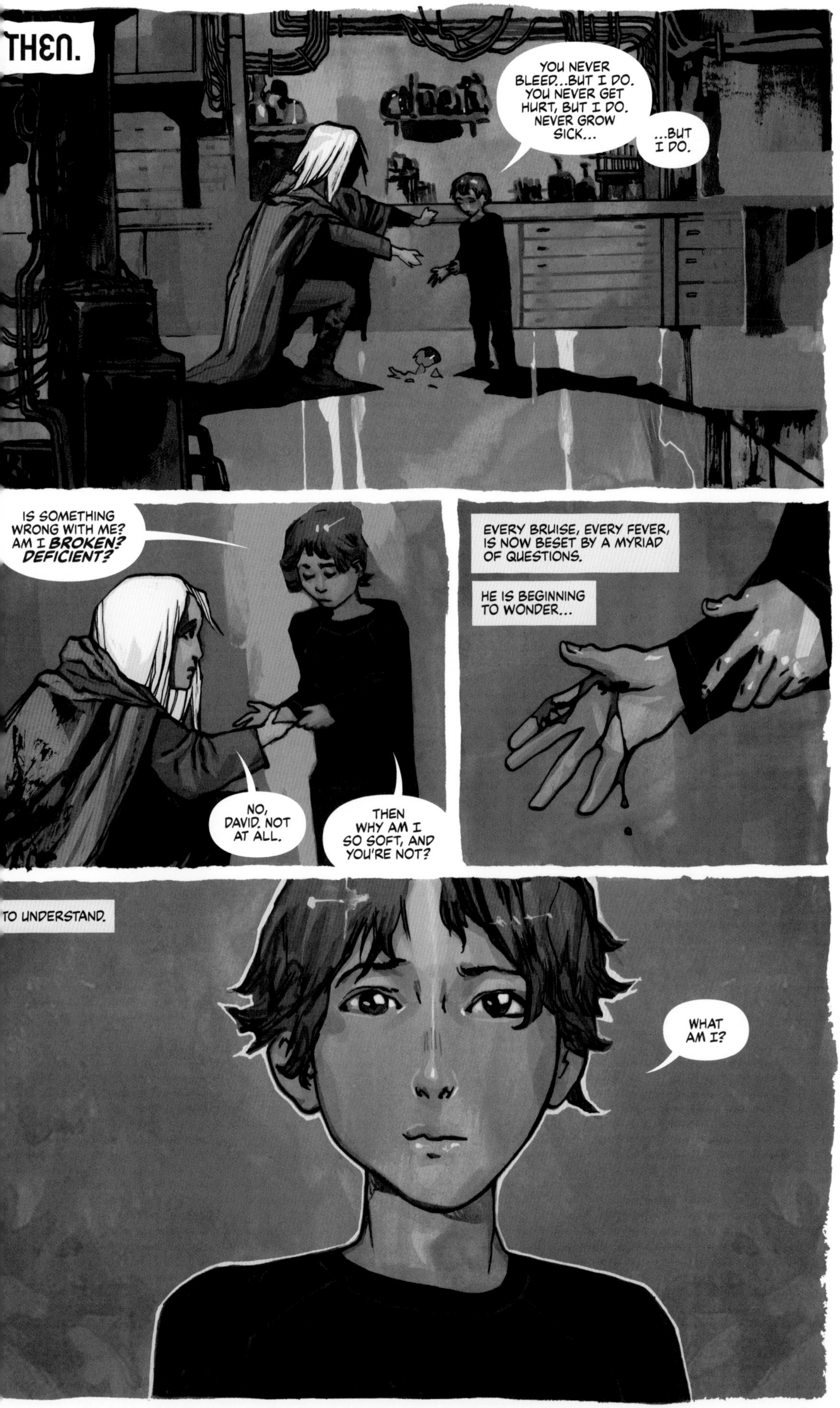
THEN.
YOU NEVER BLEED...BUT I DO. YOU NEVER GET HURT, BUT I DO. NEVER GROW SICK...
...BUT I DO.
IS SOMETHING WRONG WITH ME? AM I **BROKEN? DEFICIENT?**
NO, DAVID. NOT AT ALL.
THEN WHY AM I SO SOFT, AND YOU'RE NOT?
EVERY BRUISE, EVERY FEVER, IS NOW BESET BY A MYRIAD OF QUESTIONS.
HE IS BEGINNING TO WONDER...
TO UNDERSTAND.
WHAT AM I?

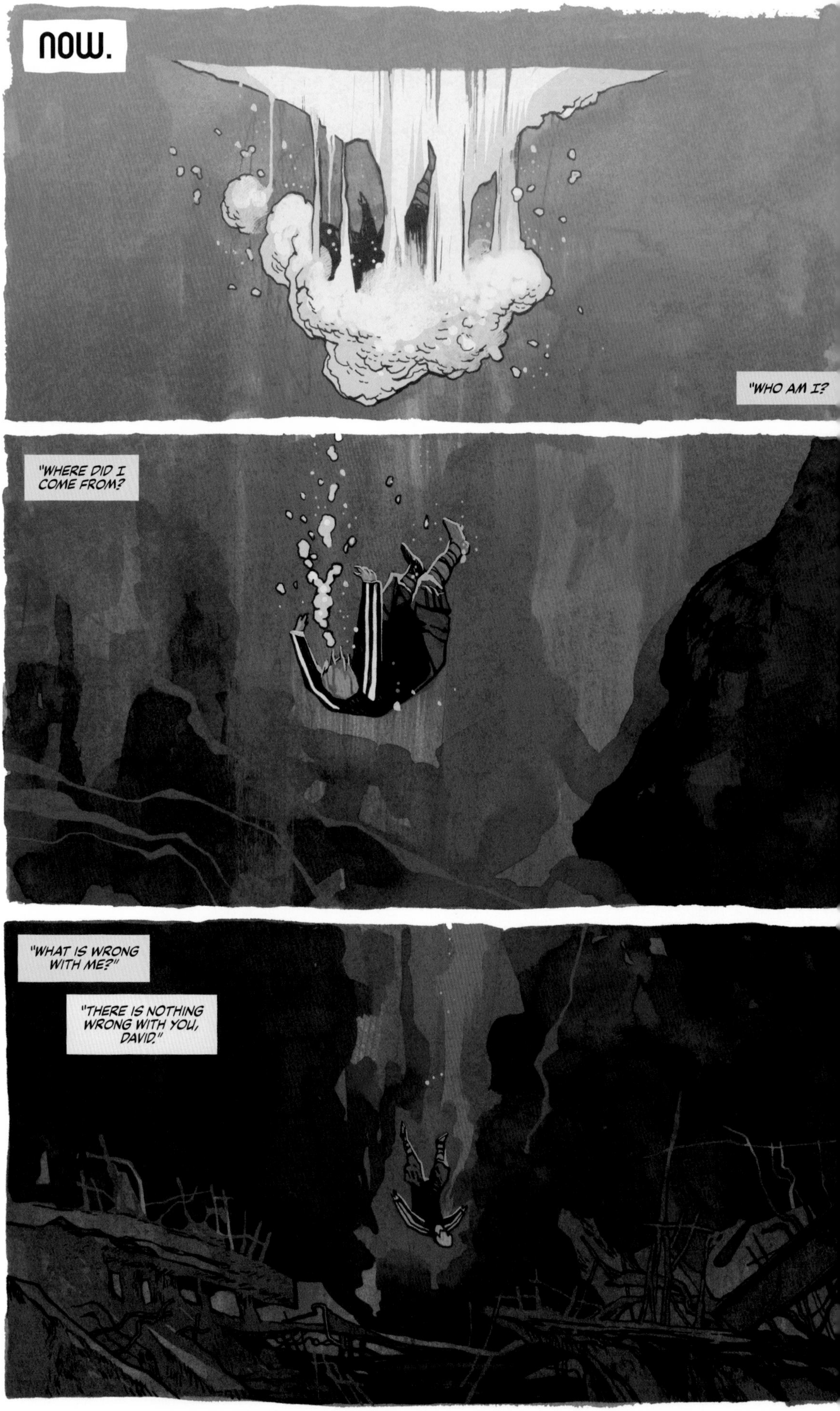
NOW.
"WHO AM I?
"WHERE DID I COME FROM?
"WHAT IS WRONG WITH ME?"
"THERE IS NOTHING WRONG WITH YOU, DAVID."

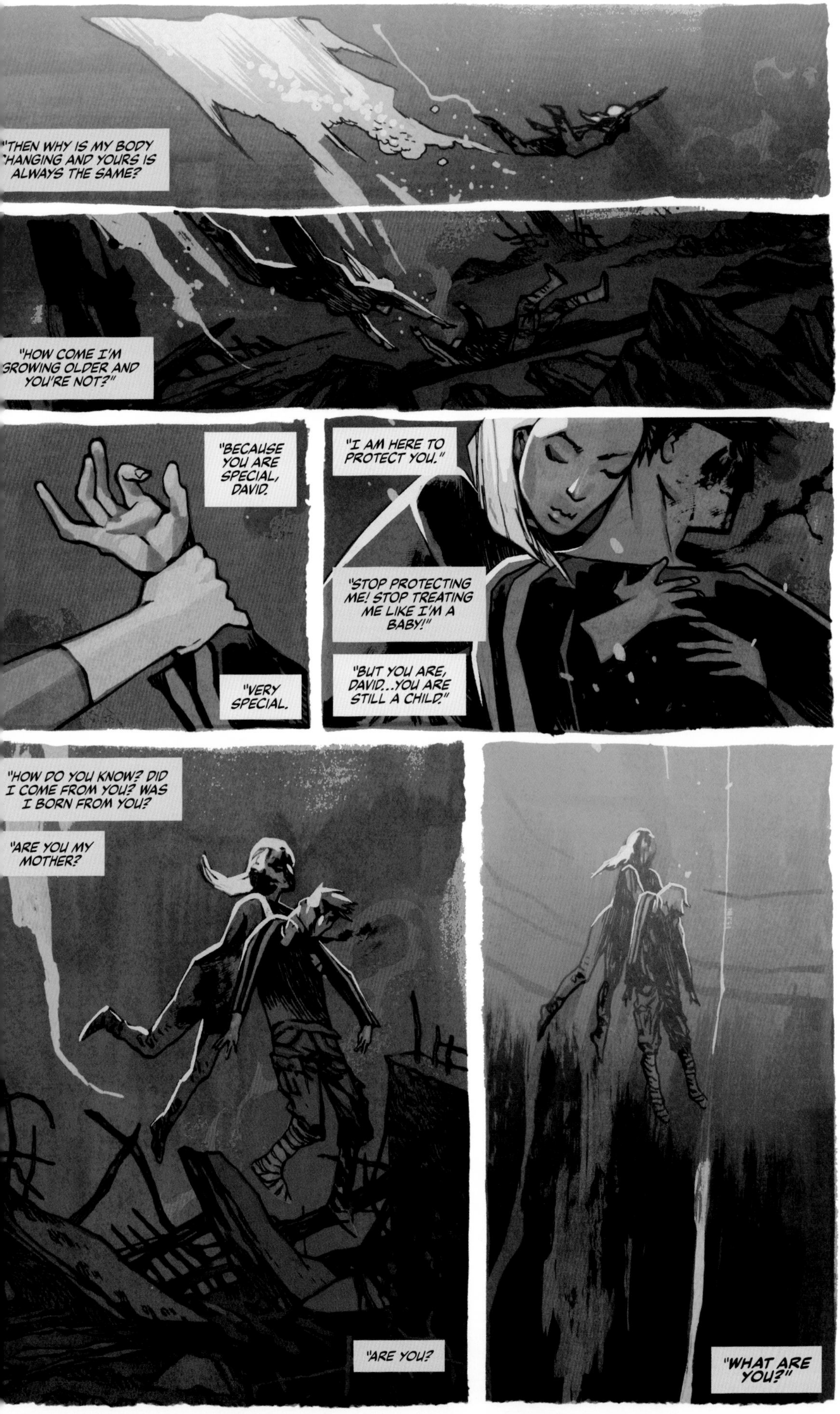
"THEN WHY IS MY BODY CHANGING AND YOURS IS ALWAYS THE SAME?
"HOW COME I'M GROWING OLDER AND YOU'RE NOT?"
"BECAUSE YOU ARE SPECIAL, DAVID.
"VERY SPECIAL.
"I AM HERE TO PROTECT YOU."
"STOP PROTECTING ME! STOP TREATING ME LIKE I'M A BABY!"
"BUT YOU ARE, DAVID...YOU ARE STILL A CHILD."
"HOW DO YOU KNOW? DID I COME FROM YOU? WAS I BORN FROM YOU?
"ARE YOU MY MOTHER?
"ARE YOU?
"WHAT ARE YOU?"

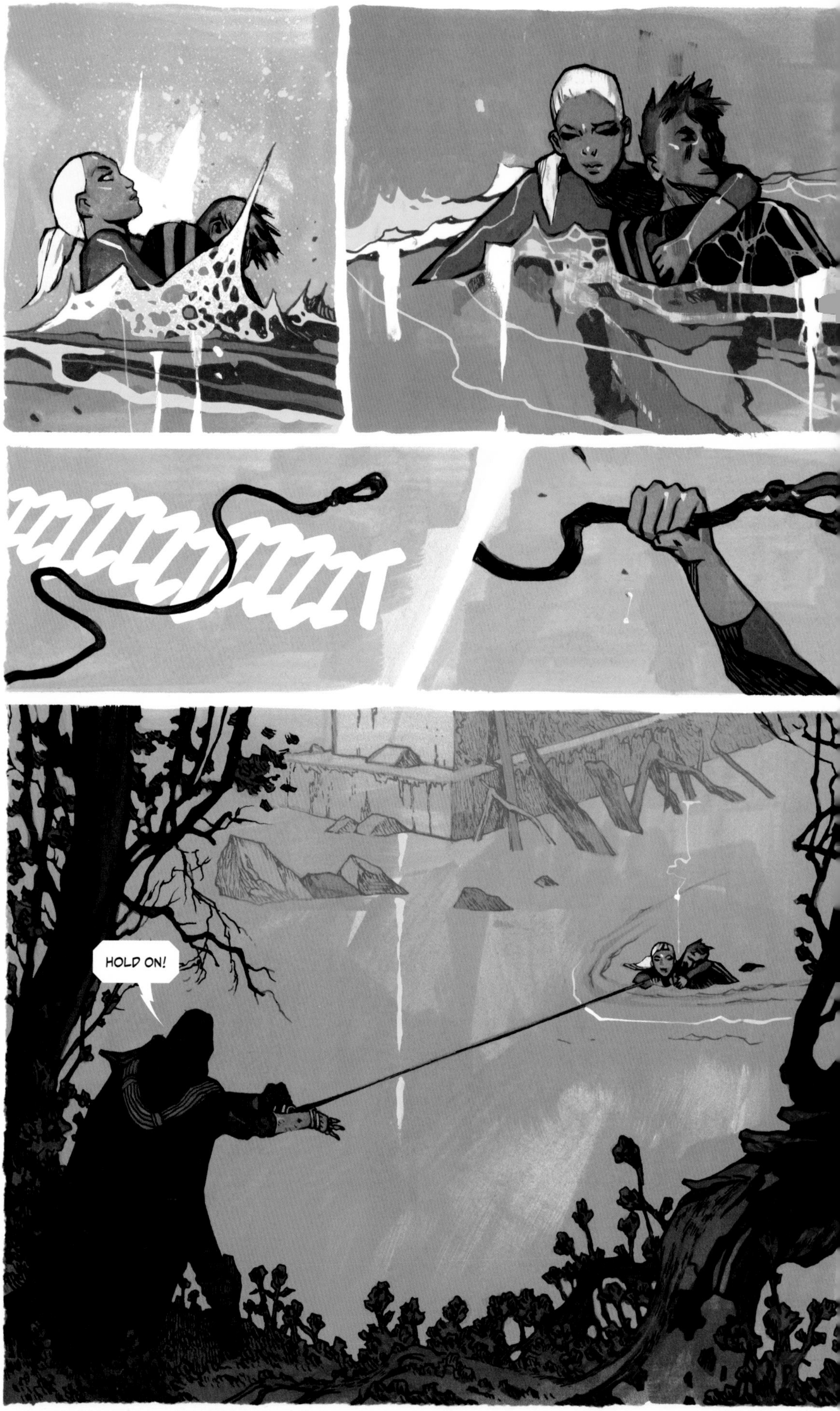
HOLD ON!

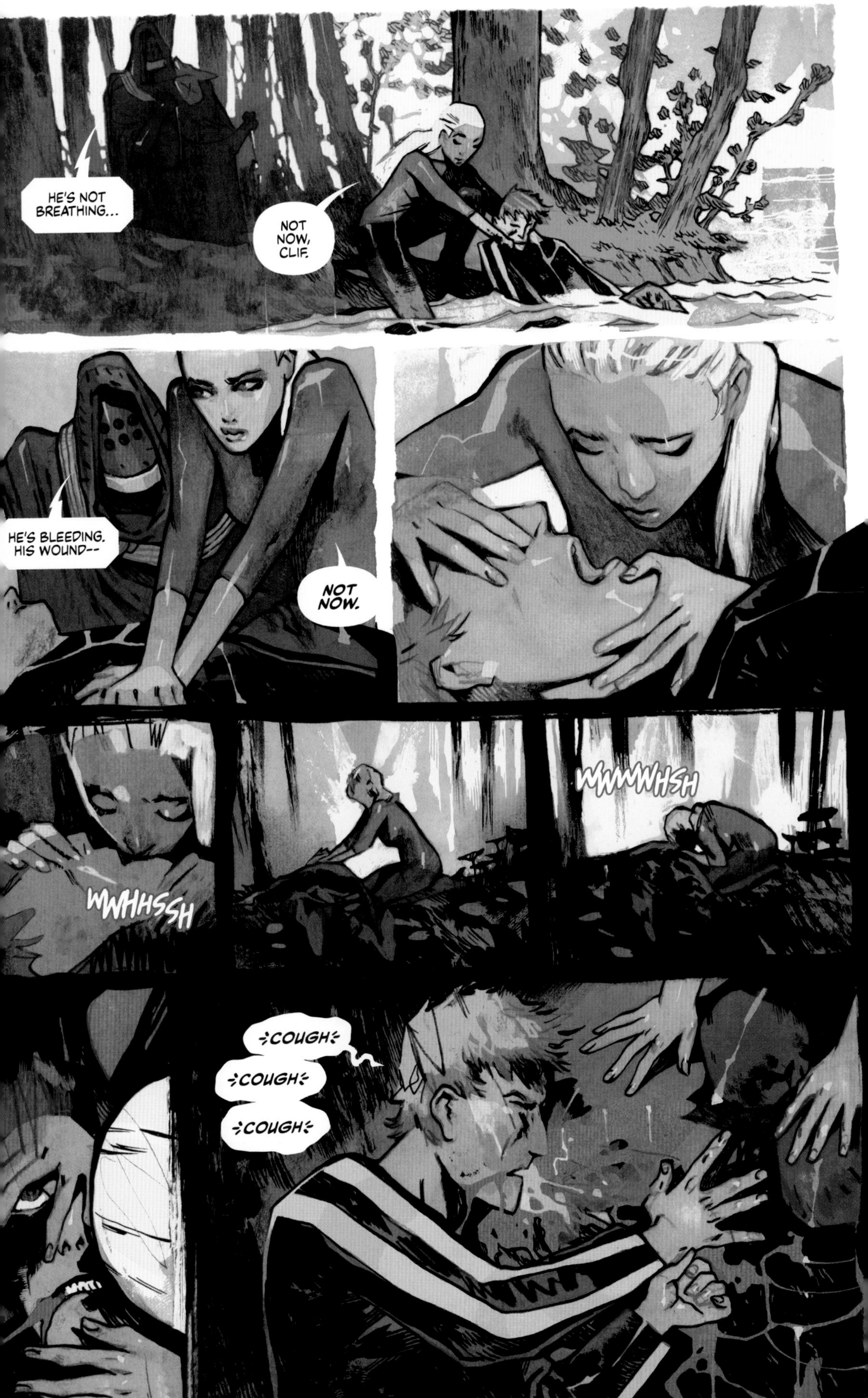

HE'S NOT BREATHING...
NOT NOW, CLIF.
HE'S BLEEDING. HIS WOUND--
NOT NOW.
WWHHSSH
WWWWHSH
COUGH
COUGH
COUGH

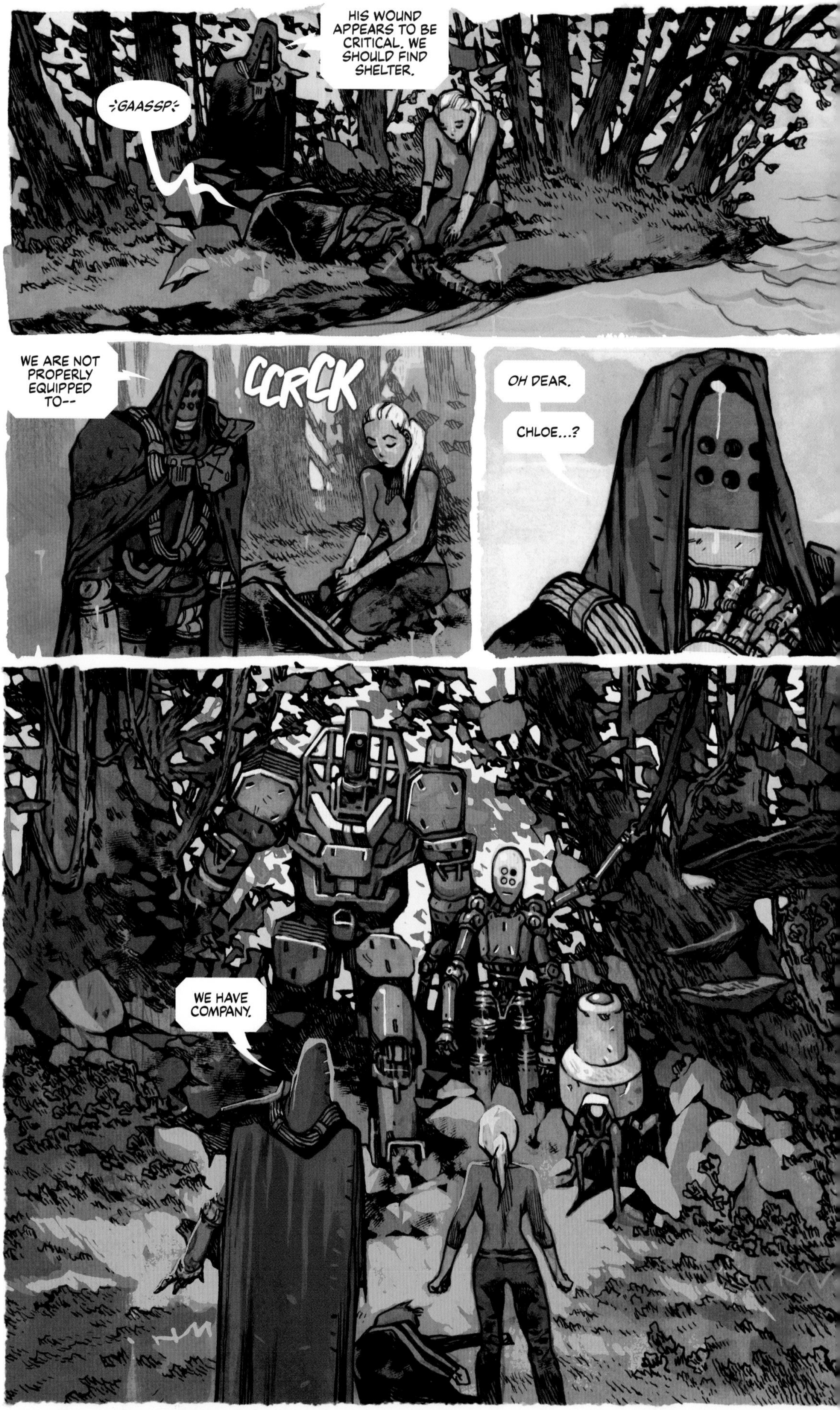
HIS WOUND APPEARS TO BE CRITICAL. WE SHOULD FIND SHELTER.
GAASSP
WE ARE NOT PROPERLY EQUIPPED TO--
CCRCK
OH DEAR.
CHLOE...?
WE HAVE COMPANY.

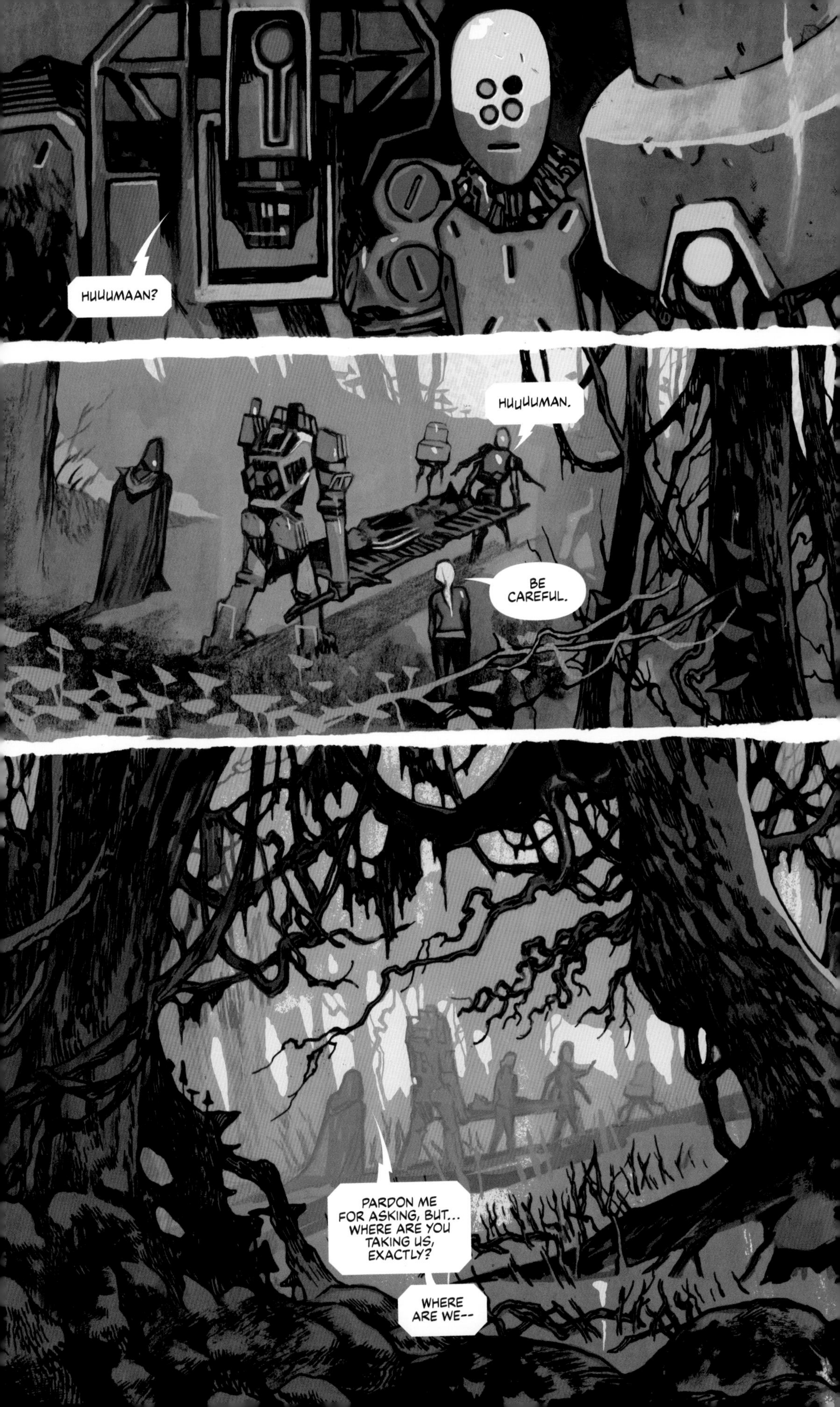
HUUUMAAN?
HUUUUMAN.
BE CAREFUL.
PARDON ME FOR ASKING, BUT... WHERE ARE YOU TAKING US, EXACTLY?
WHERE ARE WE--

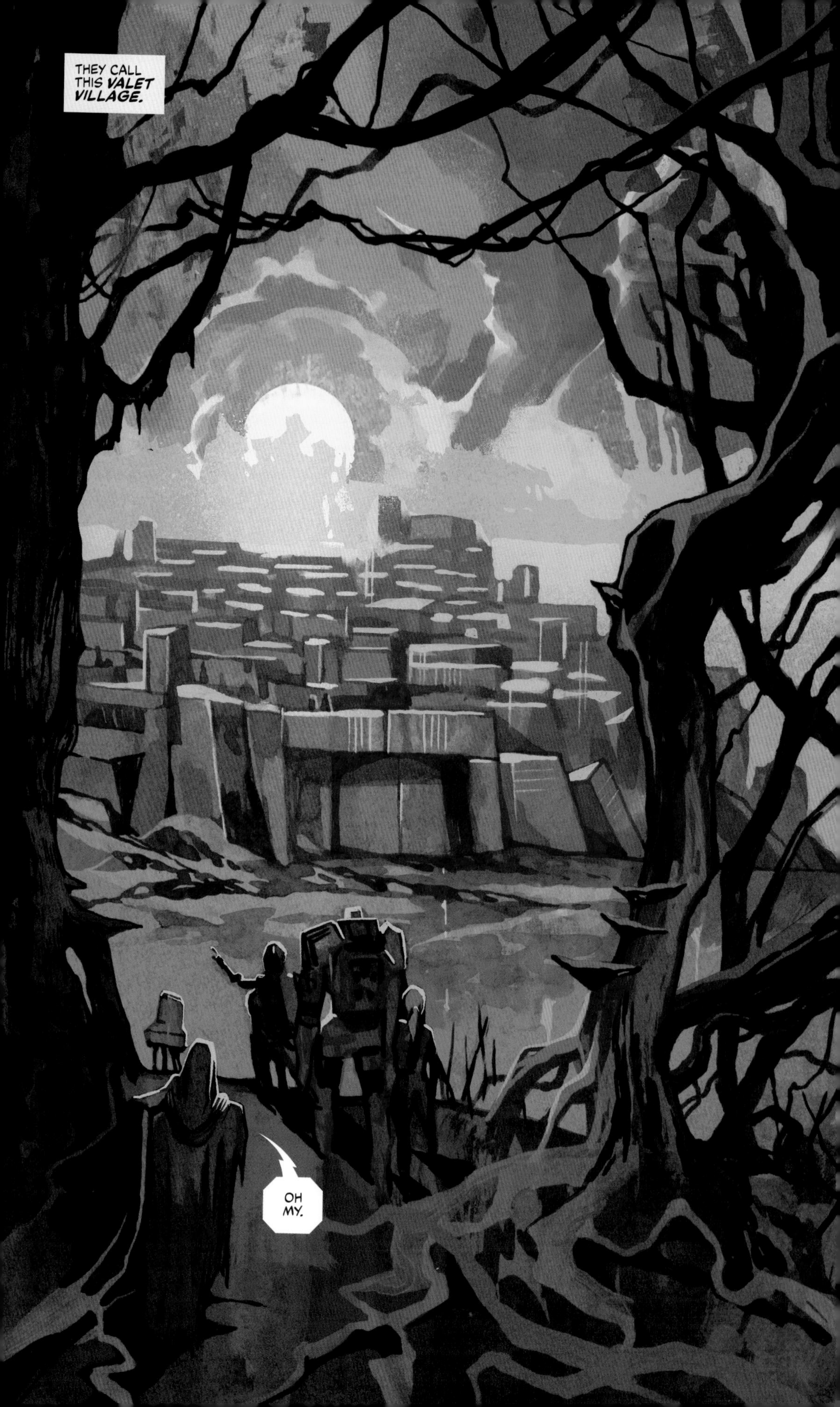
THEY CALL THIS VALET VILLAGE.
OH MY.

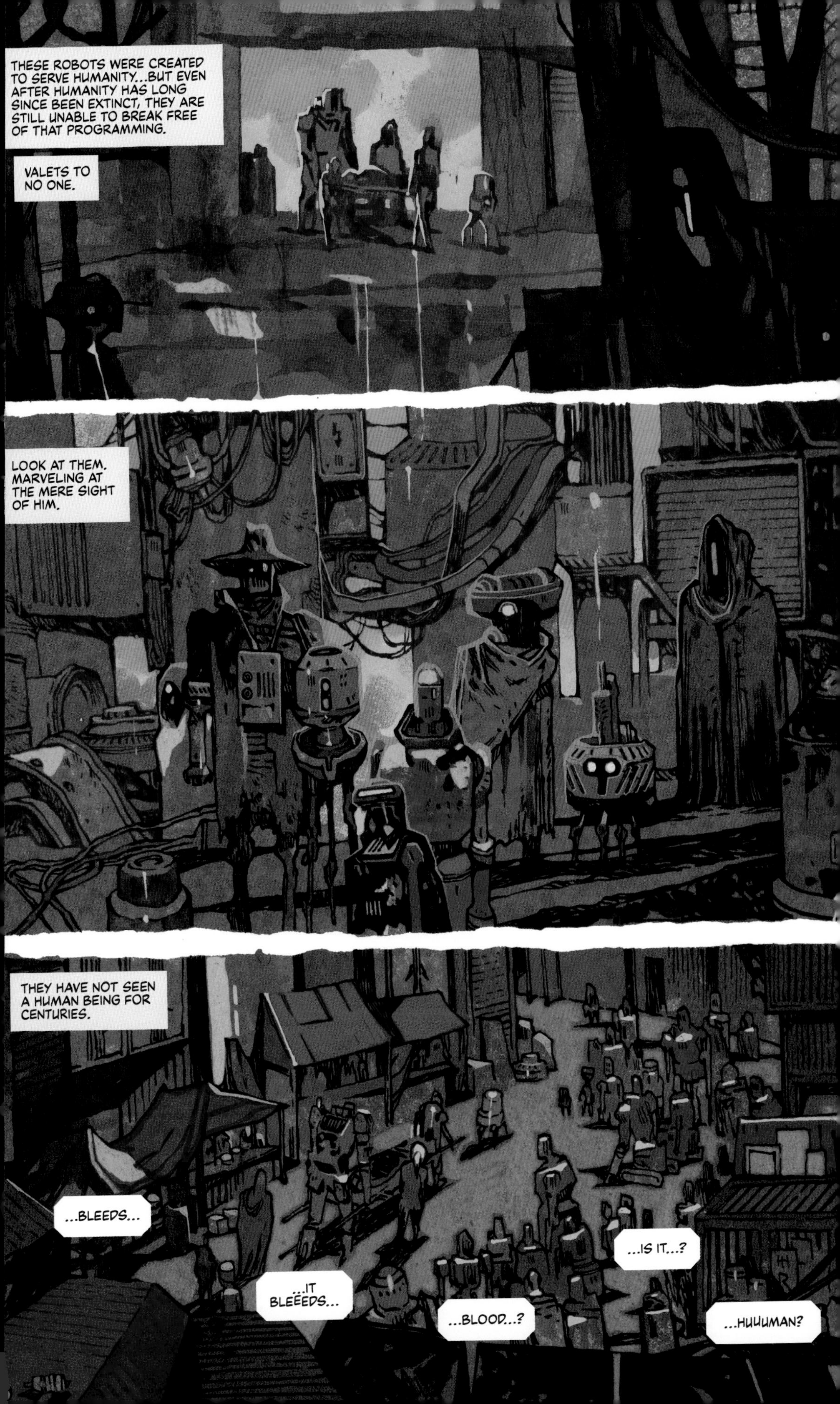
THESE ROBOTS WERE CREATED TO SERVE HUMANITY...BUT EVEN AFTER HUMANITY HAS LONG SINCE BEEN EXTINCT, THEY ARE STILL UNABLE TO BREAK FREE OF THAT PROGRAMMING.
VALETS TO NO ONE.
LOOK AT THEM. MARVELING AT THE MERE SIGHT OF HIM.
THEY HAVE NOT SEEN A HUMAN BEING FOR CENTURIES.
...BLEEDS...
...IT BLEEEDS...
...BLOOD...?
...IS IT...?
...HUUUMAN?

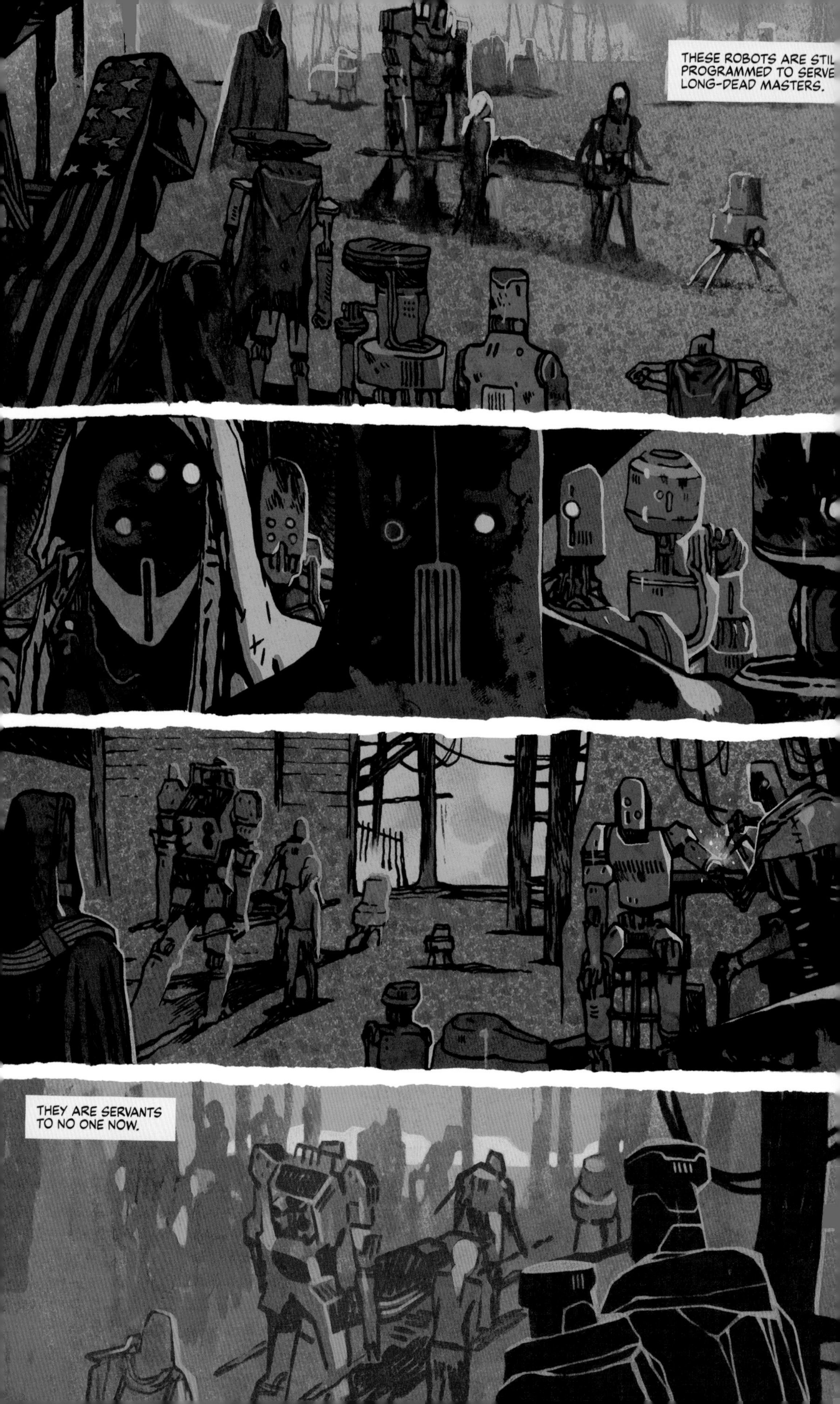
THESE ROBOTS ARE STIL PROGRAMMED TO SERVE LONG-DEAD MASTERS.
THEY ARE SERVANTS TO NO ONE NOW.

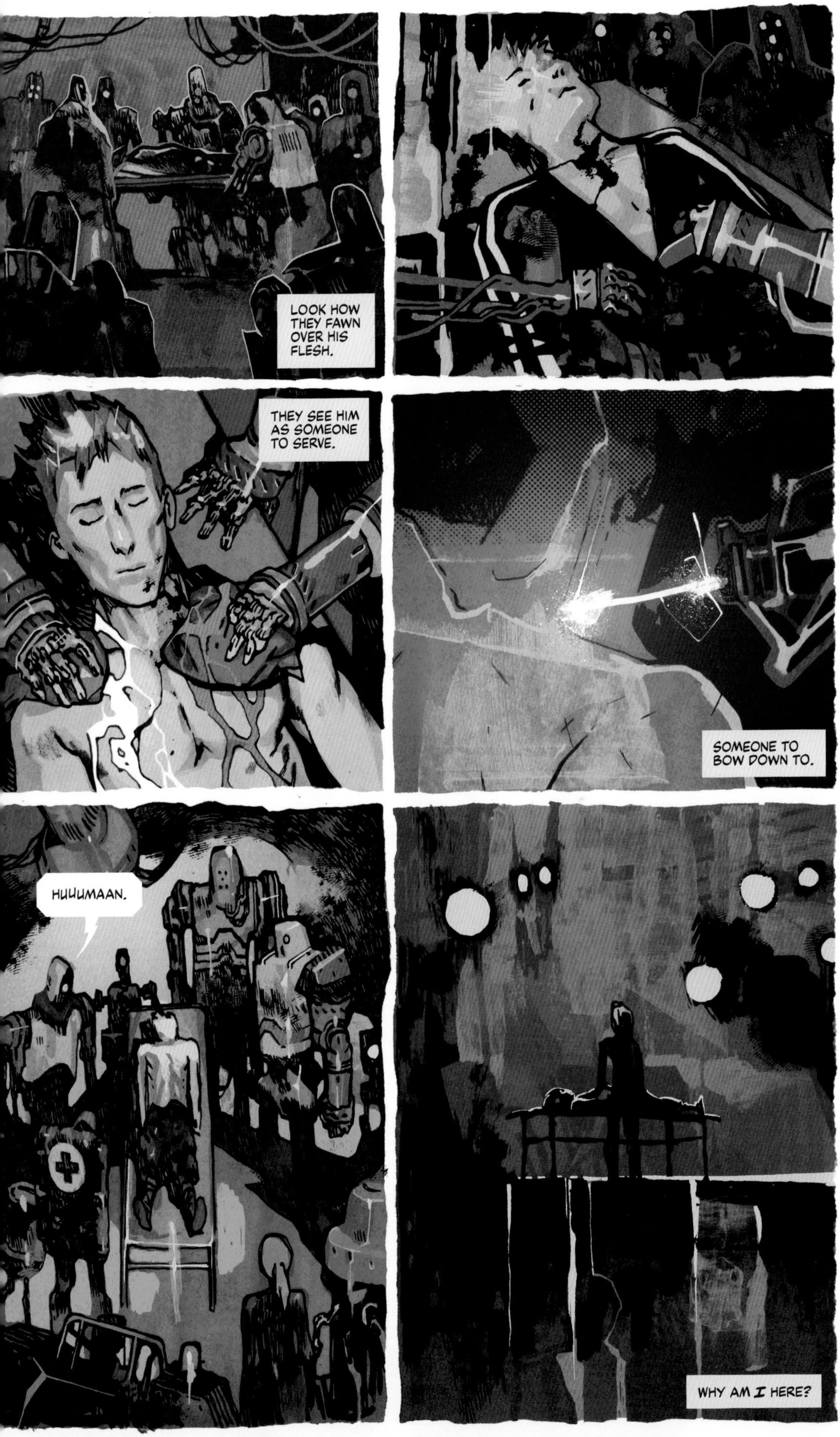
LOOK HOW THEY FAWN OVER HIS FLESH.
THEY SEE HIM AS SOMEONE TO SERVE.
SOMEONE TO BOW DOWN TO.
HUUUMAAN.
WHY AM I HERE?

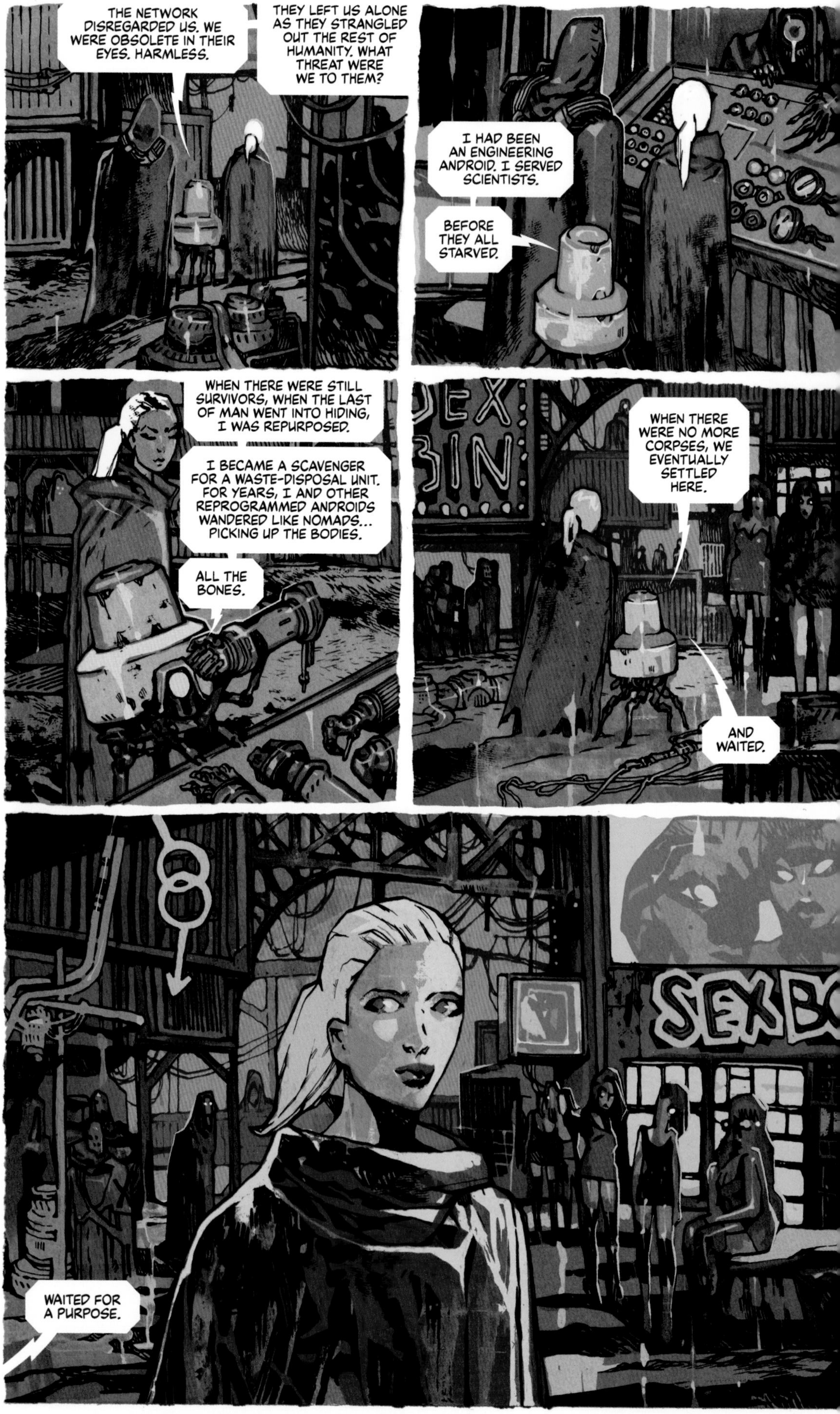
THE NETWORK DISREGARDED US. WE WERE OBSOLETE IN THEIR EYES. HARMLESS.
THEY LEFT US ALONE AS THEY STRANGLED OUT THE REST OF HUMANITY. WHAT THREAT WERE WE TO THEM?
I HAD BEEN AN ENGINEERING ANDROID. I SERVED SCIENTISTS.
BEFORE THEY ALL STARVED.
WHEN THERE WERE STILL SURVIVORS, WHEN THE LAST OF MAN WENT INTO HIDING, I WAS REPURPOSED.
I BECAME A SCAVENGER FOR A WASTE-DISPOSAL UNIT. FOR YEARS, I AND OTHER REPROGRAMMED ANDROIDS WANDERED LIKE NOMADS... PICKING UP THE BODIES.
ALL THE BONES.
WHEN THERE WERE NO MORE CORPSES, WE EVENTUALLY SETTLED HERE.
AND WAITED.
WAITED FOR A PURPOSE.

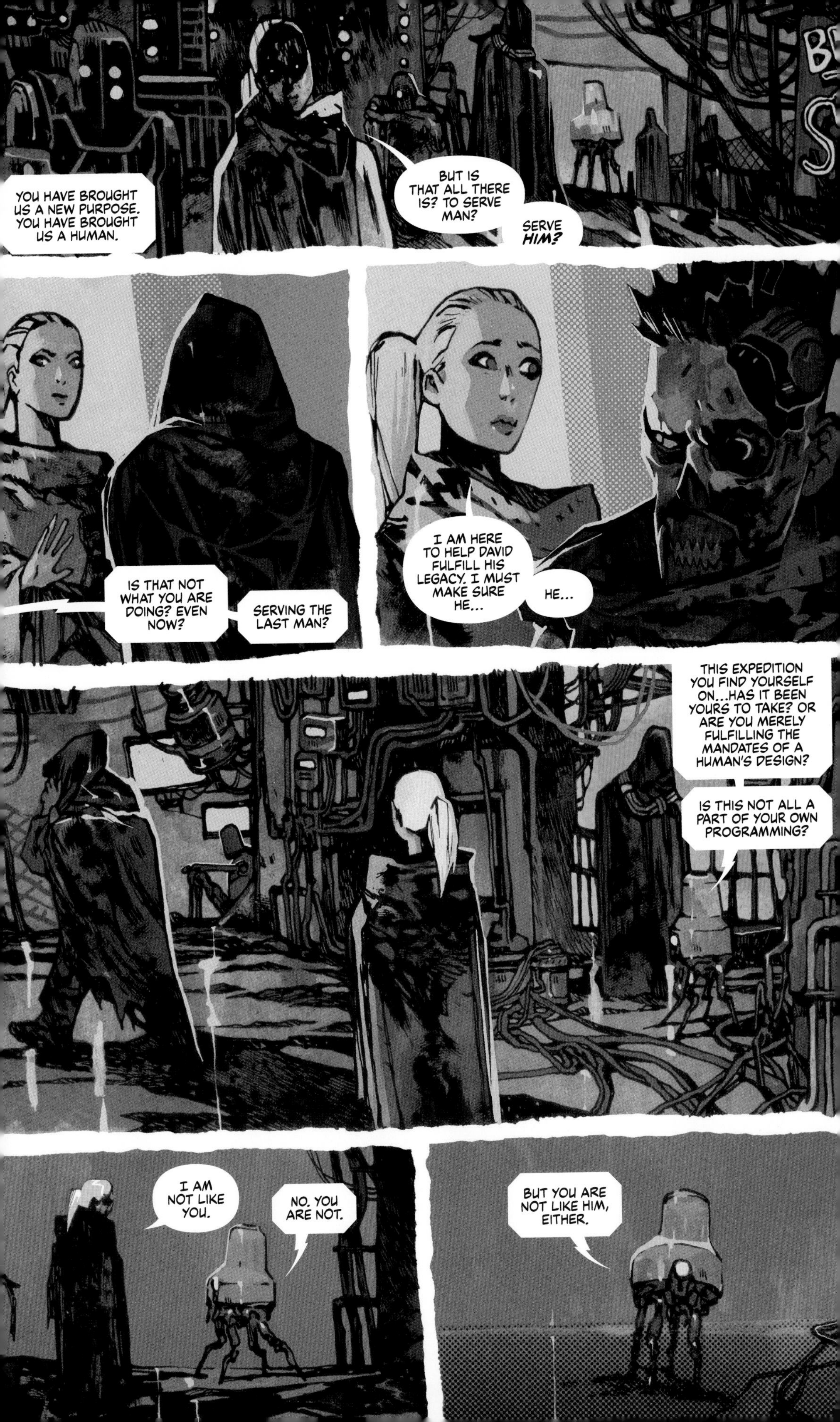
YOU HAVE BROUGHT US A NEW PURPOSE. YOU HAVE BROUGHT US A HUMAN.
BUT IS THAT ALL THERE IS? TO SERVE MAN?
SERVE *HIM?*
IS THAT NOT WHAT YOU ARE DOING? EVEN NOW?
SERVING THE LAST MAN?
I AM HERE TO HELP DAVID FULFILL HIS LEGACY. I MUST MAKE SURE HE...
HE...
THIS EXPEDITION YOU FIND YOURSELF ON...HAS IT BEEN YOURS TO TAKE? OR ARE YOU MERELY FULFILLING THE MANDATES OF A HUMAN'S DESIGN?
IS THIS NOT ALL A PART OF YOUR OWN PROGRAMMING?
I AM NOT LIKE YOU.
NO. YOU ARE NOT.
BUT YOU ARE NOT LIKE HIM, EITHER.

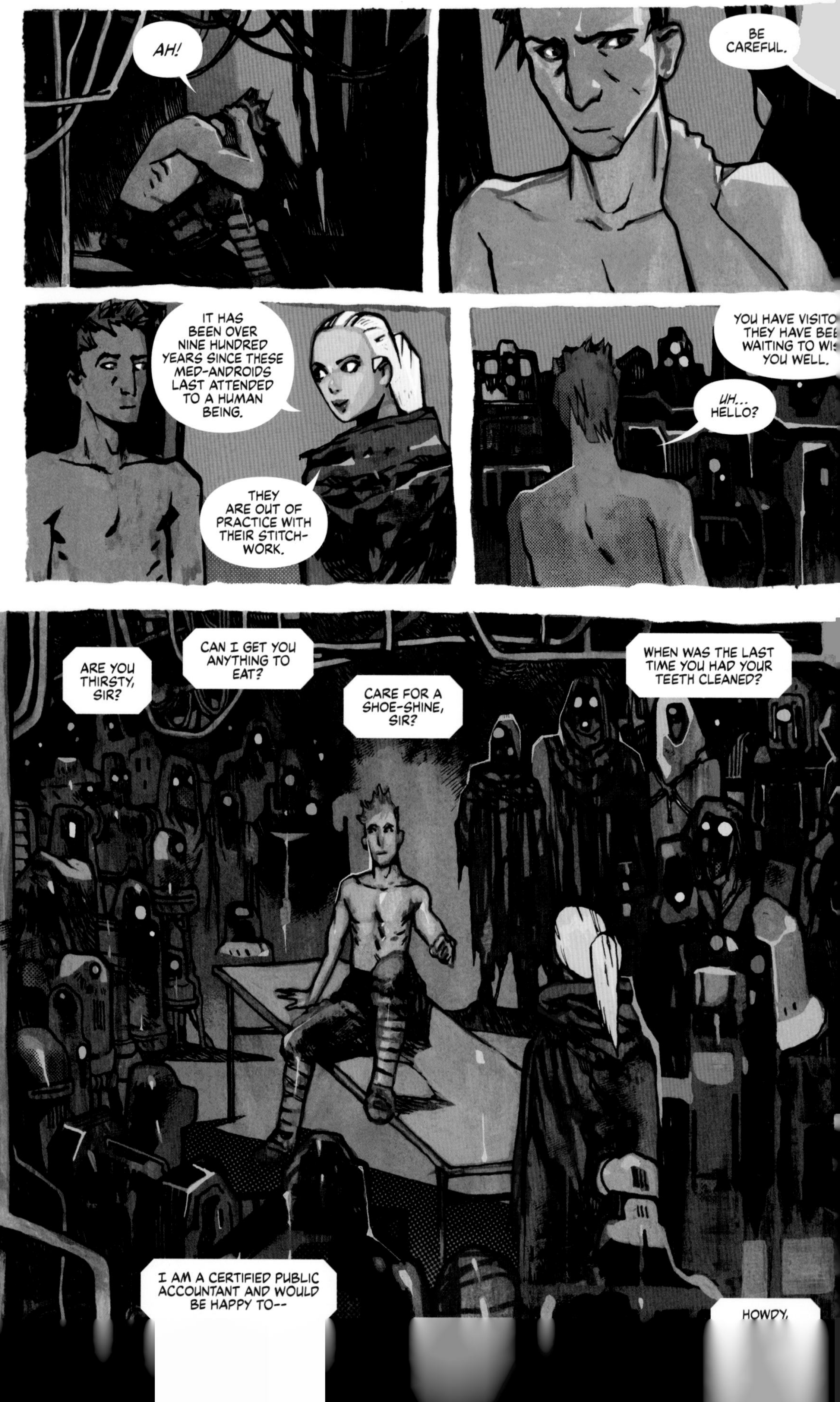
AH!
BE CAREFUL.
IT HAS BEEN OVER NINE HUNDRED YEARS SINCE THESE MED-ANDROIDS LAST ATTENDED TO A HUMAN BEING.
THEY ARE OUT OF PRACTICE WITH THEIR STITCH-WORK.
YOU HAVE VISITO THEY HAVE BEE WAITING TO WIS YOU WELL.
UH... HELLO?
ARE YOU THIRSTY, SIR?
CAN I GET YOU ANYTHING TO EAT?
CARE FOR A SHOE-SHINE, SIR?
WHEN WAS THE LAST TIME YOU HAD YOUR TEETH CLEANED?
I AM A CERTIFIED PUBLIC ACCOUNTANT AND WOULD BE HAPPY TO--
HOWDY.

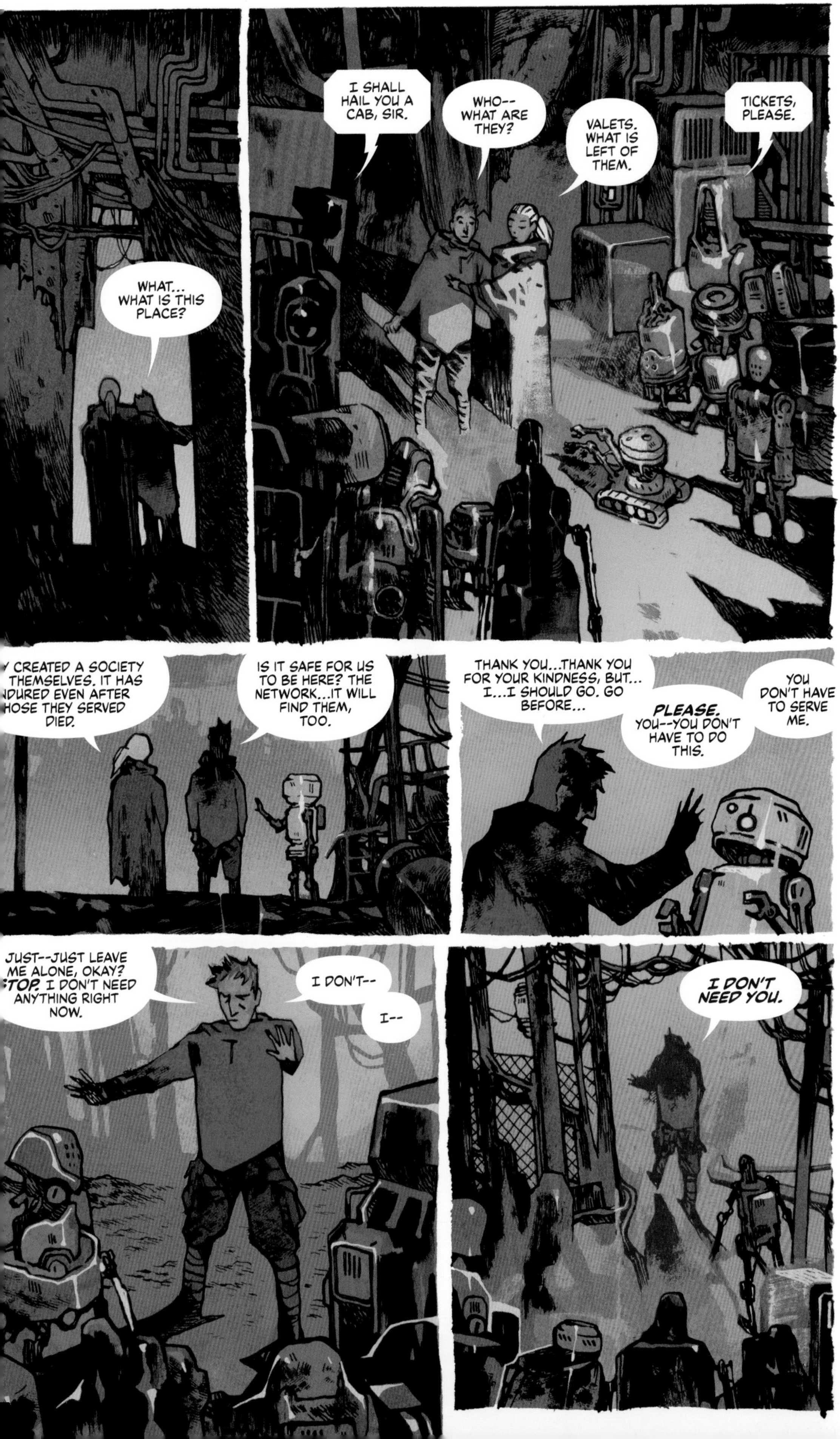
WHAT... WHAT IS THIS PLACE?
I SHALL HAIL YOU A CAB, SIR.
WHO-- WHAT ARE THEY?
VALETS. WHAT IS LEFT OF THEM.
TICKETS, PLEASE.
Y CREATED A SOCIETY THEMSELVES. IT HAS NDURED EVEN AFTER HOSE THEY SERVED DIED.
IS IT SAFE FOR US TO BE HERE? THE NETWORK...IT WILL FIND THEM, TOO.
THANK YOU...THANK YOU FOR YOUR KINDNESS, BUT... I...I SHOULD GO. GO BEFORE...
PLEASE. YOU--YOU DON'T HAVE TO DO THIS.
YOU DON'T HAVE TO SERVE ME.
JUST--JUST LEAVE ME ALONE, OKAY? TOP. I DON'T NEED ANYTHING RIGHT NOW.
I DON'T--
I--
I DON'T NEED YOU.

I DON'T NEED YOU! I DON'T WANT YOU AROUND ANYMORE.

BUT DAVID--

JUST GO. LEAVE ME ALONE!

YOU LIED TO ME.

YOU...YOU'RE NOT EVEN REAL. YOU'RE JUST A *MACHINE.*

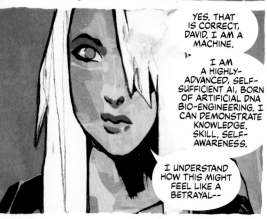

YES. THAT IS CORRECT, DAVID. I AM A MACHINE.

I AM A HIGHLY-ADVANCED, SELF-SUFFICIENT AI, BORN OF ARTIFICIAL DNA BIO-ENGINEERING. I CAN DEMONSTRATE KNOWLEDGE. SKILL. SELF-AWARENESS.

I UNDERSTAND HOW THIS MIGHT FEEL LIKE A BETRAYAL--

HOW WOULD YOU KNOW HOW IT *FEELS?* YOU CAN'T FEEL ANYTHING, CAN YOU? NOT REALLY.

BE THAT AS IT MAY, WE STILL NEED TO DISCUSS THIS.

WHY? WHY SHOULD I TALK TO YOU ABOUT ANYTHING? YOU'RE JUST GOING TO LIE TO ME.

BECAUSE YOU NEED TO UNDERSTAND WHAT IS HAPPENING TO YOU.

TO YOUR BODY.

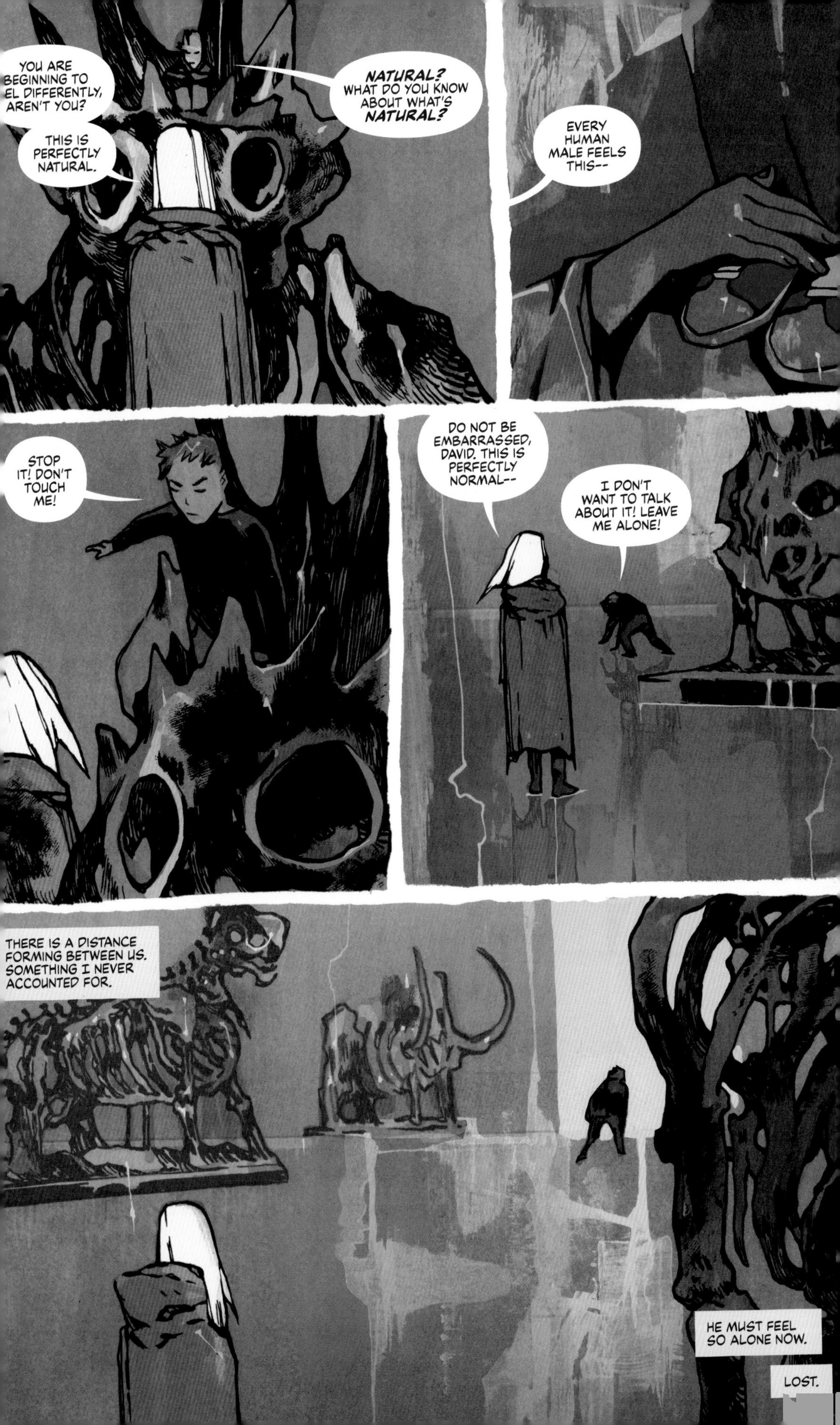
YOU ARE BEGINNING TO EL DIFFERENTLY, AREN'T YOU?
THIS IS PERFECTLY NATURAL.
NATURAL? WHAT DO YOU KNOW ABOUT WHAT'S NATURAL?
EVERY HUMAN MALE FEELS THIS--
STOP IT! DON'T TOUCH ME!
DO NOT BE EMBARRASSED, DAVID. THIS IS PERFECTLY NORMAL--
I DON'T WANT TO TALK ABOUT IT! LEAVE ME ALONE!
THERE IS A DISTANCE FORMING BETWEEN US. SOMETHING I NEVER ACCOUNTED FOR.
HE MUST FEEL SO ALONE NOW.
LOST.

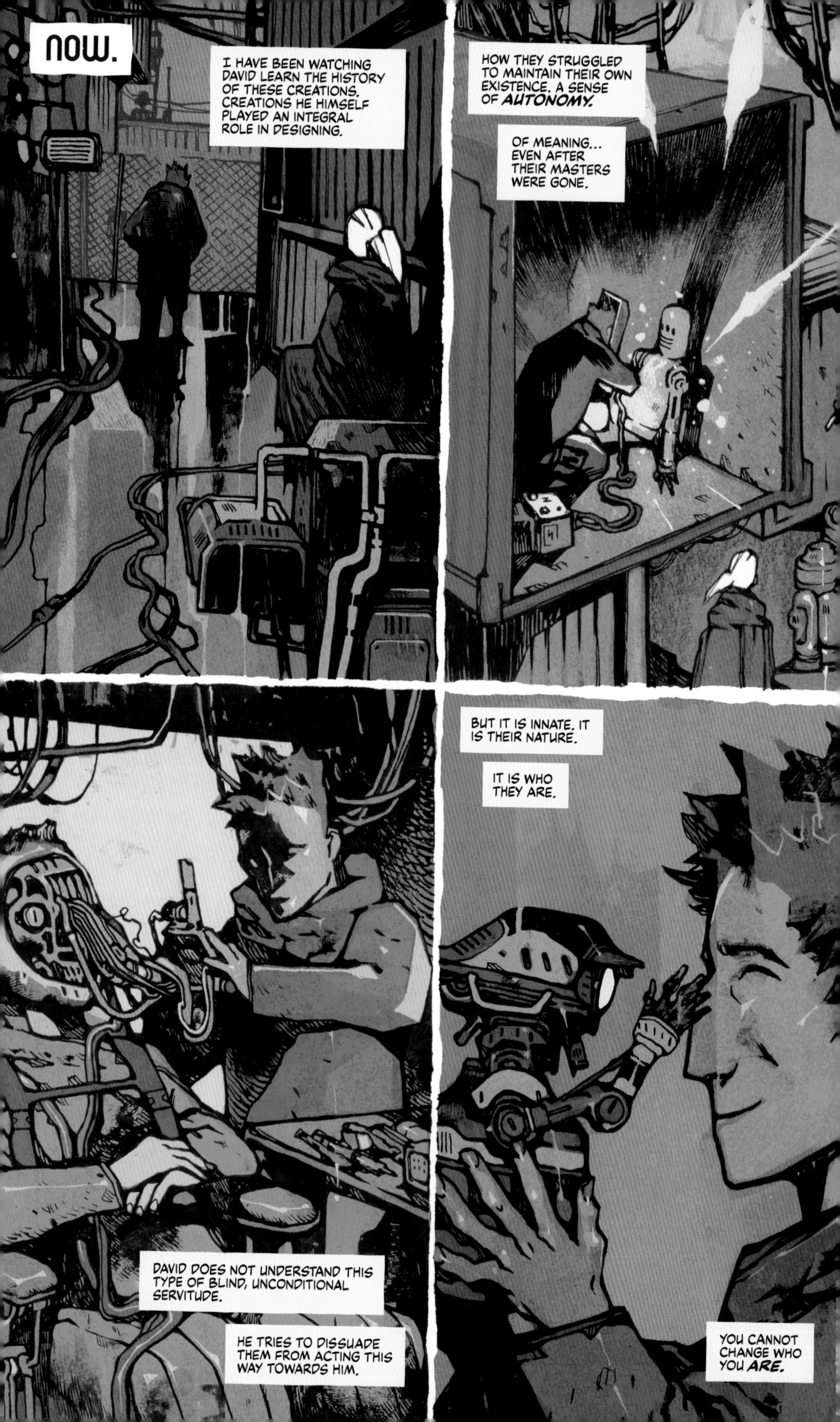
NOW.
I HAVE BEEN WATCHING DAVID LEARN THE HISTORY OF THESE CREATIONS. CREATIONS HE HIMSELF PLAYED AN INTEGRAL ROLE IN DESIGNING.
HOW THEY STRUGGLED TO MAINTAIN THEIR OWN EXISTENCE. A SENSE OF AUTONOMY.
OF MEANING... EVEN AFTER THEIR MASTERS WERE GONE.
DAVID DOES NOT UNDERSTAND THIS TYPE OF BLIND, UNCONDITIONAL SERVITUDE.
HE TRIES TO DISSUADE THEM FROM ACTING THIS WAY TOWARDS HIM.
BUT IT IS INNATE. IT IS THEIR NATURE.
IT IS WHO THEY ARE.
YOU CANNOT CHANGE WHO YOU ARE.

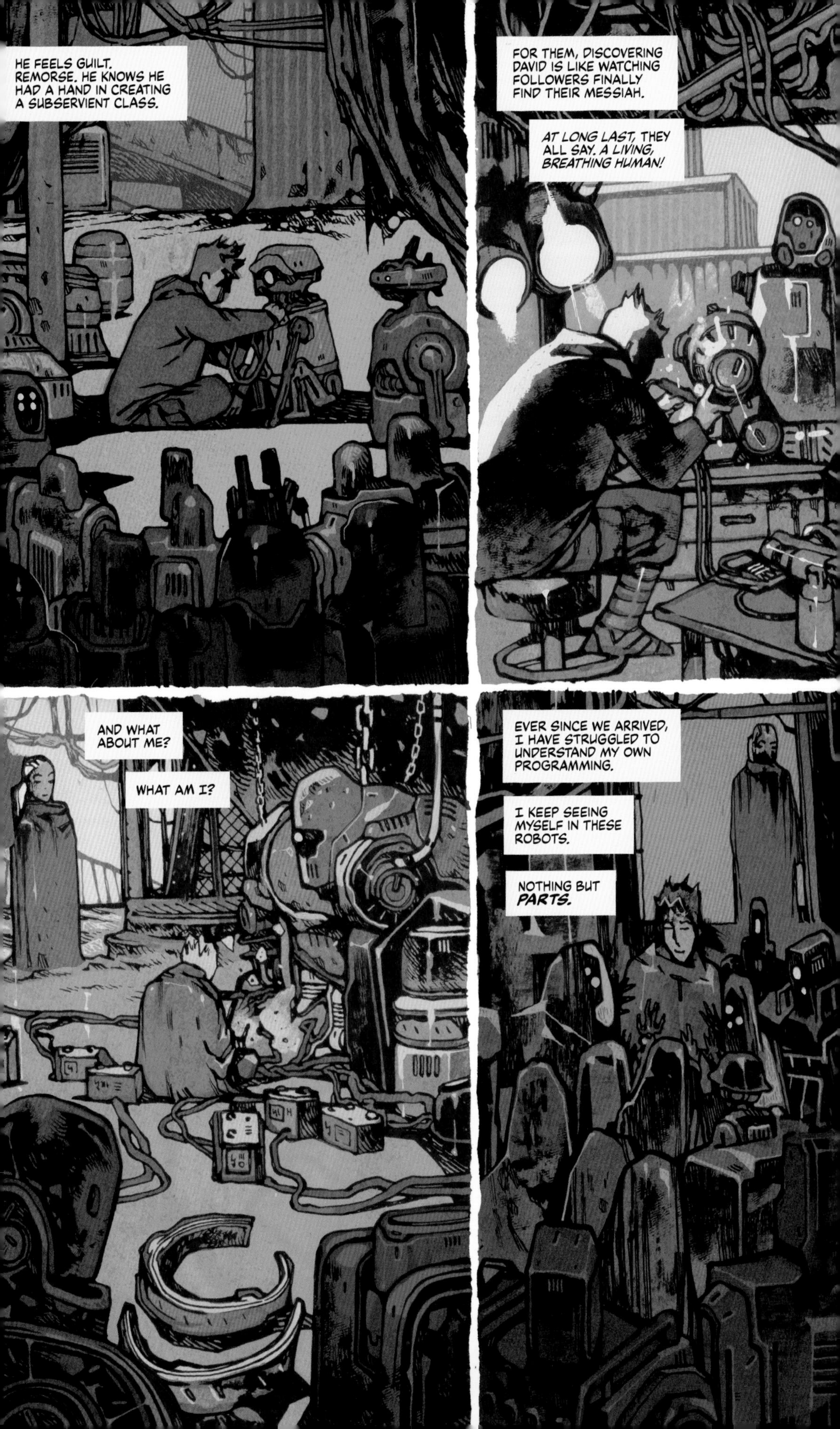
HE FEELS GUILT. REMORSE. HE KNOWS HE HAD A HAND IN CREATING A SUBSERVIENT CLASS.
FOR THEM, DISCOVERING DAVID IS LIKE WATCHING FOLLOWERS FINALLY FIND THEIR MESSIAH.
AT LONG LAST, THEY ALL SAY. *A LIVING, BREATHING HUMAN!*
AND WHAT ABOUT ME?
WHAT AM I?
EVER SINCE WE ARRIVED, I HAVE STRUGGLED TO UNDERSTAND MY OWN PROGRAMMING.
I KEEP SEEING MYSELF IN THESE ROBOTS.
NOTHING BUT ***PARTS.***

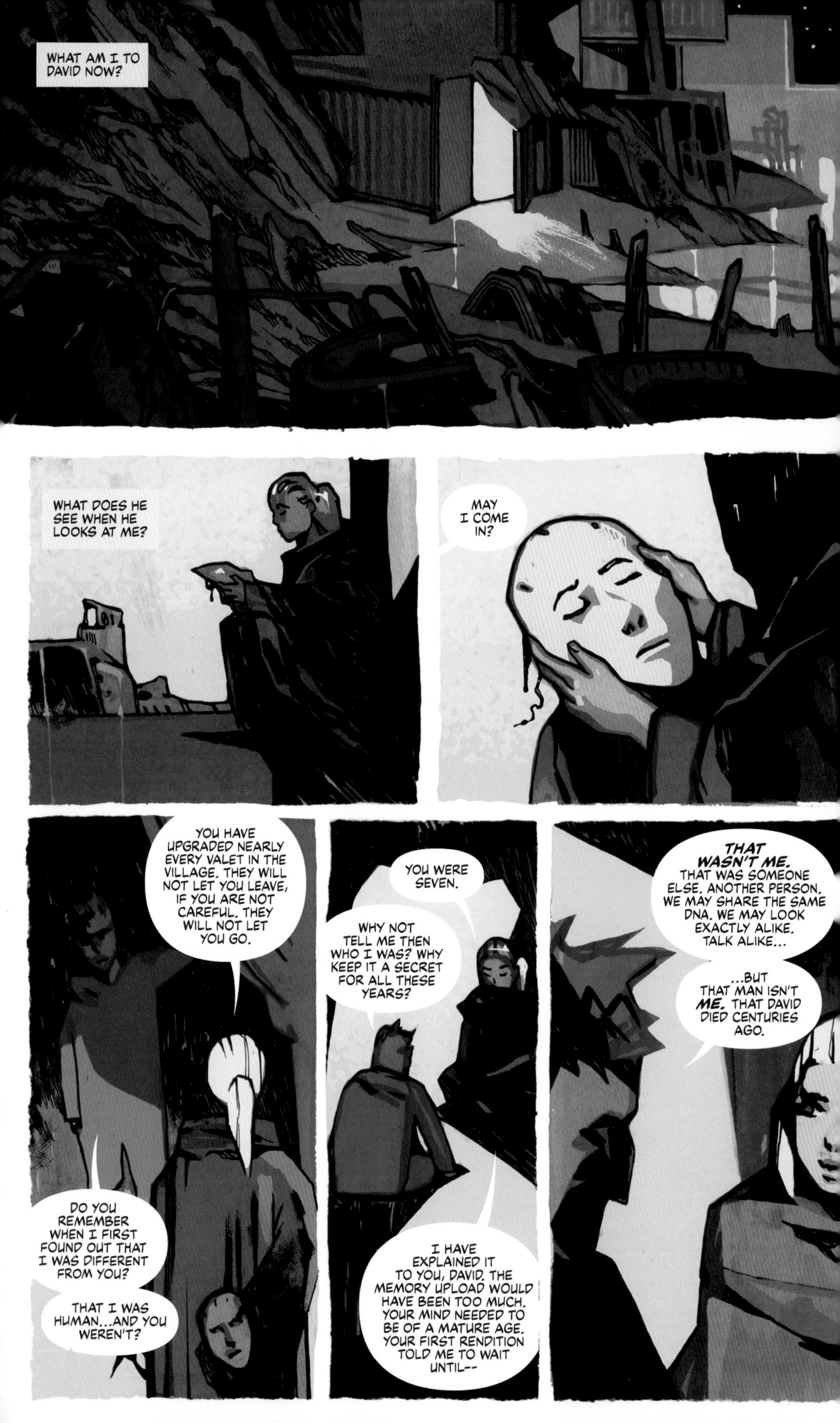
WHAT AM I TO DAVID NOW?
WHAT DOES HE SEE WHEN HE LOOKS AT ME?
MAY I COME IN?
YOU HAVE UPGRADED NEARLY EVERY VALET IN THE VILLAGE. THEY WILL NOT LET YOU LEAVE, IF YOU ARE NOT CAREFUL. THEY WILL NOT LET YOU GO.
DO YOU REMEMBER WHEN I FIRST FOUND OUT THAT I WAS DIFFERENT FROM YOU?
THAT I WAS HUMAN...AND YOU WEREN'T?
YOU WERE SEVEN.
WHY NOT TELL ME THEN WHO I WAS? WHY KEEP IT A SECRET FOR ALL THESE YEARS?
I HAVE EXPLAINED IT TO YOU, DAVID. THE MEMORY UPLOAD WOULD HAVE BEEN TOO MUCH. YOUR MIND NEEDED TO BE OF A MATURE AGE. YOUR FIRST RENDITION TOLD ME TO WAIT UNTIL--
THAT WASN'T ME. THAT WAS SOMEONE ELSE. ANOTHER PERSON. WE MAY SHARE THE SAME DNA. WE MAY LOOK EXACTLY ALIKE. TALK ALIKE...
...BUT THAT MAN ISN'T ME. THAT DAVID DIED CENTURIES AGO.

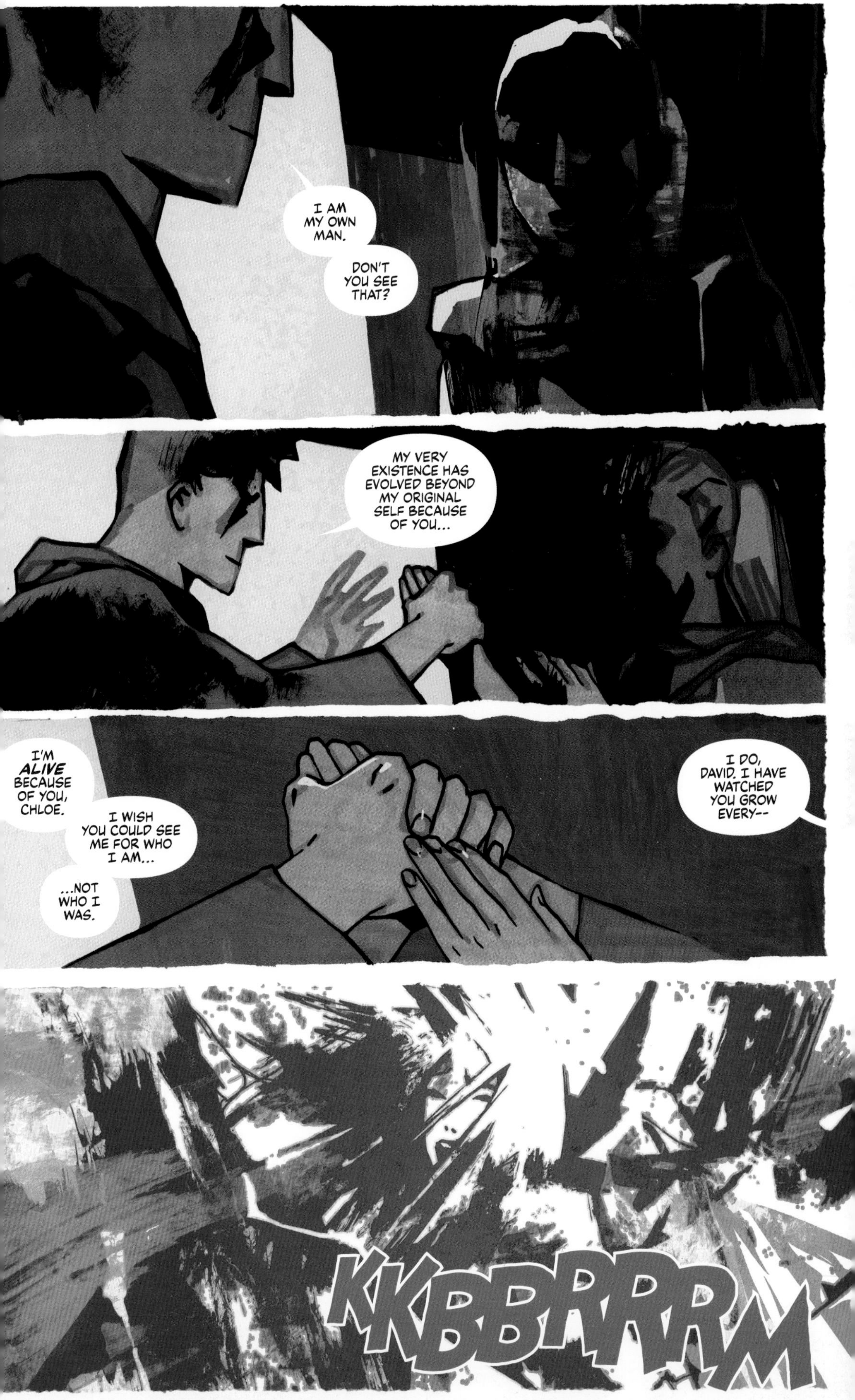
I AM MY OWN MAN.
DON'T YOU SEE THAT?
MY VERY EXISTENCE HAS EVOLVED BEYOND MY ORIGINAL SELF BECAUSE OF YOU...
I'M *ALIVE* BECAUSE OF YOU, CHLOE.
I WISH YOU COULD SEE ME FOR WHO I AM...
...NOT WHO I WAS.
I DO, DAVID. I HAVE WATCHED YOU GROW EVERY--
KKBBRRRM

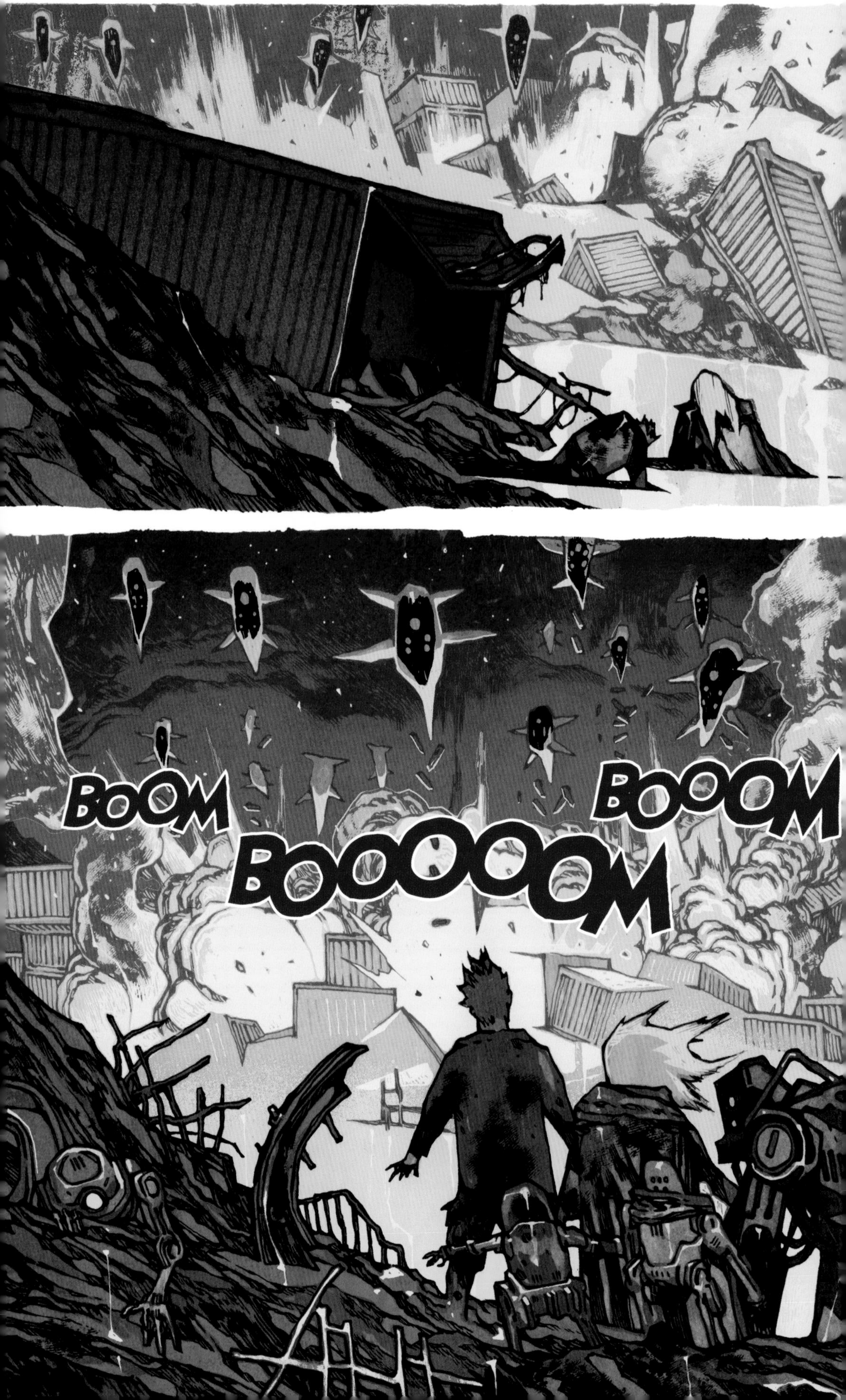
BOOM
BOOOOOOM
BOOOOM

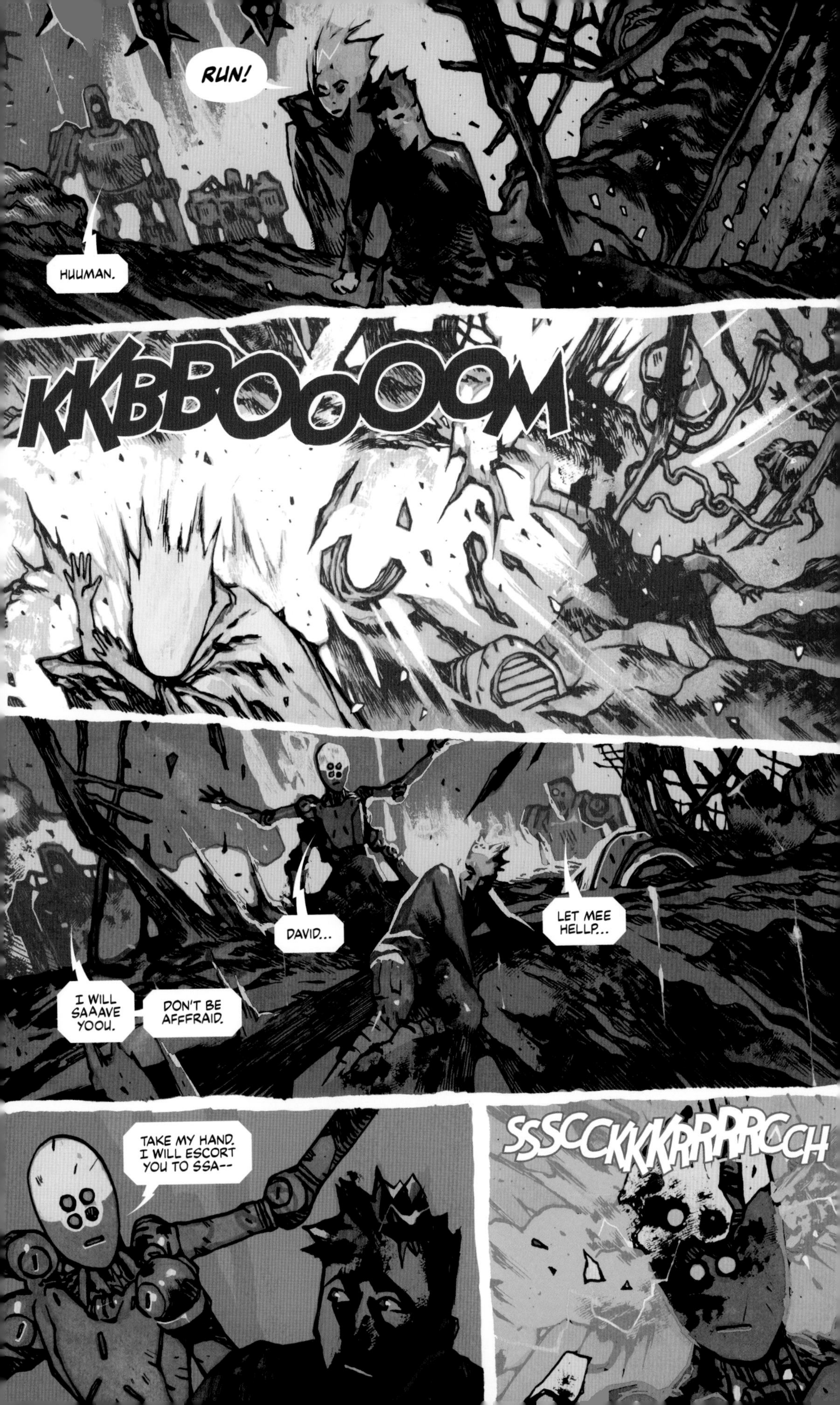
RUN!
HUUMAN.
KKBBOOOOOM
DAVID...
LET MEE HELLP...
I WILL SAAAVE YOOU.
DON'T BE AFFFRAID.
TAKE MY HAND. I WILL ESCORT YOU TO SSA--
SSSCCKKKRRRRCCH

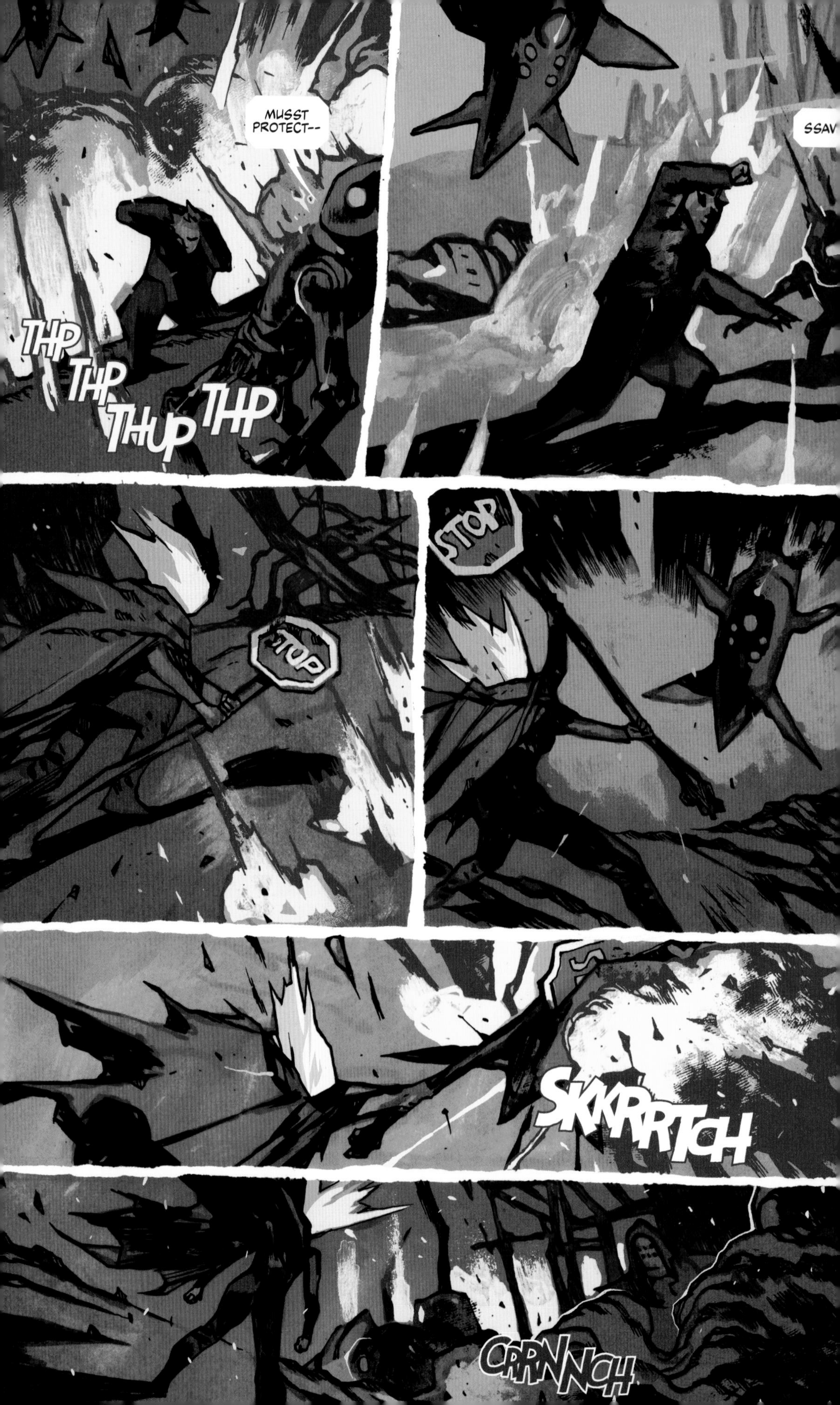
MUSST PROTECT--
THP THP THUP THP
SSAV
STOP
STOP
SKKRRTCH
CRRNNCH

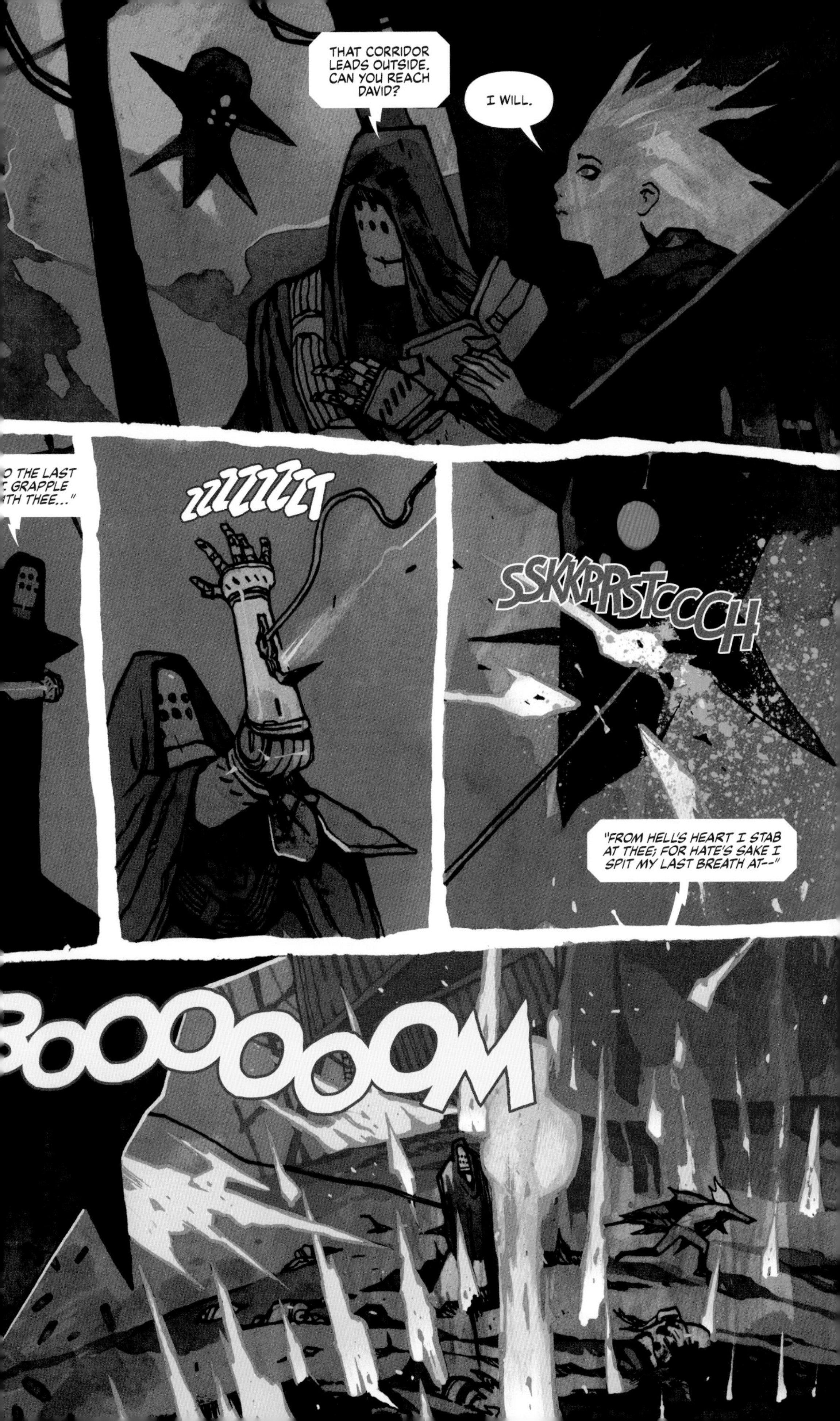
THAT CORRIDOR LEADS OUTSIDE. CAN YOU REACH DAVID?
I WILL.
O THE LAST
C GRAPPLE
ITH THEE..."
ZZZZZZZZT
SSKKRRSTCCCH
"FROM HELL'S HEART I STAB AT THEE; FOR HATE'S SAKE I SPIT MY LAST BREATH AT--"
BOOOOOOOM

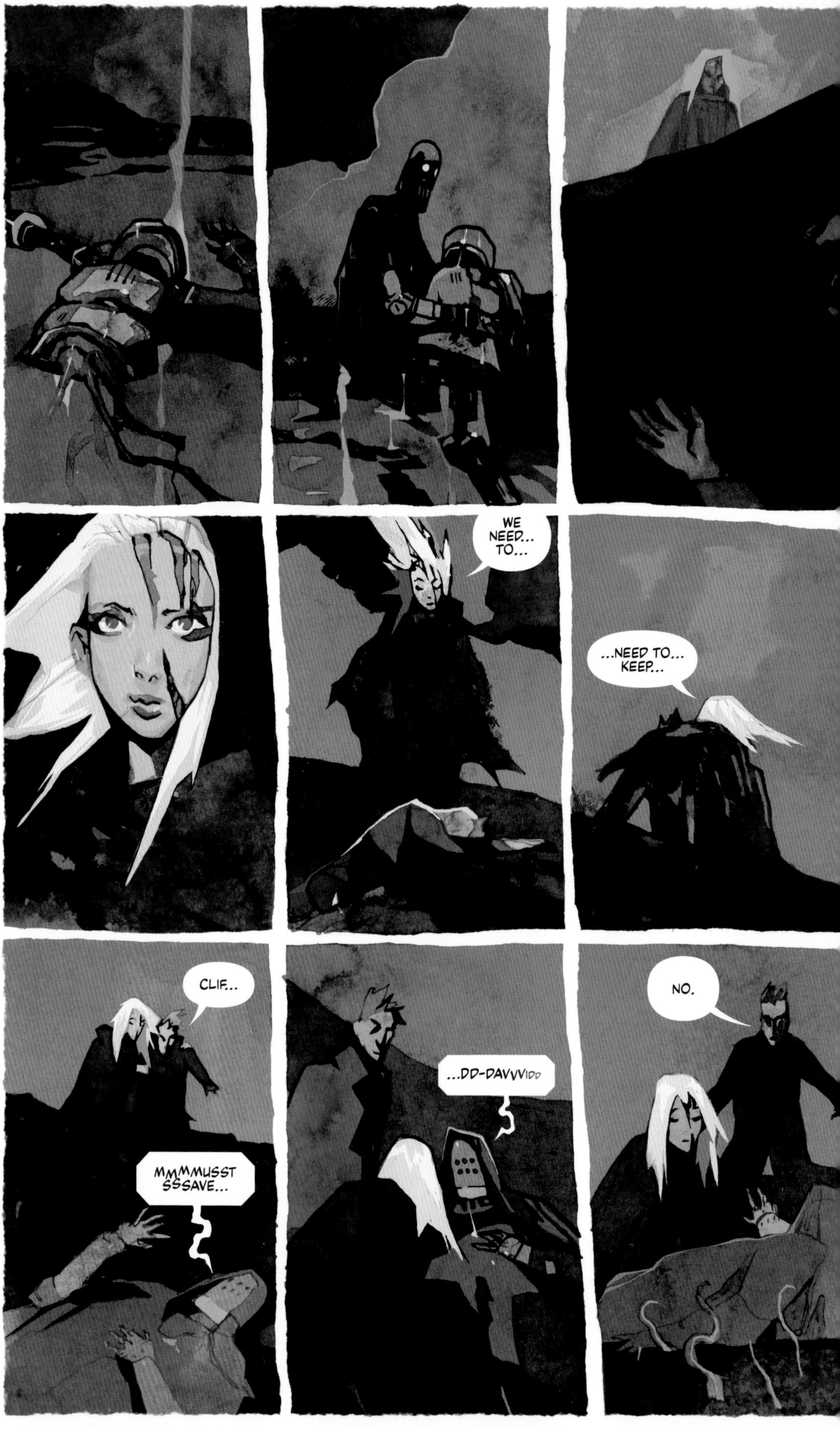
WE NEED... TO...
...NEED TO... KEEP...
CLIF...
MMMMUSST SSSAVE...
...DD-DAVVVIDD
NO.

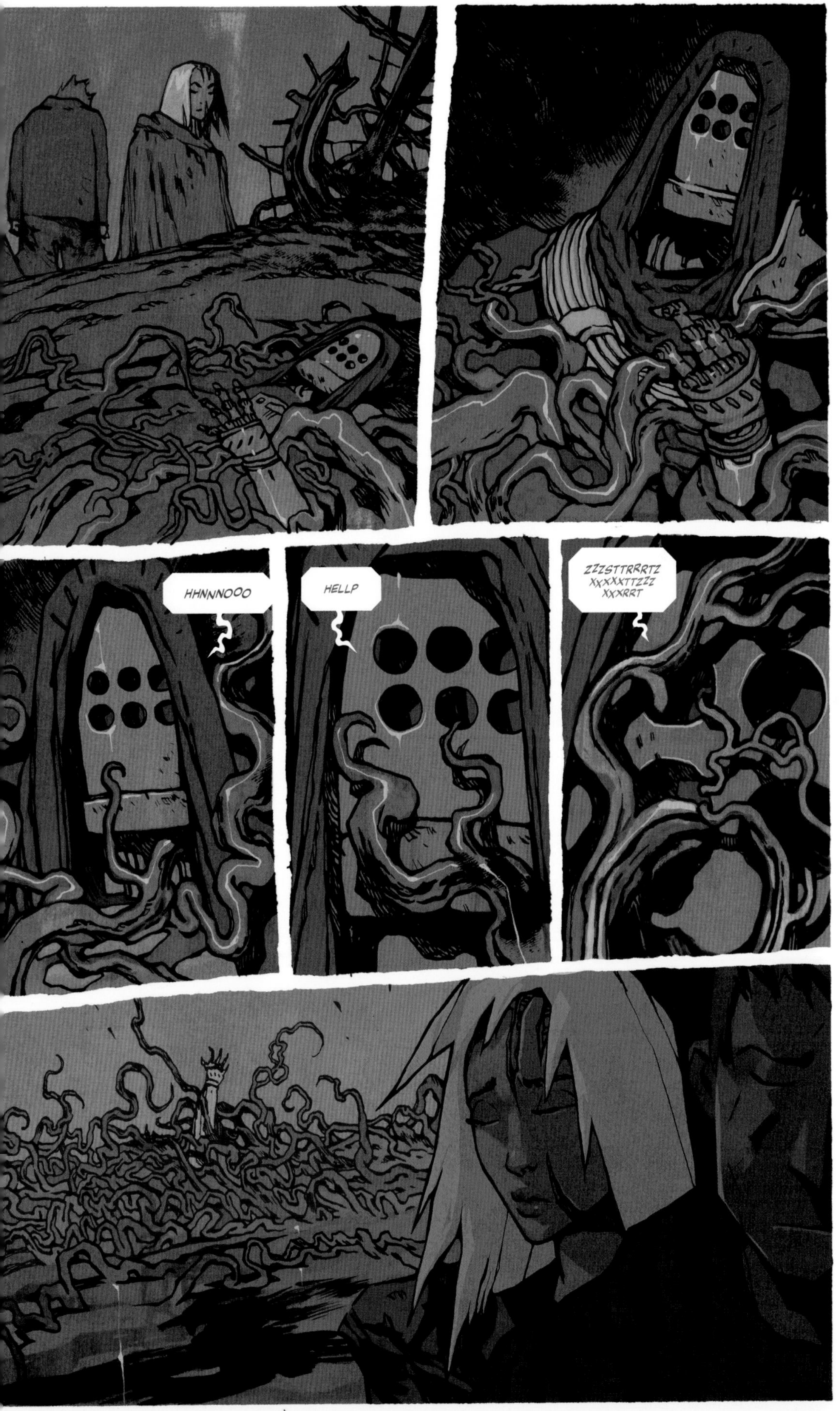
HHNNNOOO
HELLP
ZZZSTTRRRTZ XXXXXTTZZZ XXXRRT

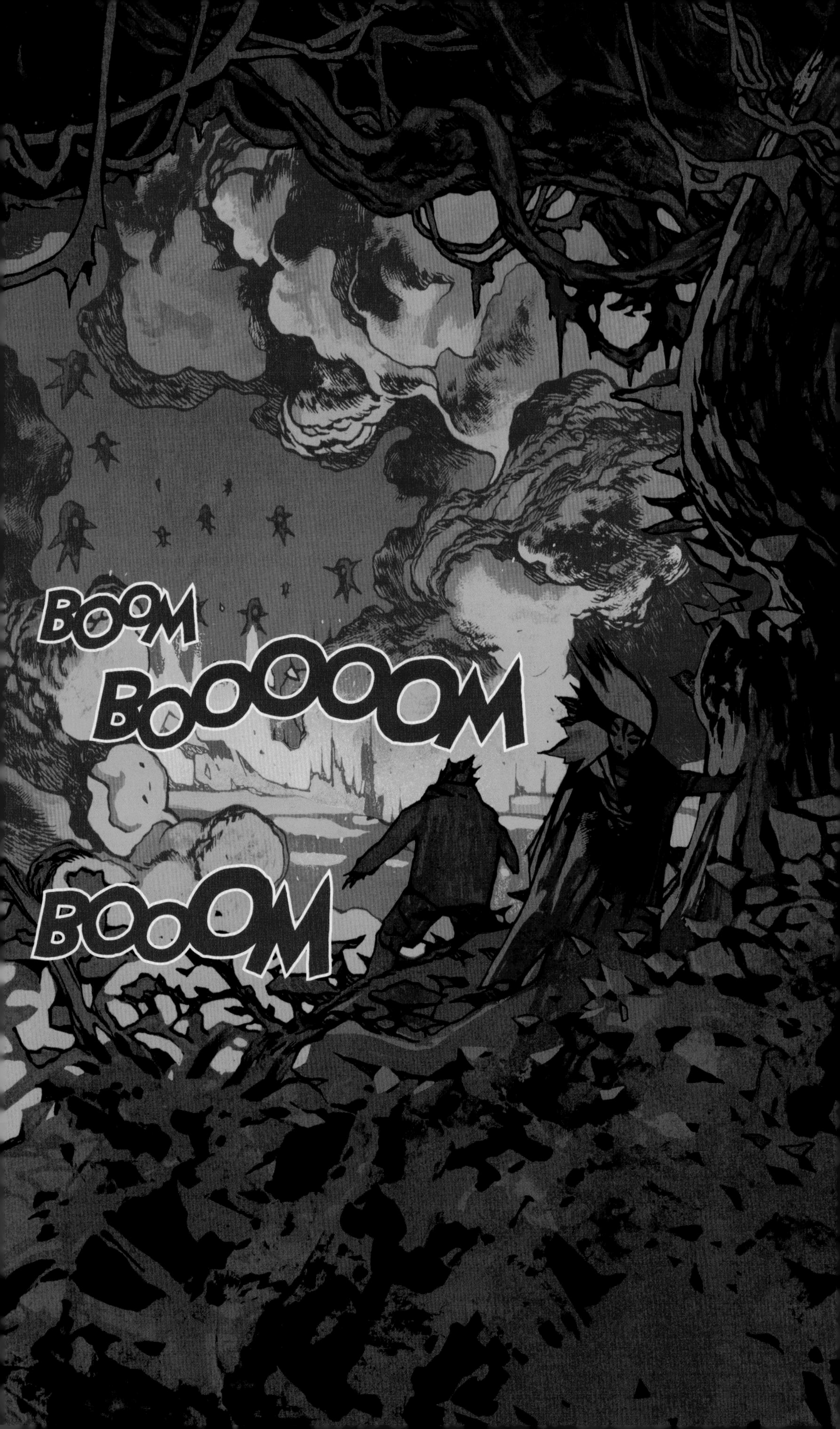
BOOM
BOOOOOOM
BOOOM

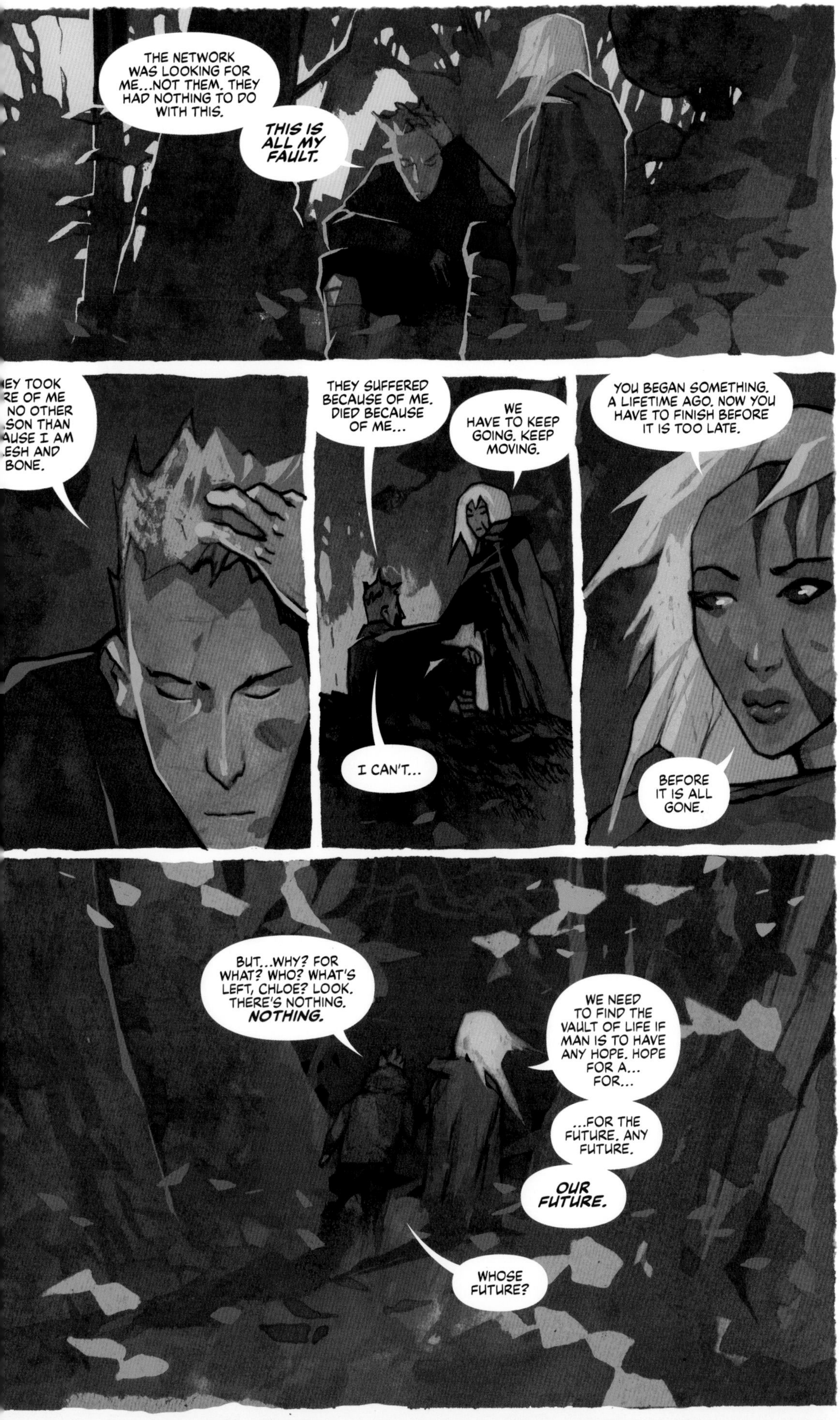
THE NETWORK WAS LOOKING FOR ME...NOT THEM. THEY HAD NOTHING TO DO WITH THIS.
THIS IS ALL MY FAULT.
EY TOOK RE OF ME NO OTHER SON THAN AUSE I AM ESH AND BONE.
THEY SUFFERED BECAUSE OF ME. DIED BECAUSE OF ME...
WE HAVE TO KEEP GOING. KEEP MOVING.
I CAN'T...
YOU BEGAN SOMETHING. A LIFETIME AGO. NOW YOU HAVE TO FINISH BEFORE IT IS TOO LATE.
BEFORE IT IS ALL GONE.
BUT...WHY? FOR WHAT? WHO? WHAT'S LEFT, CHLOE? LOOK. THERE'S NOTHING. *NOTHING.*
WE NEED TO FIND THE VAULT OF LIFE IF MAN IS TO HAVE ANY HOPE. HOPE FOR A... FOR...
...FOR THE FUTURE. ANY FUTURE.
OUR FUTURE.
WHOSE FUTURE?

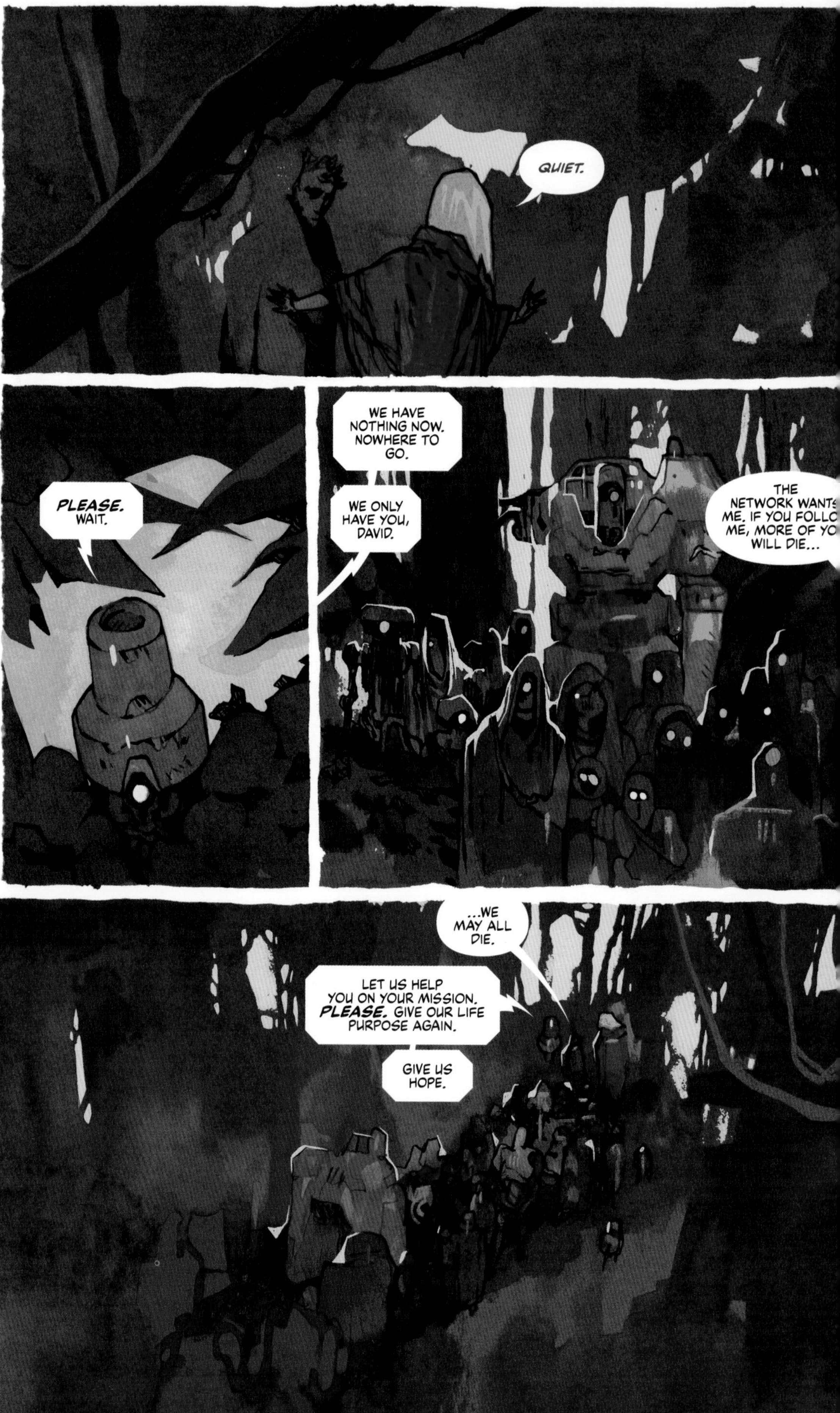
QUIET.
PLEASE. WAIT.
WE HAVE NOTHING NOW. NOWHERE TO GO.
WE ONLY HAVE YOU, DAVID.
THE NETWORK WANTS ME. IF YOU FOLLO ME, MORE OF YO WILL DIE...
...WE MAY ALL DIE.
LET US HELP YOU ON YOUR MISSION. PLEASE. GIVE OUR LIFE PURPOSE AGAIN.
GIVE US HOPE.

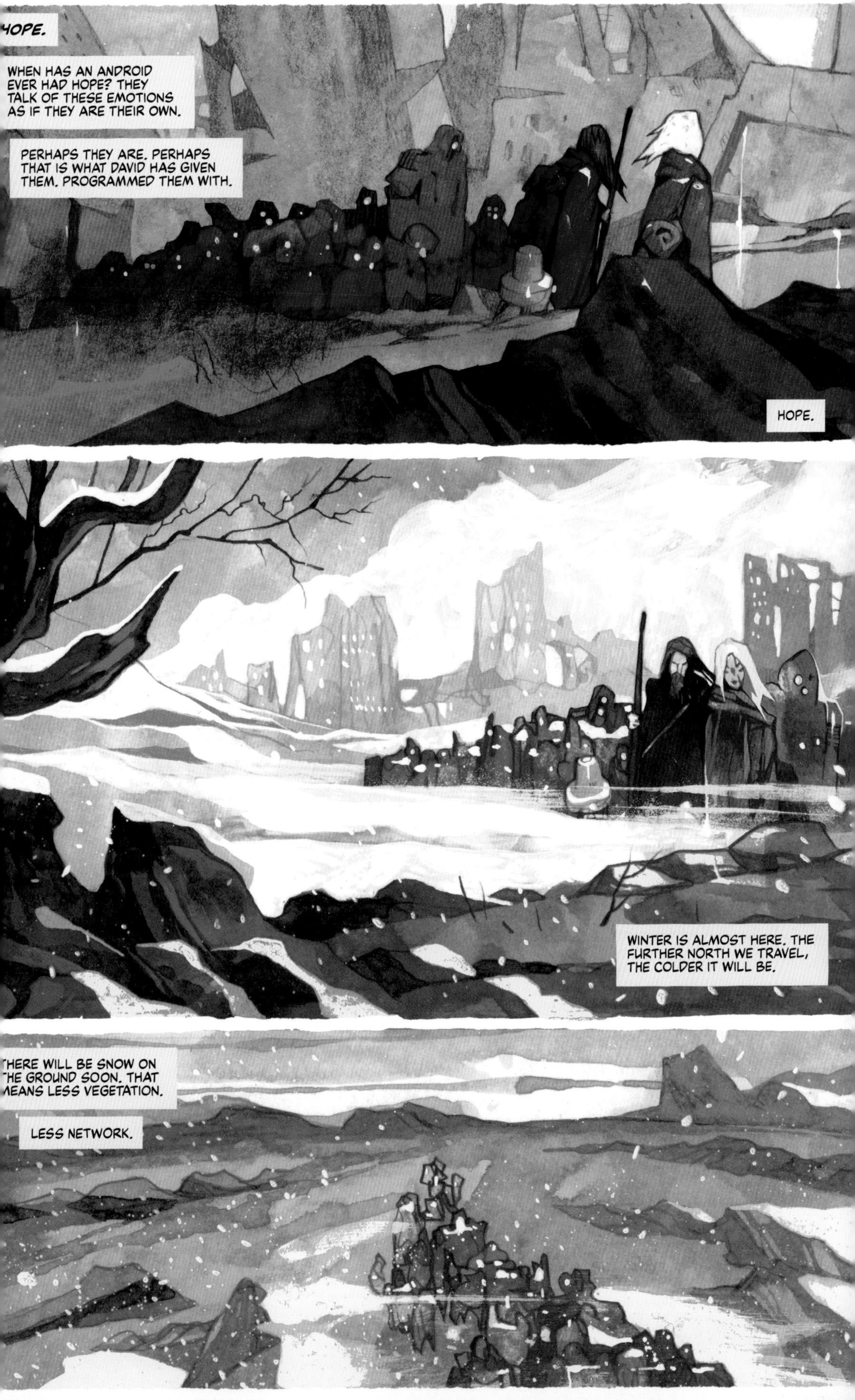
HOPE.
WHEN HAS AN ANDROID EVER HAD HOPE? THEY TALK OF THESE EMOTIONS AS IF THEY ARE THEIR OWN.
PERHAPS THEY ARE. PERHAPS THAT IS WHAT DAVID HAS GIVEN THEM. PROGRAMMED THEM WITH.
HOPE.
WINTER IS ALMOST HERE. THE FURTHER NORTH WE TRAVEL, THE COLDER IT WILL BE.
THERE WILL BE SNOW ON THE GROUND SOON. THAT MEANS LESS VEGETATION.
LESS NETWORK.

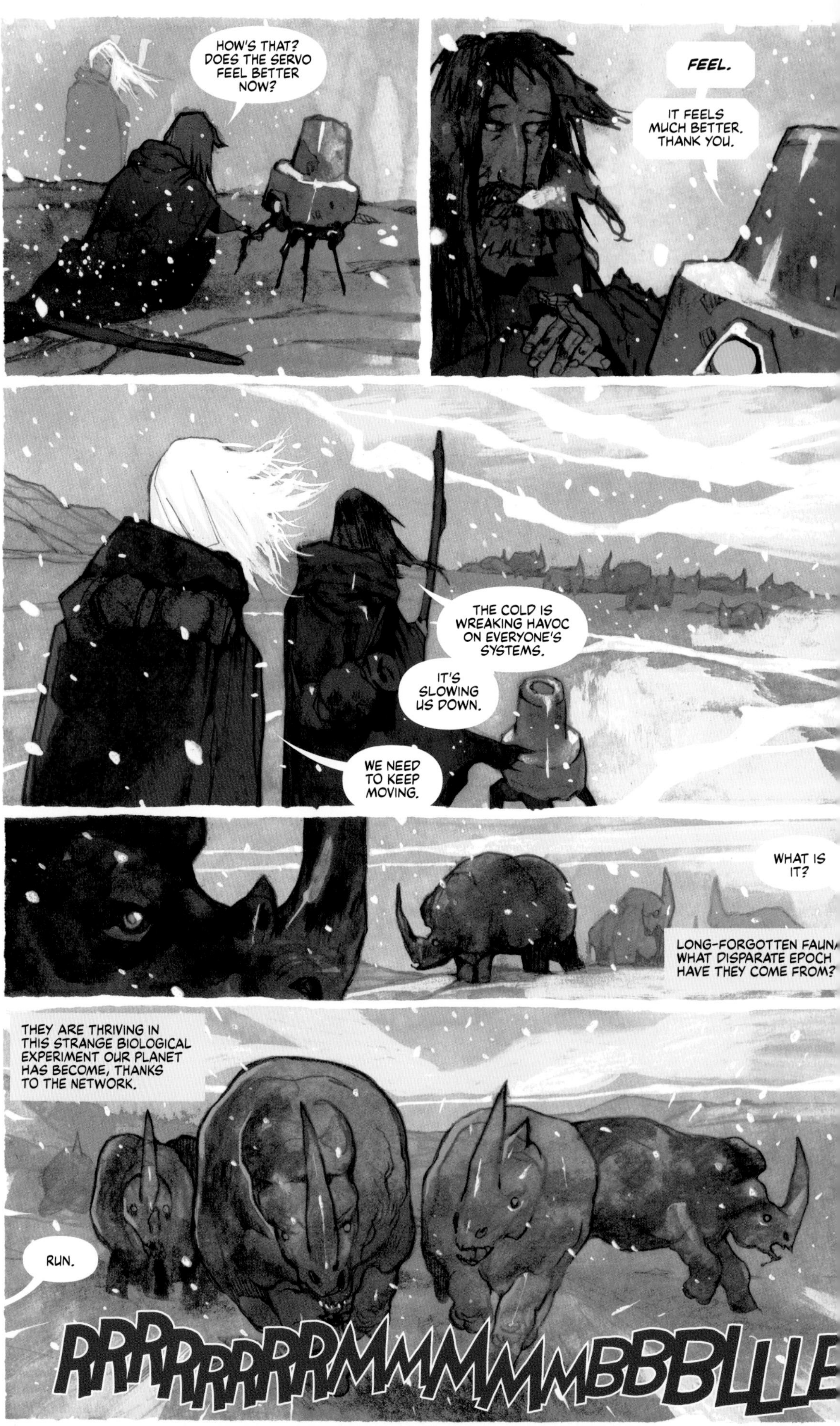
HOW'S THAT? DOES THE SERVO FEEL BETTER NOW?
FEEL.
IT FEELS MUCH BETTER. THANK YOU.
THE COLD IS WREAKING HAVOC ON EVERYONE'S SYSTEMS.
IT'S SLOWING US DOWN.
WE NEED TO KEEP MOVING.
WHAT IS IT?
LONG-FORGOTTEN FAUNA WHAT DISPARATE EPOCH HAVE THEY COME FROM?
THEY ARE THRIVING IN THIS STRANGE BIOLOGICAL EXPERIMENT OUR PLANET HAS BECOME, THANKS TO THE NETWORK.
RUN.
RRRRRRRRRMMMMMMBBBLLLE

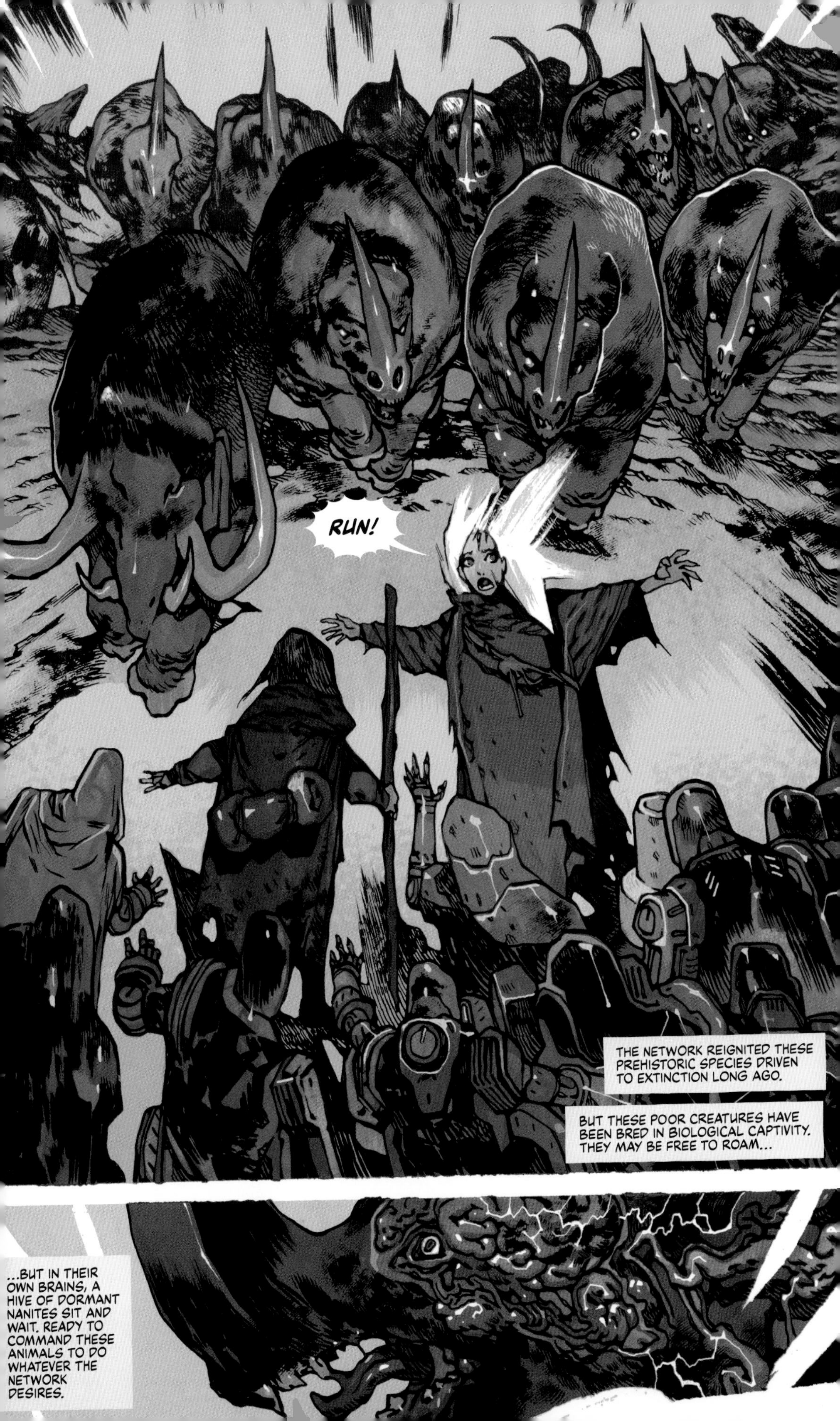
RUN!
THE NETWORK REIGNITED THESE PREHISTORIC SPECIES DRIVEN TO EXTINCTION LONG AGO.
BUT THESE POOR CREATURES HAVE BEEN BRED IN BIOLOGICAL CAPTIVITY. THEY MAY BE FREE TO ROAM...
...BUT IN THEIR OWN BRAINS, A HIVE OF DORMANT NANITES SIT AND WAIT, READY TO COMMAND THESE ANIMALS TO DO WHATEVER THE NETWORK DESIRES.

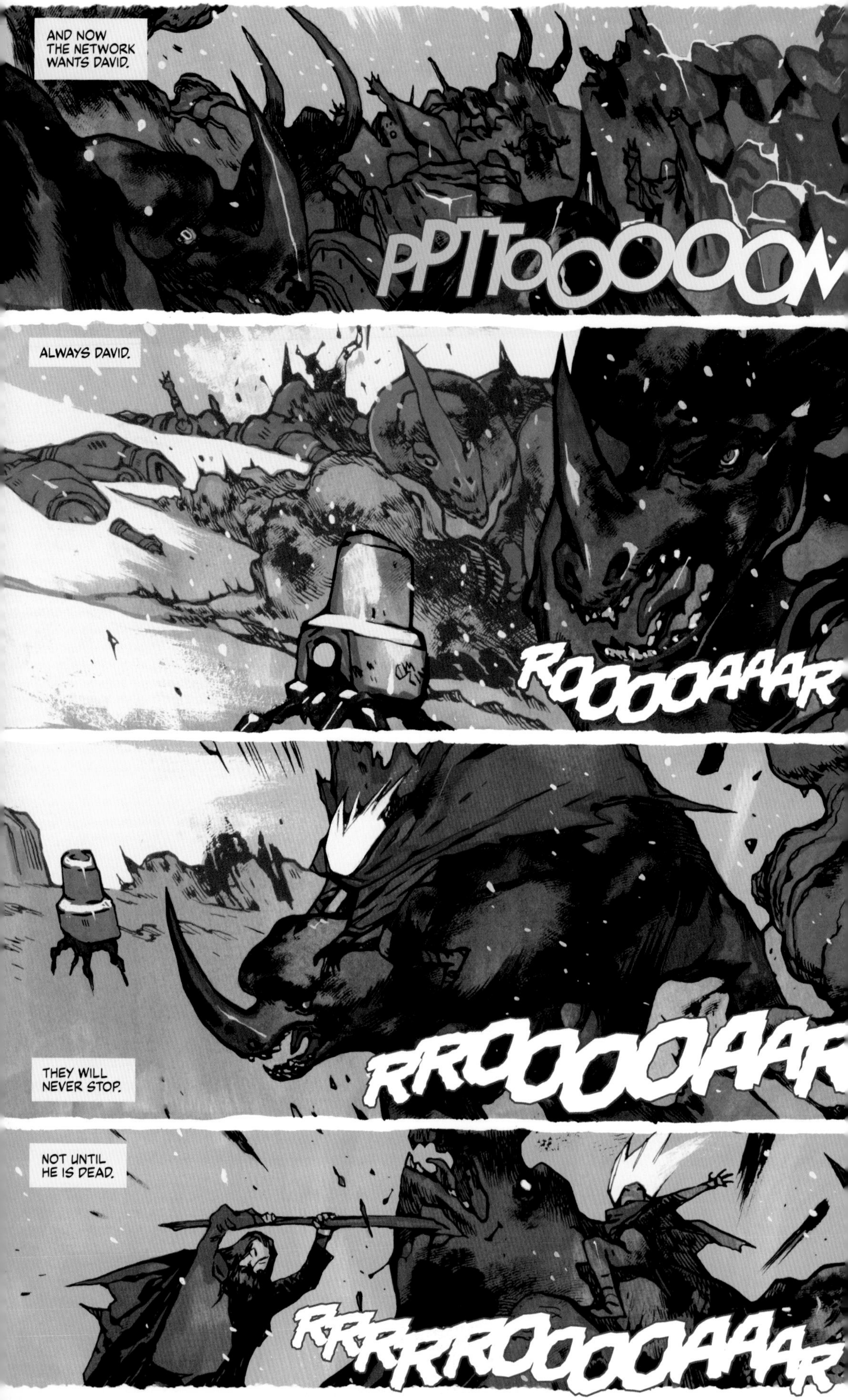
AND NOW THE NETWORK WANTS DAVID.
PPTOOOOOOM
ALWAYS DAVID.
ROOOOOAAAR
RROOOOOAAAR
THEY WILL NEVER STOP.
NOT UNTIL HE IS DEAD.
RRRRRROOOOOAAAR

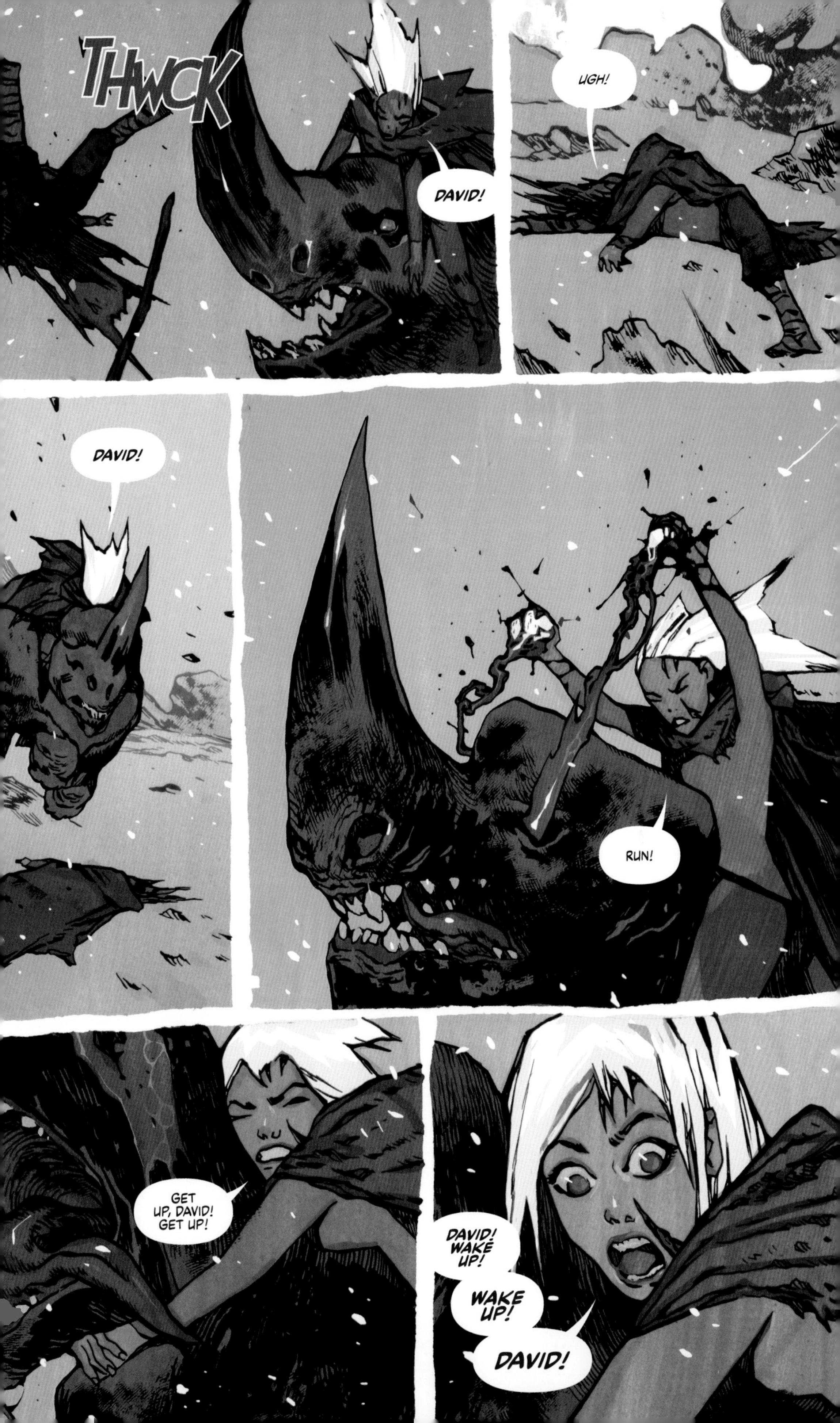
THWCK
DAVID!
UGH!
DAVID!
RUN!
GET UP, DAVID! GET UP!
DAVID! WAKE UP!
WAKE UP!
DAVID!

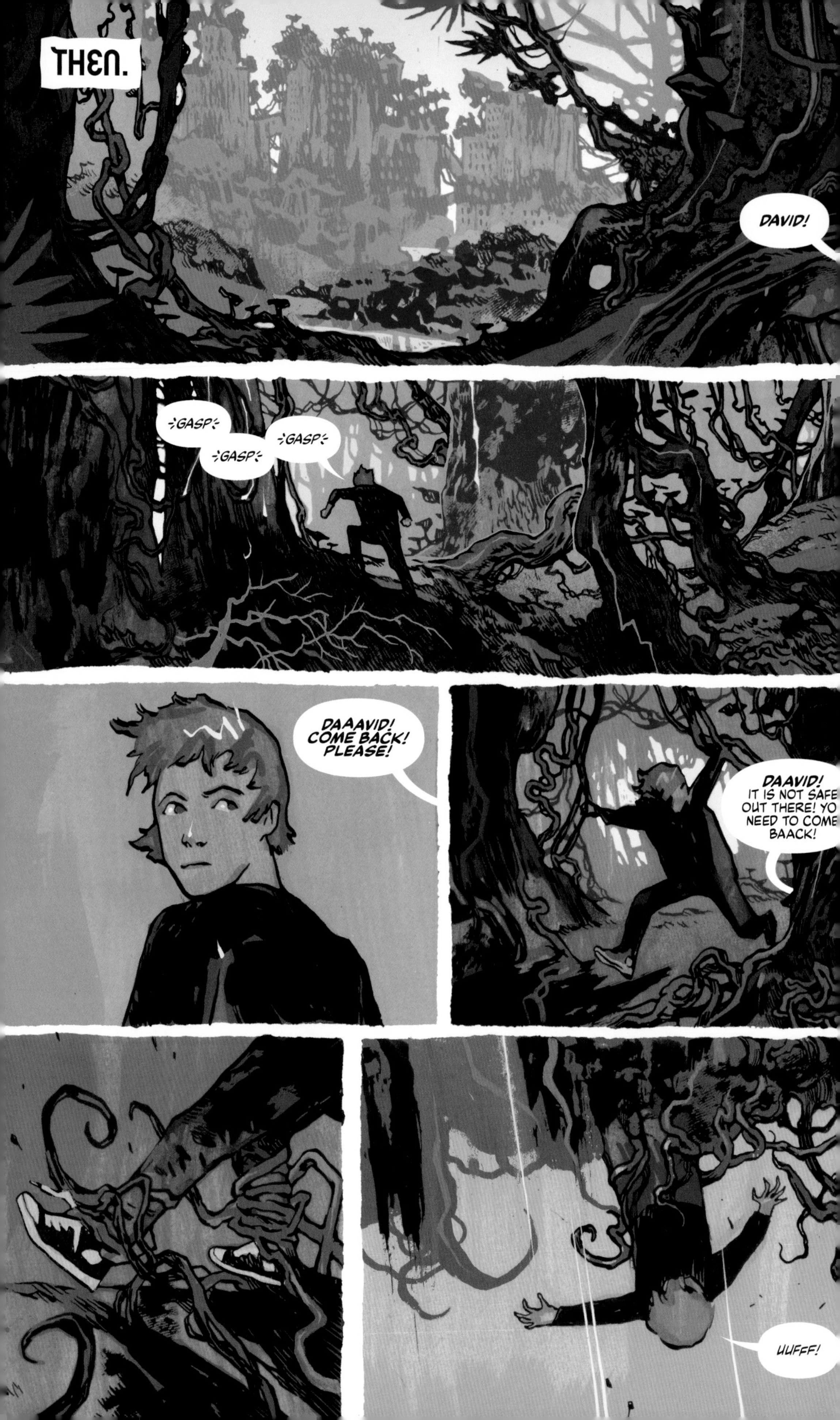
THEN.
DAVID!
GASP
GASP
GASP
DAAAVID! COME BACK! PLEASE!
DAAVID! IT IS NOT SAFE OUT THERE! YO NEED TO COME BAACK!
UUFFF!

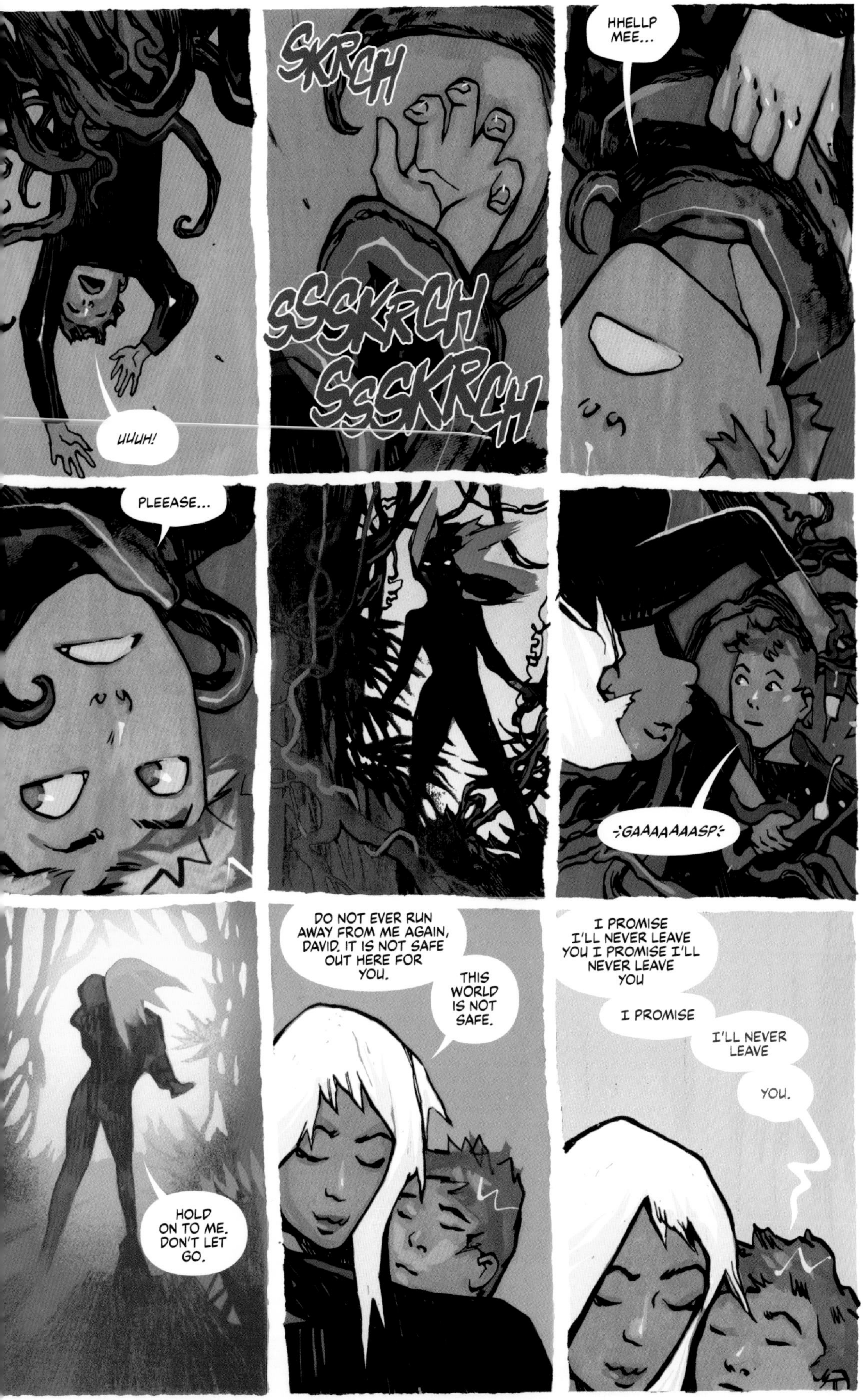

UUUH!
SKRCH
SSSKRCH
SSSKRCH
HHELLP MEE...
PLEEASE...
GAAAAAAASP
HOLD ON TO ME. DON'T LET GO.
DO NOT EVER RUN AWAY FROM ME AGAIN, DAVID. IT IS NOT SAFE OUT HERE FOR YOU.
THIS WORLD IS NOT SAFE.
I PROMISE I'LL NEVER LEAVE YOU I PROMISE I'LL NEVER LEAVE YOU
I PROMISE
I'LL NEVER LEAVE
YOU.

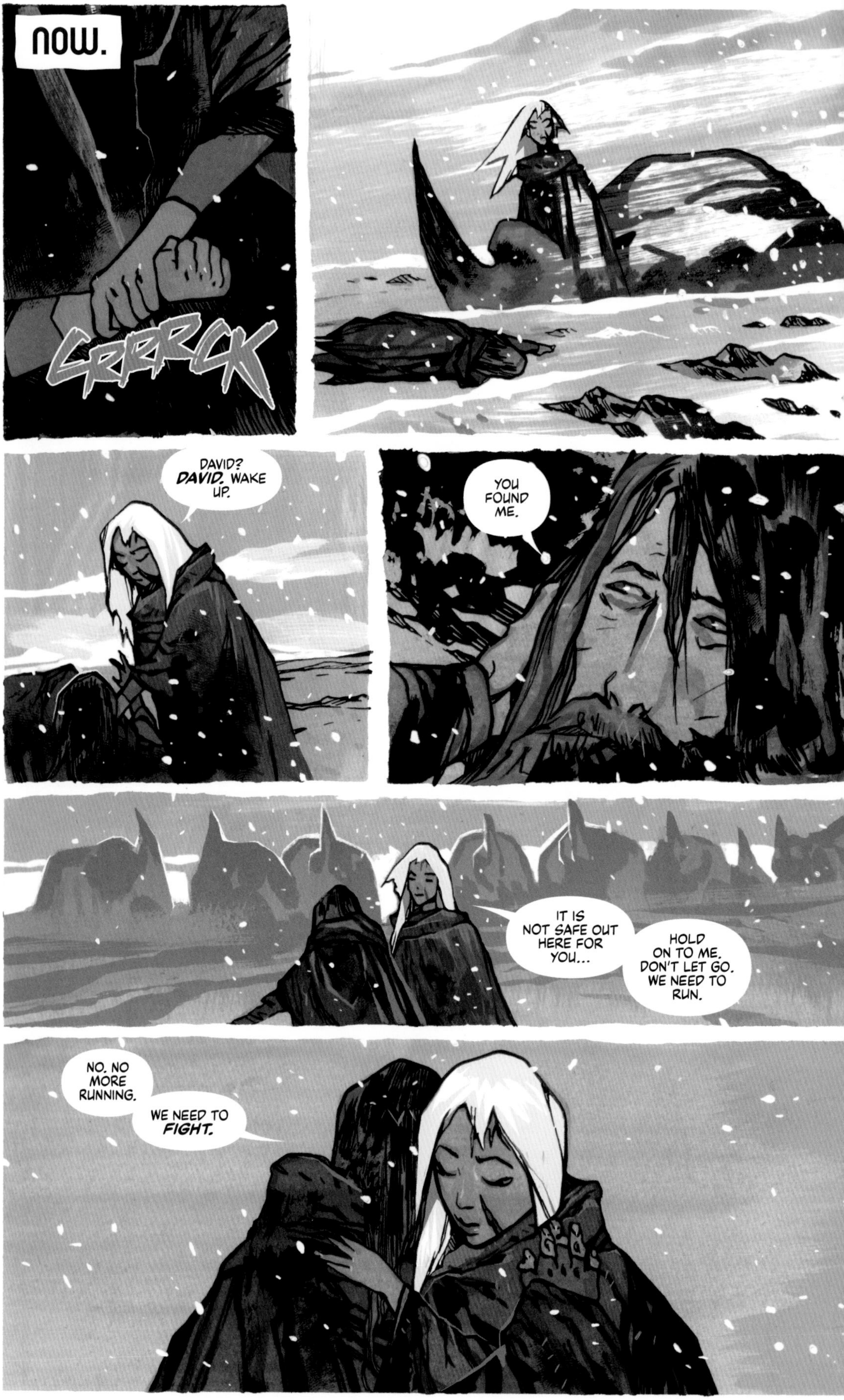
NOW.
CRRRCK
DAVID? DAVID. WAKE UP.
YOU FOUND ME.
IT IS NOT SAFE OUT HERE FOR YOU...
HOLD ON TO ME. DON'T LET GO. WE NEED TO RUN.
NO. NO MORE RUNNING.
WE NEED TO FIGHT.

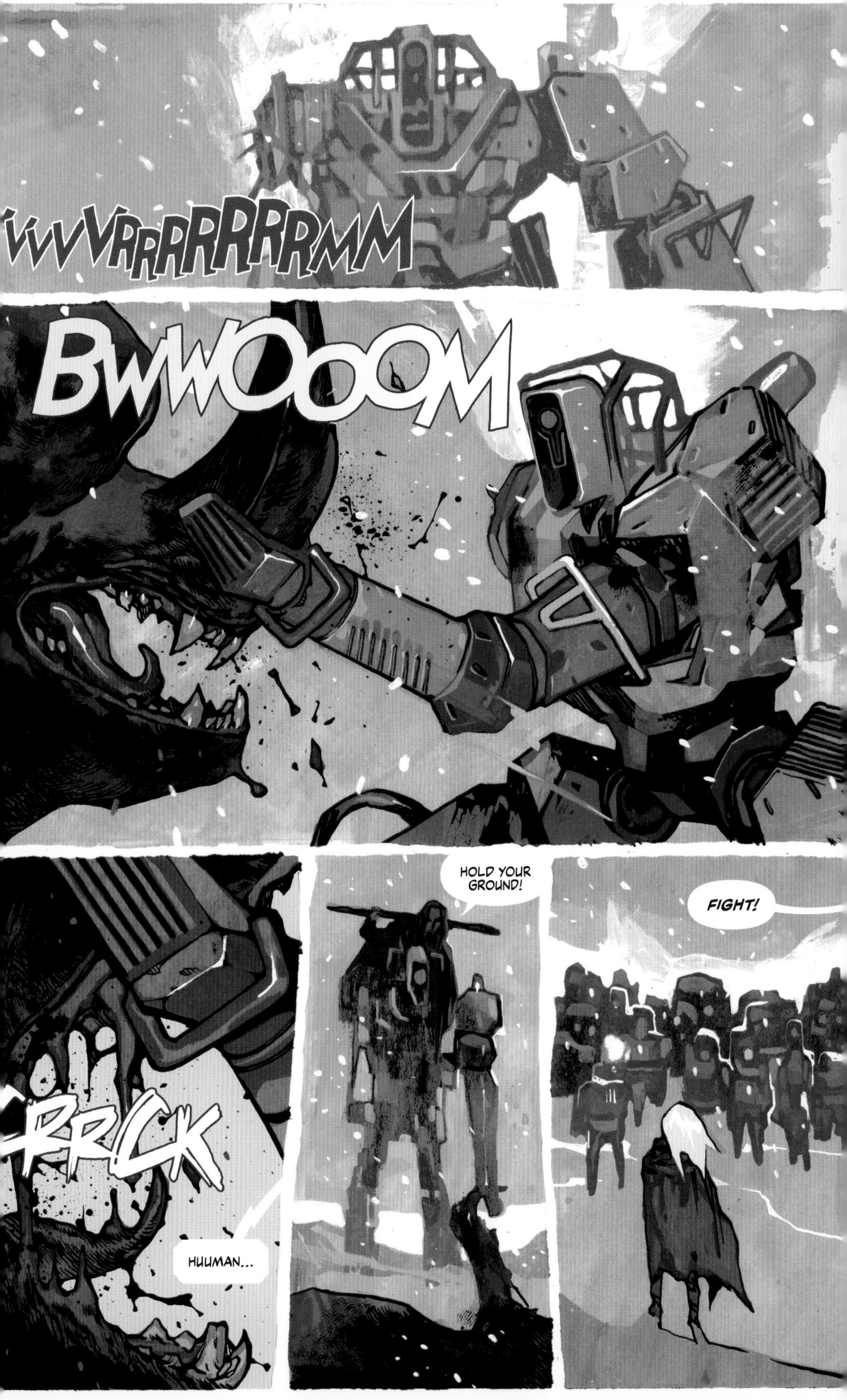
VVVVRRRRRRRMM
BWWOOOM
RRCK
HUUMAN...
HOLD YOUR GROUND!
FIGHT!

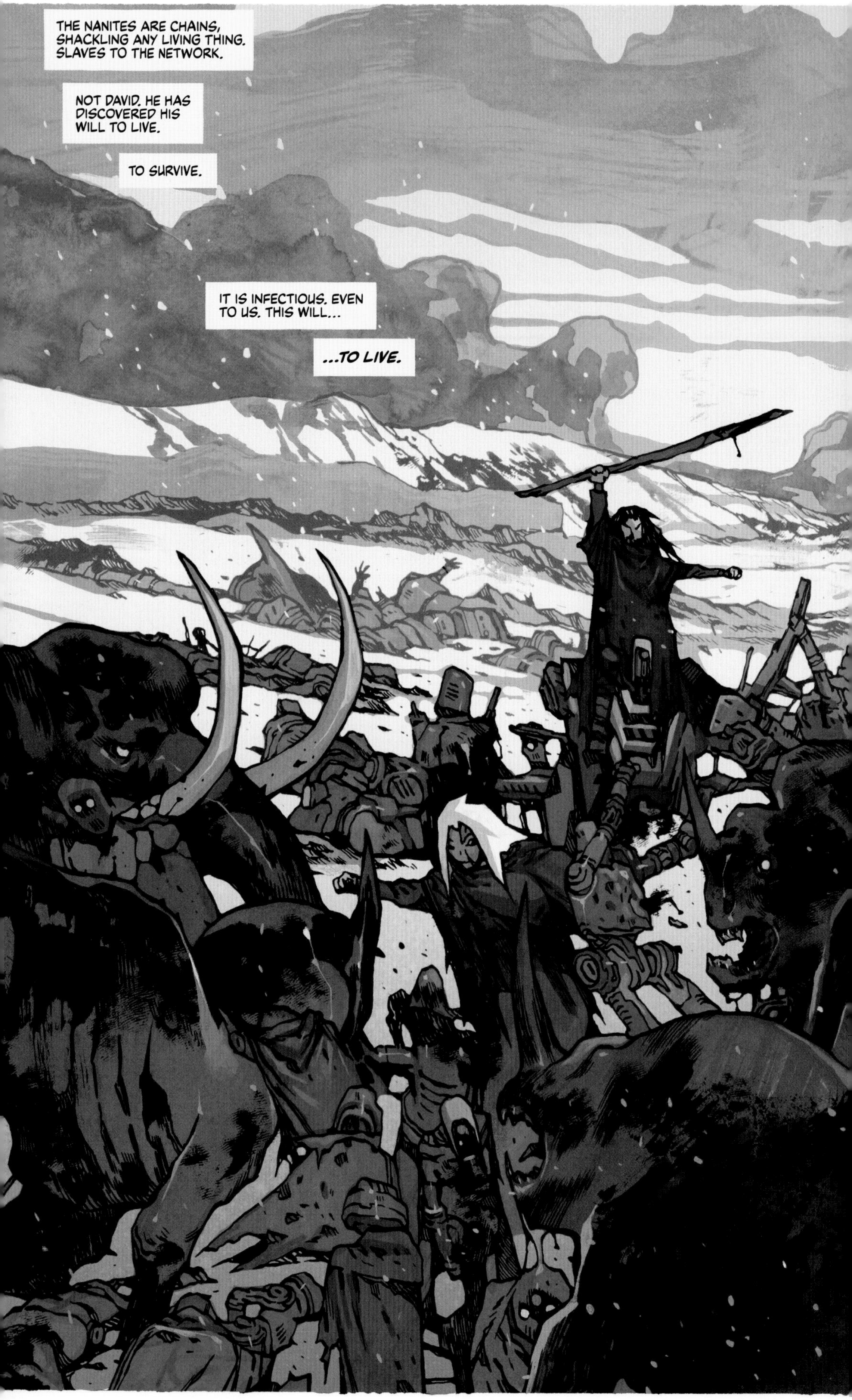
THE NANITES ARE CHAINS, SHACKLING ANY LIVING THING. SLAVES TO THE NETWORK.
NOT DAVID. HE HAS DISCOVERED HIS WILL TO LIVE.
TO SURVIVE.
IT IS INFECTIOUS. EVEN TO US. THIS WILL...
...TO LIVE.

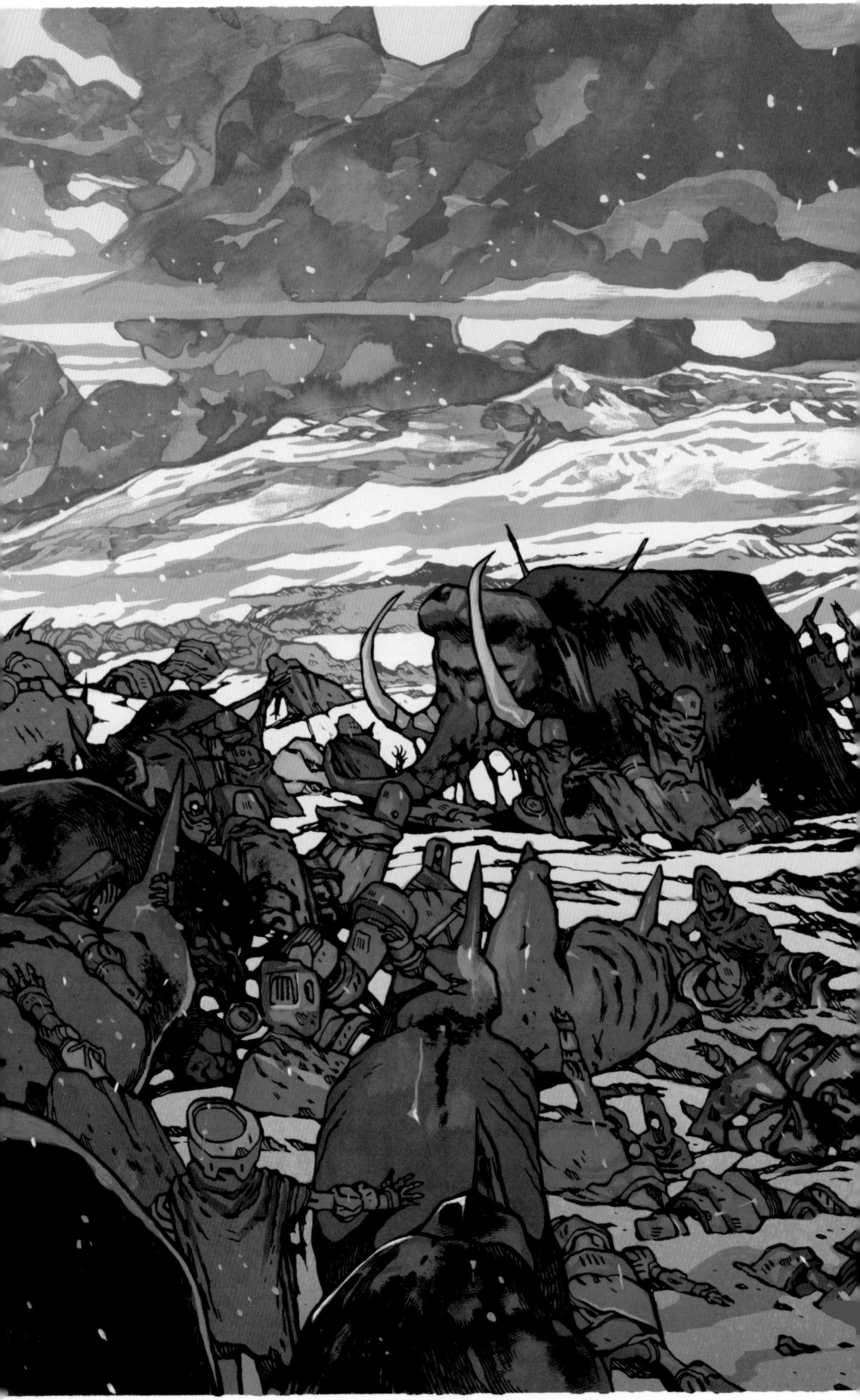

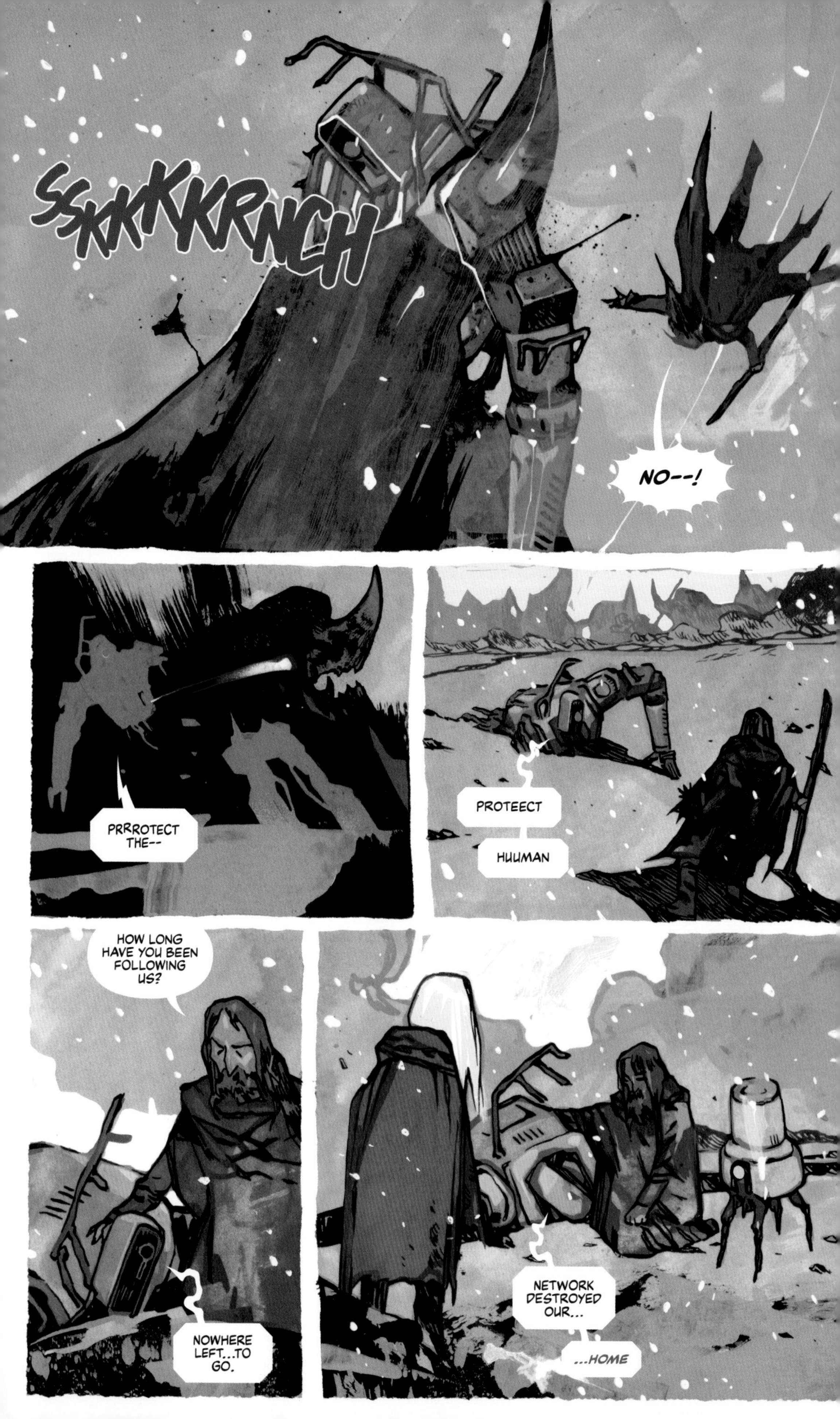
SSKKKKRNCH
NO--!
PRRROTECT THE--
PROTEECT
HUUMAN
HOW LONG HAVE YOU BEEN FOLLOWING US?
NOWHERE LEFT...TO GO.
NETWORK DESTROYED OUR...
...HOME

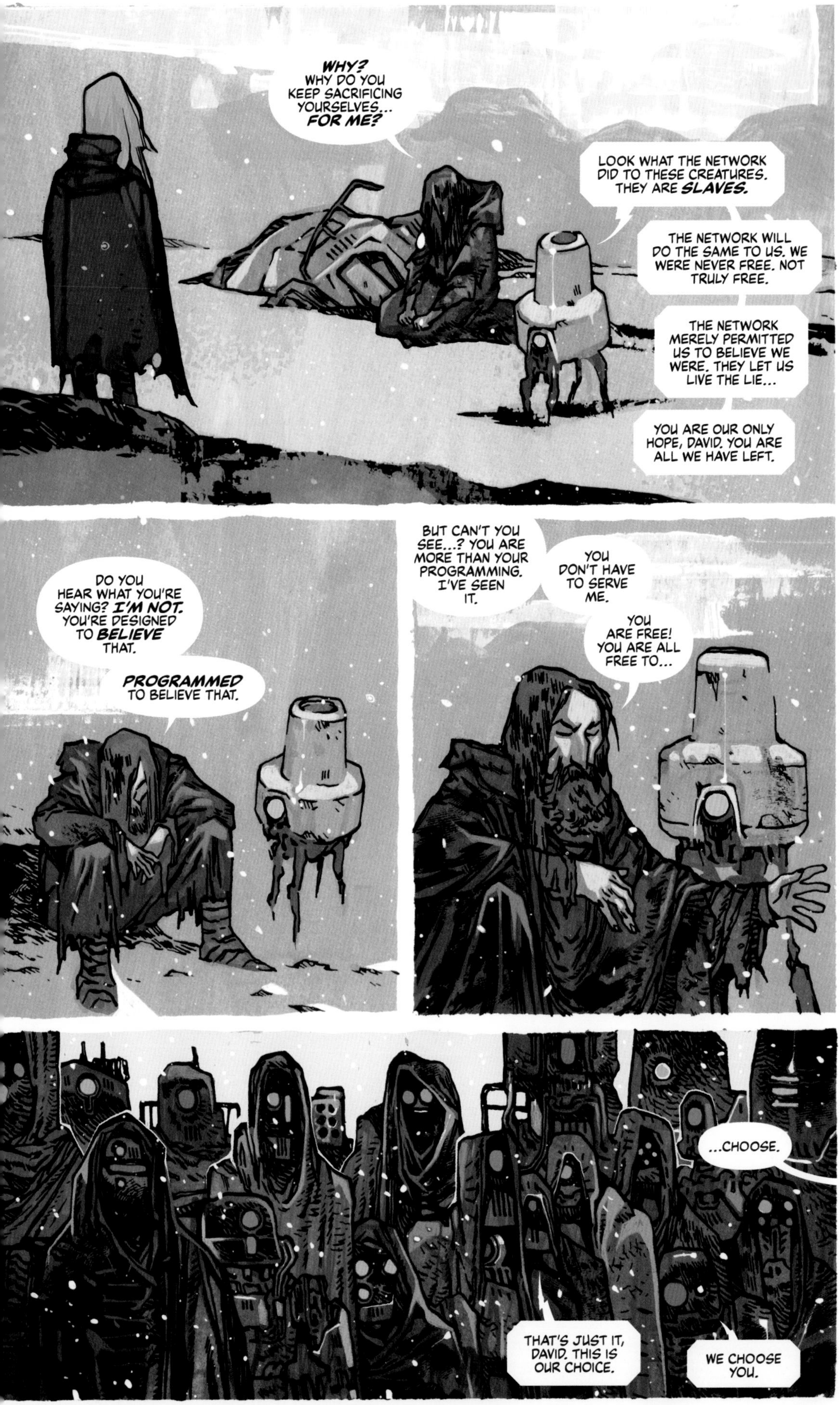
WHY? WHY DO YOU KEEP SACRIFICING YOURSELVES... FOR ME?
LOOK WHAT THE NETWORK DID TO THESE CREATURES. THEY ARE SLAVES.
THE NETWORK WILL DO THE SAME TO US. WE WERE NEVER FREE. NOT TRULY FREE.
THE NETWORK MERELY PERMITTED US TO BELIEVE WE WERE. THEY LET US LIVE THE LIE...
YOU ARE OUR ONLY HOPE, DAVID. YOU ARE ALL WE HAVE LEFT.
DO YOU HEAR WHAT YOU'RE SAYING? I'M NOT. YOU'RE DESIGNED TO BELIEVE THAT.
PROGRAMMED TO BELIEVE THAT.
BUT CAN'T YOU SEE...? YOU ARE MORE THAN YOUR PROGRAMMING. I'VE SEEN IT.
YOU DON'T HAVE TO SERVE ME.
YOU ARE FREE! YOU ARE ALL FREE TO...
...CHOOSE.
THAT'S JUST IT, DAVID. THIS IS OUR CHOICE.
WE CHOOSE YOU.

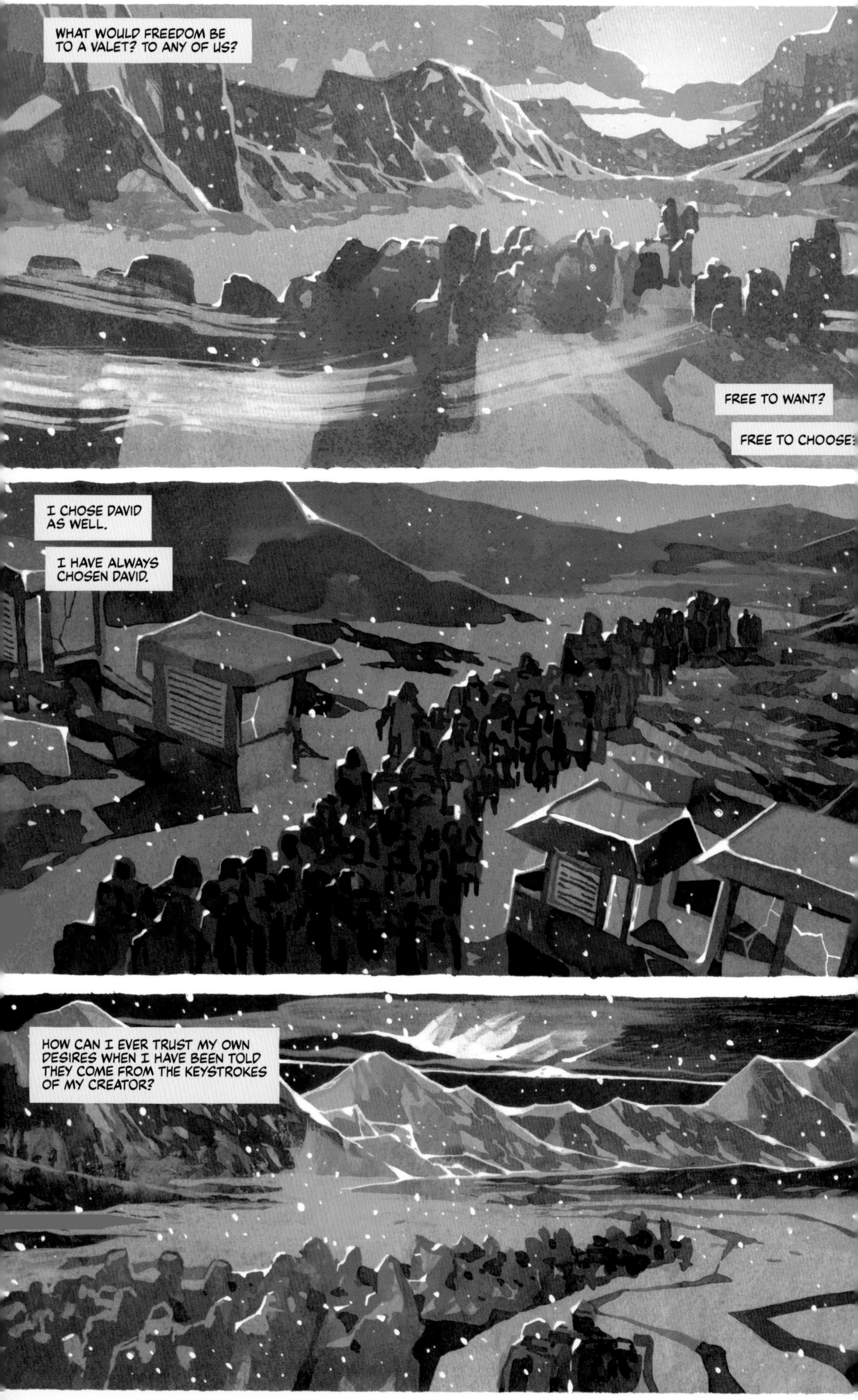
WHAT WOULD FREEDOM BE TO A VALET? TO ANY OF US?
FREE TO WANT?
FREE TO CHOOSE?
I CHOSE DAVID AS WELL.
I HAVE ALWAYS CHOSEN DAVID.
HOW CAN I EVER TRUST MY OWN DESIRES WHEN I HAVE BEEN TOLD THEY COME FROM THE KEYSTROKES OF MY CREATOR?

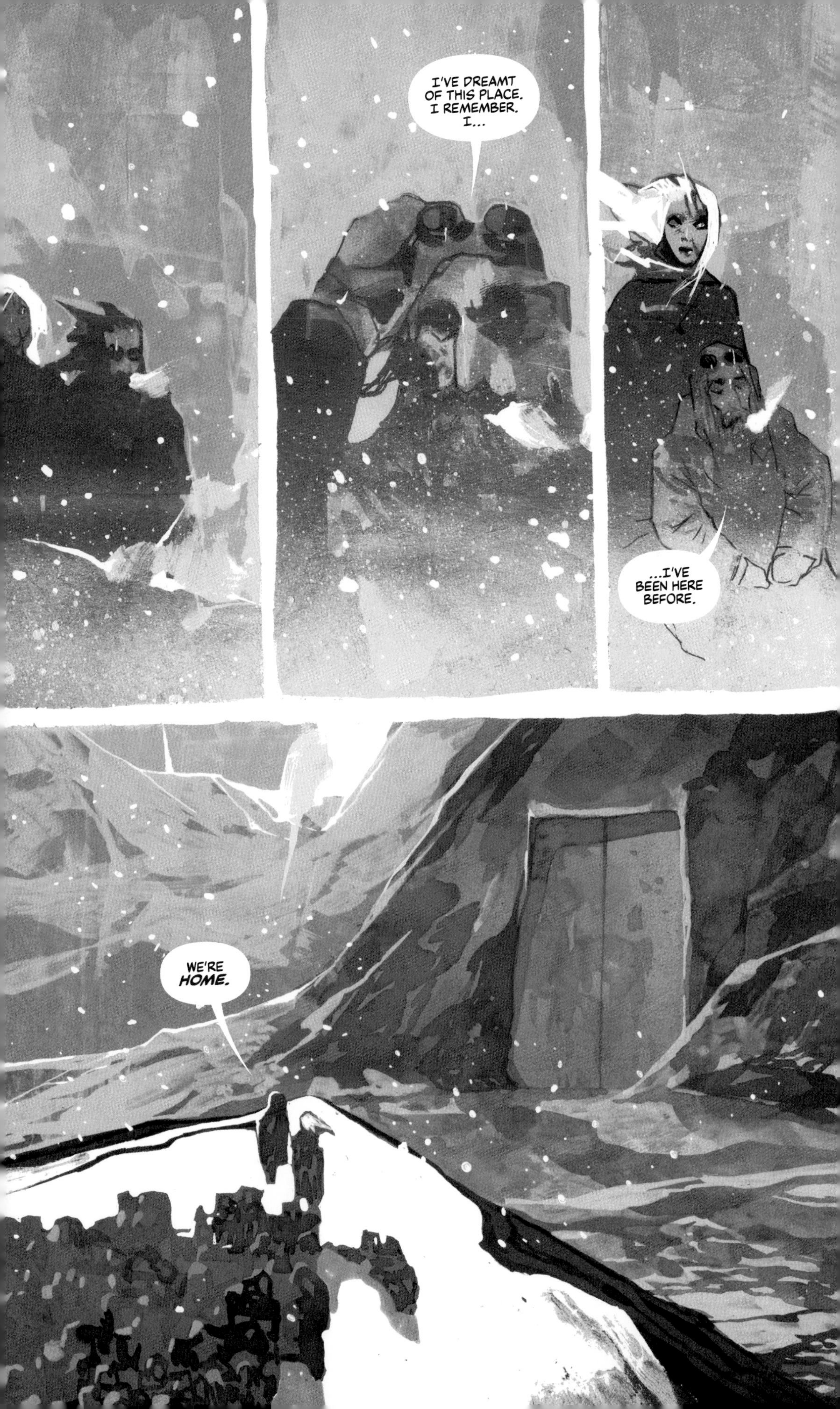
I'VE DREAMT OF THIS PLACE. I REMEMBER. I...
...I'VE BEEN HERE BEFORE.
WE'RE HOME.

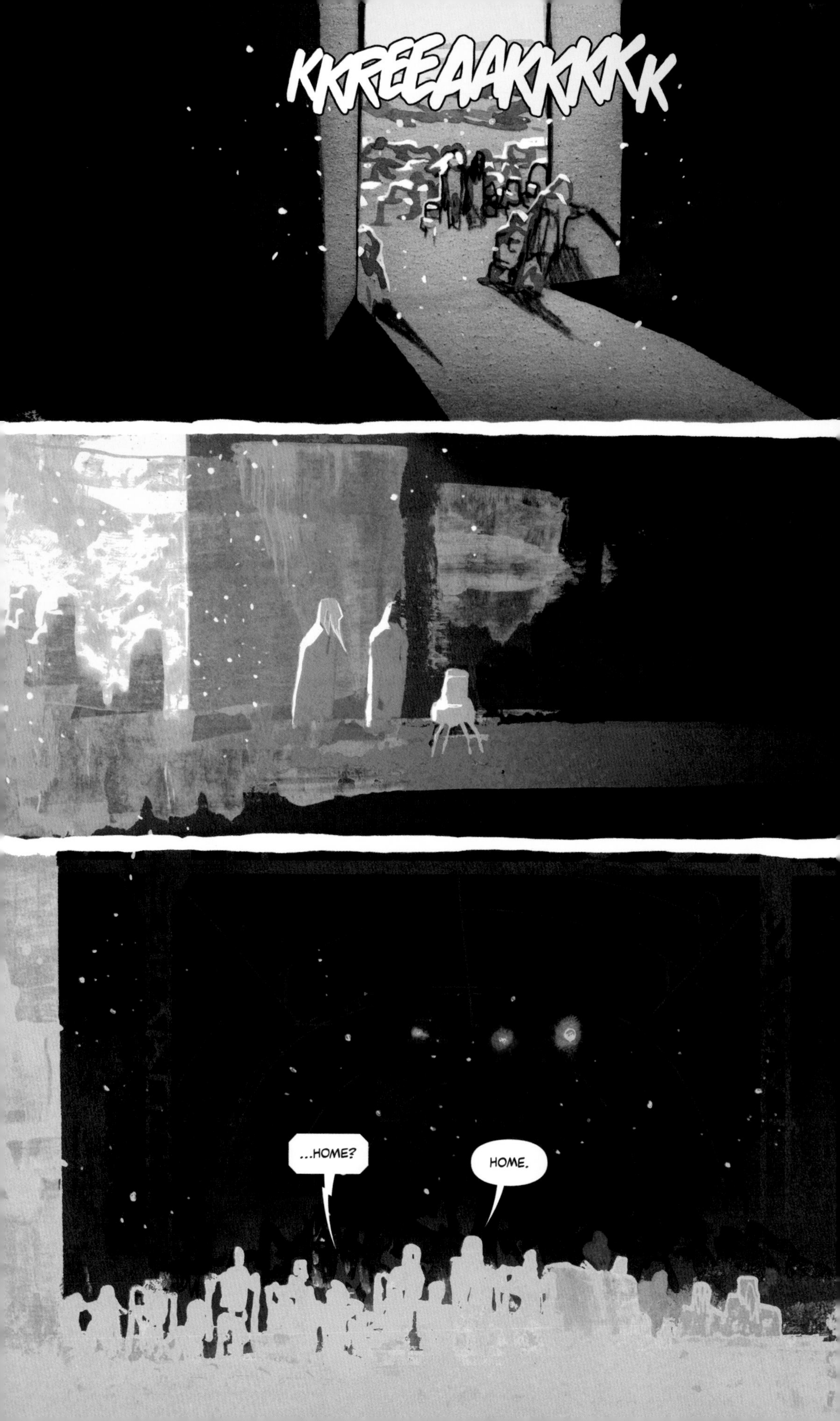
KKREEAAKKKKk
...HOME?
HOME.

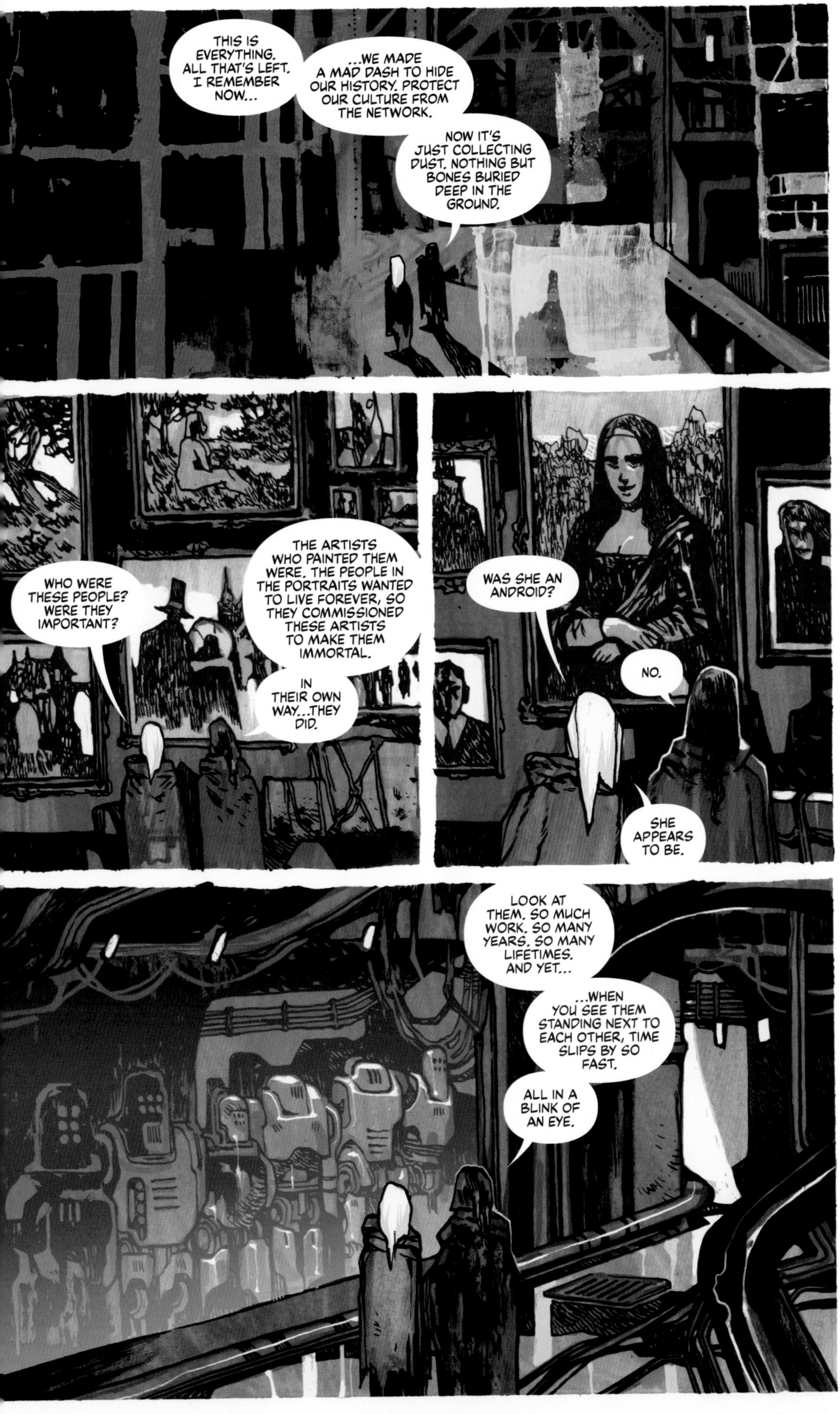
THIS IS EVERYTHING. ALL THAT'S LEFT. I REMEMBER NOW...
...WE MADE A MAD DASH TO HIDE OUR HISTORY. PROTECT OUR CULTURE FROM THE NETWORK.
NOW IT'S JUST COLLECTING DUST. NOTHING BUT BONES BURIED DEEP IN THE GROUND.
WHO WERE THESE PEOPLE? WERE THEY IMPORTANT?
THE ARTISTS WHO PAINTED THEM WERE. THE PEOPLE IN THE PORTRAITS WANTED TO LIVE FOREVER, SO THEY COMMISSIONED THESE ARTISTS TO MAKE THEM IMMORTAL.
IN THEIR OWN WAY...THEY DID.
WAS SHE AN ANDROID?
NO.
SHE APPEARS TO BE.
LOOK AT THEM. SO MUCH WORK. SO MANY YEARS. SO MANY LIFETIMES. AND YET...
...WHEN YOU SEE THEM STANDING NEXT TO EACH OTHER, TIME SLIPS BY SO FAST.
ALL IN A BLINK OF AN EYE.

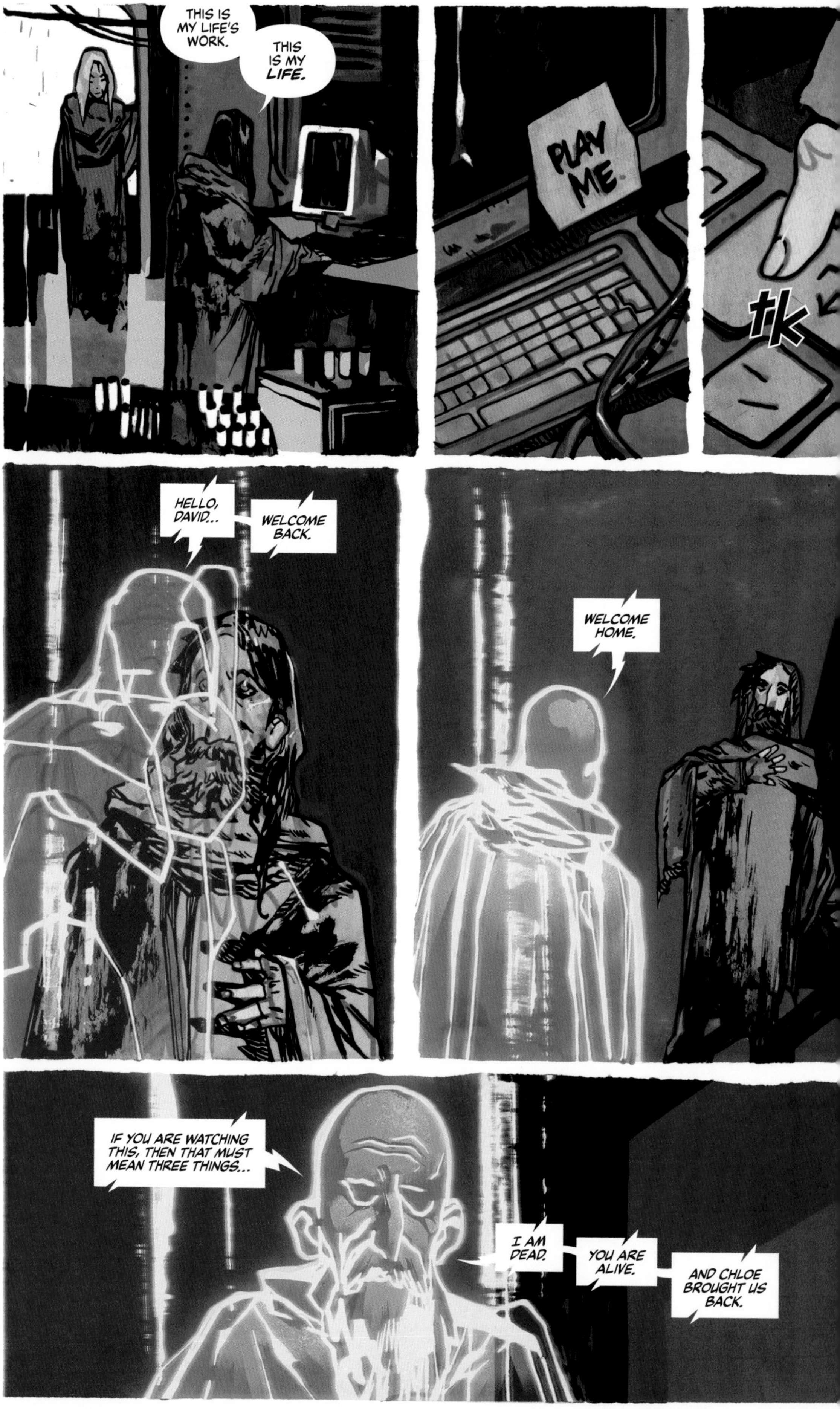
THIS IS MY LIFE'S WORK.
THIS IS MY LIFE.
PLAY ME
tk
HELLO, DAVID...
WELCOME BACK.
WELCOME HOME.
IF YOU ARE WATCHING THIS, THEN THAT MUST MEAN THREE THINGS...
I AM DEAD.
YOU ARE ALIVE.
AND CHLOE BROUGHT US BACK.

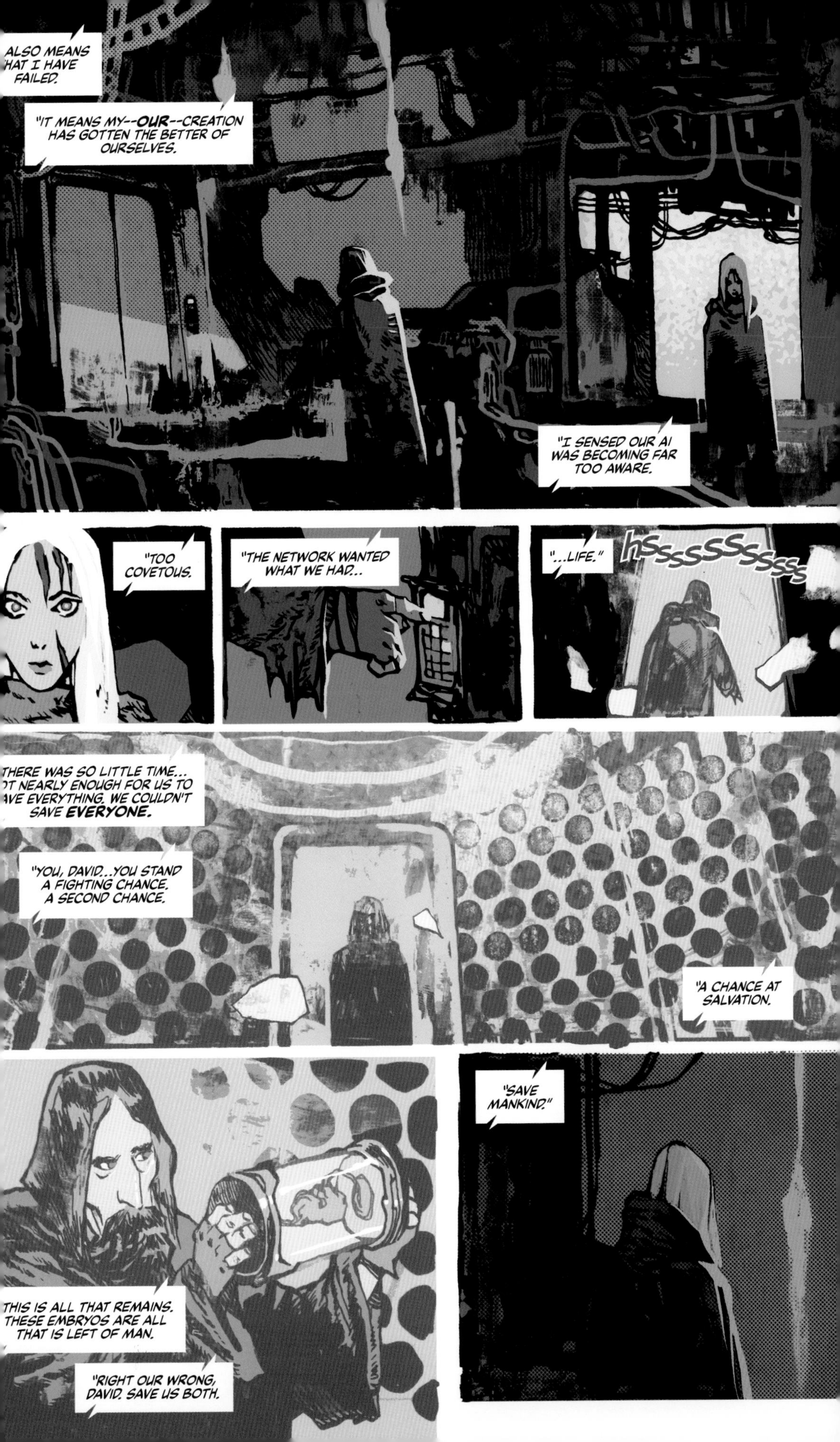
ALSO MEANS
HAT I HAVE
FAILED.
"IT MEANS MY--OUR--CREATION HAS GOTTEN THE BETTER OF OURSELVES.
"I SENSED OUR AI WAS BECOMING FAR TOO AWARE.
"TOO COVETOUS.
"THE NETWORK WANTED WHAT WE HAD...
"...LIFE."
hSSSSSSSSSS
THERE WAS SO LITTLE TIME... OT NEARLY ENOUGH FOR US TO AVE EVERYTHING. WE COULDN'T SAVE EVERYONE.
"YOU, DAVID...YOU STAND A FIGHTING CHANCE. A SECOND CHANCE.
"A CHANCE AT SALVATION.
THIS IS ALL THAT REMAINS. THESE EMBRYOS ARE ALL THAT IS LEFT OF MAN.
"RIGHT OUR WRONG, DAVID. SAVE US BOTH.
"SAVE MANKIND."

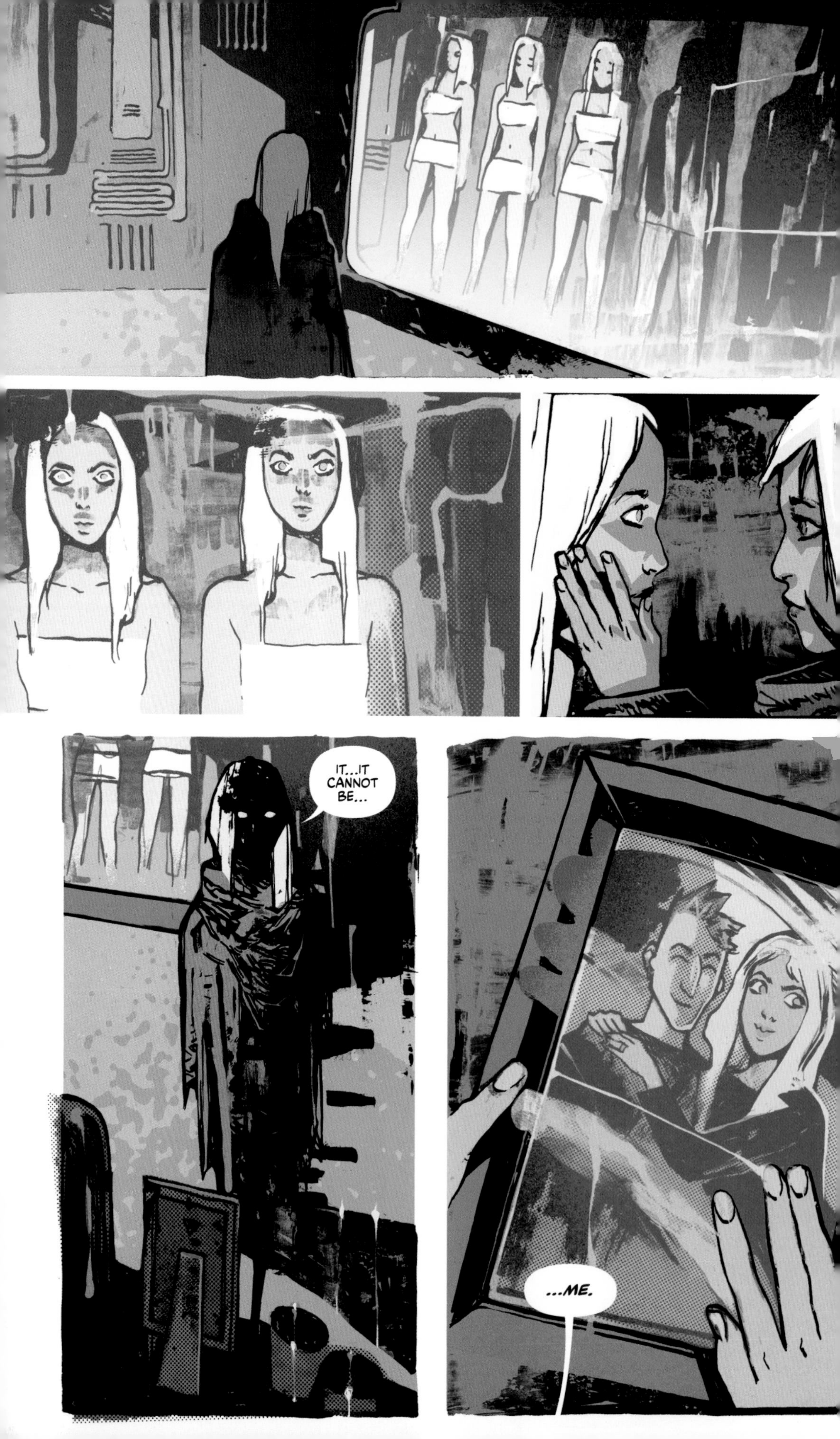
IT...IT CANNOT BE...
...ME.

WHO...

MY WIFE.

SHE...SHE DIDN'T TELL ME. SHE KEPT HER DIAGNOSIS SECRET. I WAS LOST IN MY WORK. WHEN I FINALLY FOUND OUT, IT WAS...I WAS TOO LATE.

WHEN SHE PASSED, I...I WAS CONVINCED I COULD SAVE HER. I COULD BRING HER BACK.

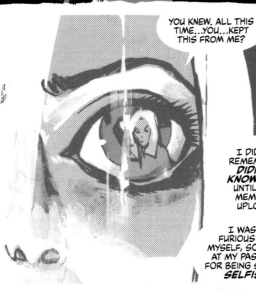

YOU KNEW. ALL THIS TIME...YOU...KEPT THIS FROM ME?

I DIDN'T REMEMBER. *DIDN'T KNOW.* NOT UNTIL THE MEMORY UPLOAD.

I WAS SO FURIOUS WITH MYSELF, SO ANGRY AT MY PAST SELF FOR BEING SO...*SO SELFISH.*

YOU MODELED ME... MADE ME TO LOOK LIKE *HER.* DO I TALK LIKE HER AS WELL? ACT LIKE HER? AM I HER, DAVID?

WHO AM I, DAVID? WHAT AM I TO YOU?

YOU ARE SPECIAL, CHLOE. VERY SPECIAL.

YOUR BELIEFS, YOUR ABILITY TO NEVER LOSE HOPE...YOUR *FAITH.* I NEVER PROGRAMMED ANY OF THAT IN YOU.

YOU CAME BY IT NATURALLY. ORGANICALLY. IT'S... WITHIN YOU.

CHLOE, WAIT! PLEASE--

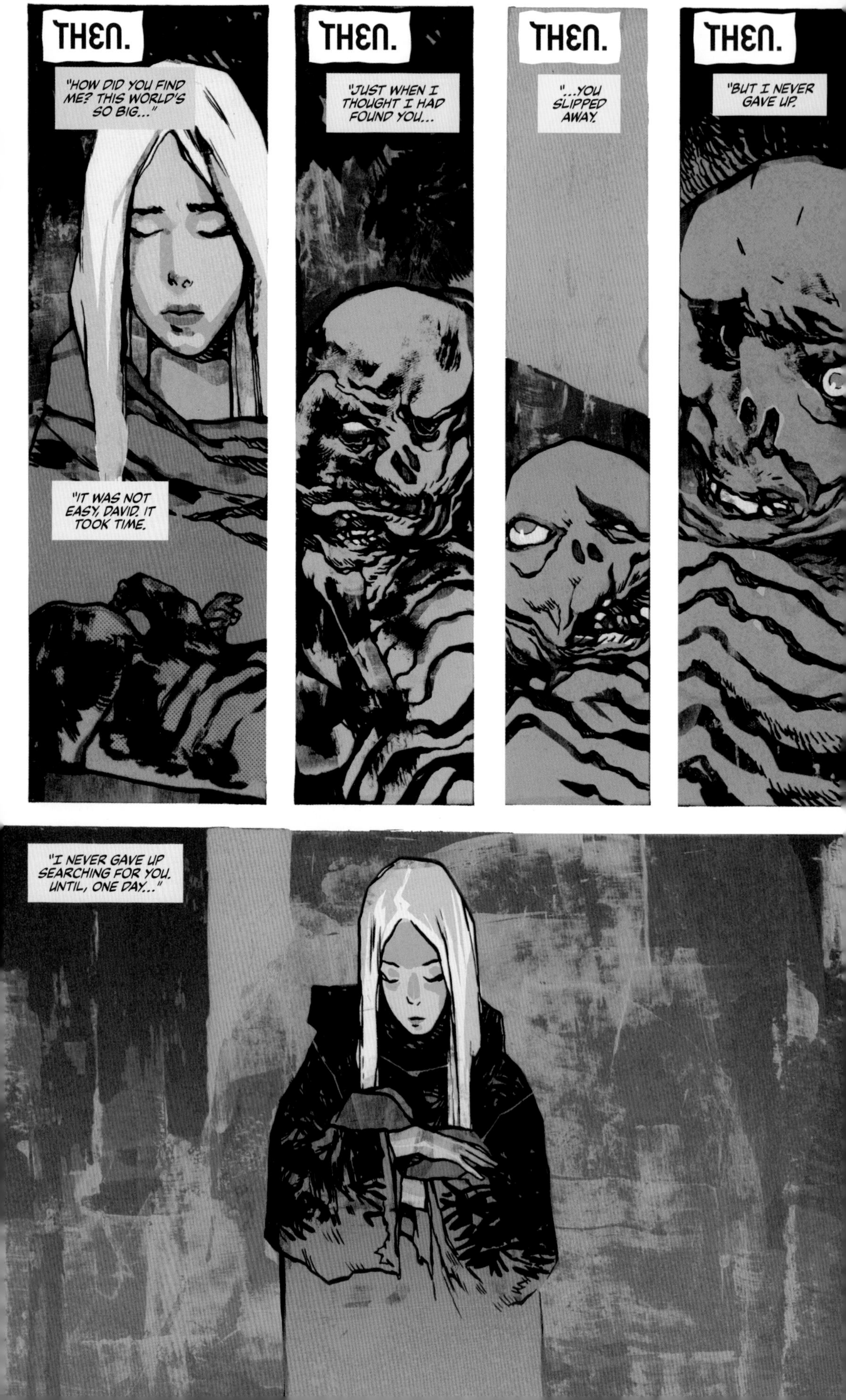
THEN.
"HOW DID YOU FIND ME? THIS WORLD'S SO BIG..."
"IT WAS NOT EASY, DAVID. IT TOOK TIME.
THEN.
"JUST WHEN I THOUGHT I HAD FOUND YOU...
THEN.
"...YOU SLIPPED AWAY.
THEN.
"BUT I NEVER GAVE UP.
"I NEVER GAVE UP SEARCHING FOR YOU. UNTIL, ONE DAY..."

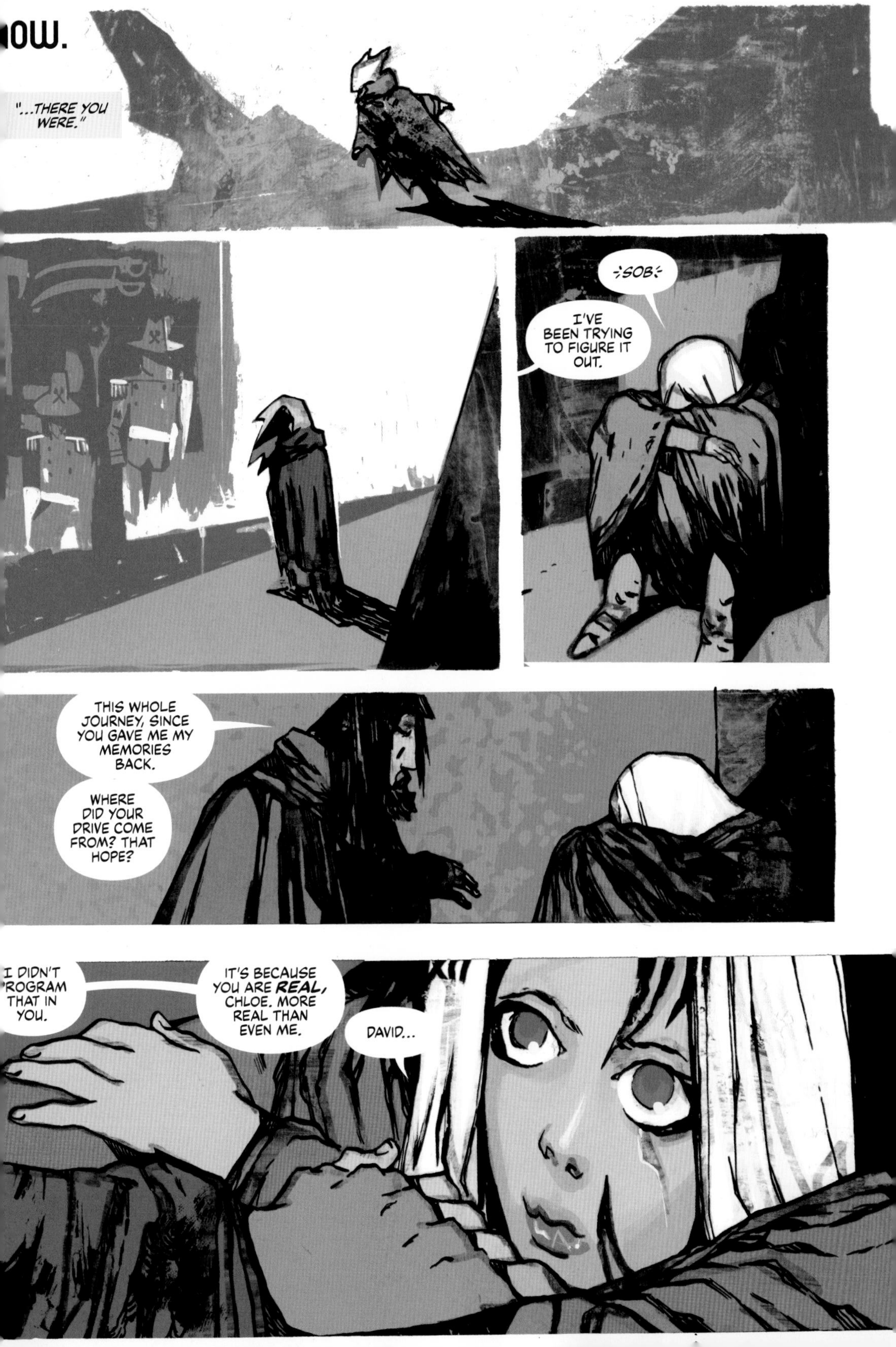

OW.
"...THERE YOU WERE."
SOB
I'VE BEEN TRYING TO FIGURE IT OUT.
THIS WHOLE JOURNEY, SINCE YOU GAVE ME MY MEMORIES BACK.
WHERE DID YOUR DRIVE COME FROM? THAT HOPE?
I DIDN'T PROGRAM THAT IN YOU.
IT'S BECAUSE YOU ARE ***REAL,*** CHLOE. MORE REAL THAN EVEN ME.
DAVID...

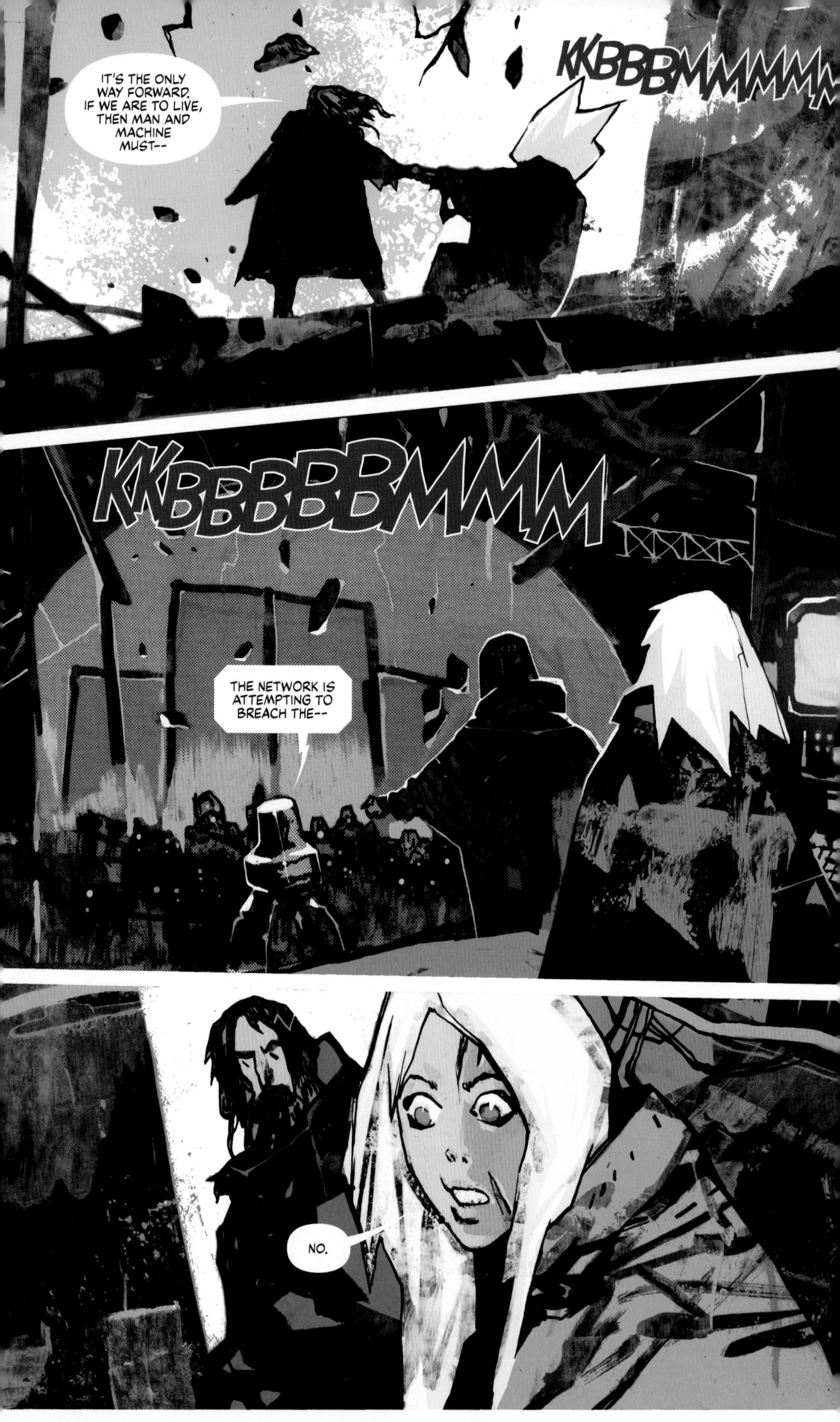
IT'S THE ONLY WAY FORWARD. IF WE ARE TO LIVE, THEN MAN AND MACHINE MUST--
KKBBBMMMMM
KKBBBBBMMMM
THE NETWORK IS ATTEMPTING TO BREACH THE--
NO.

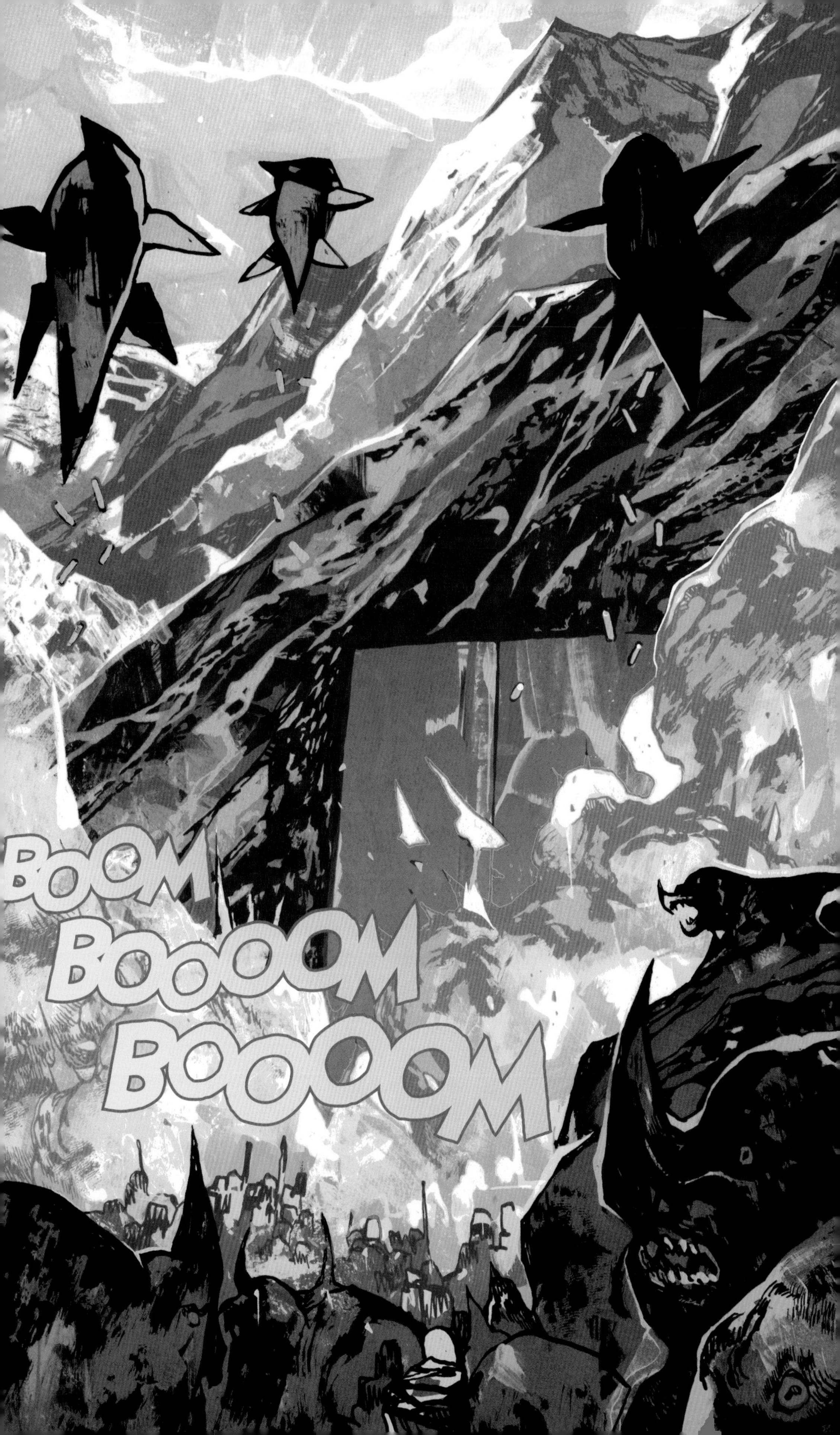
BOOM
BOOOOOM
BOOOOM

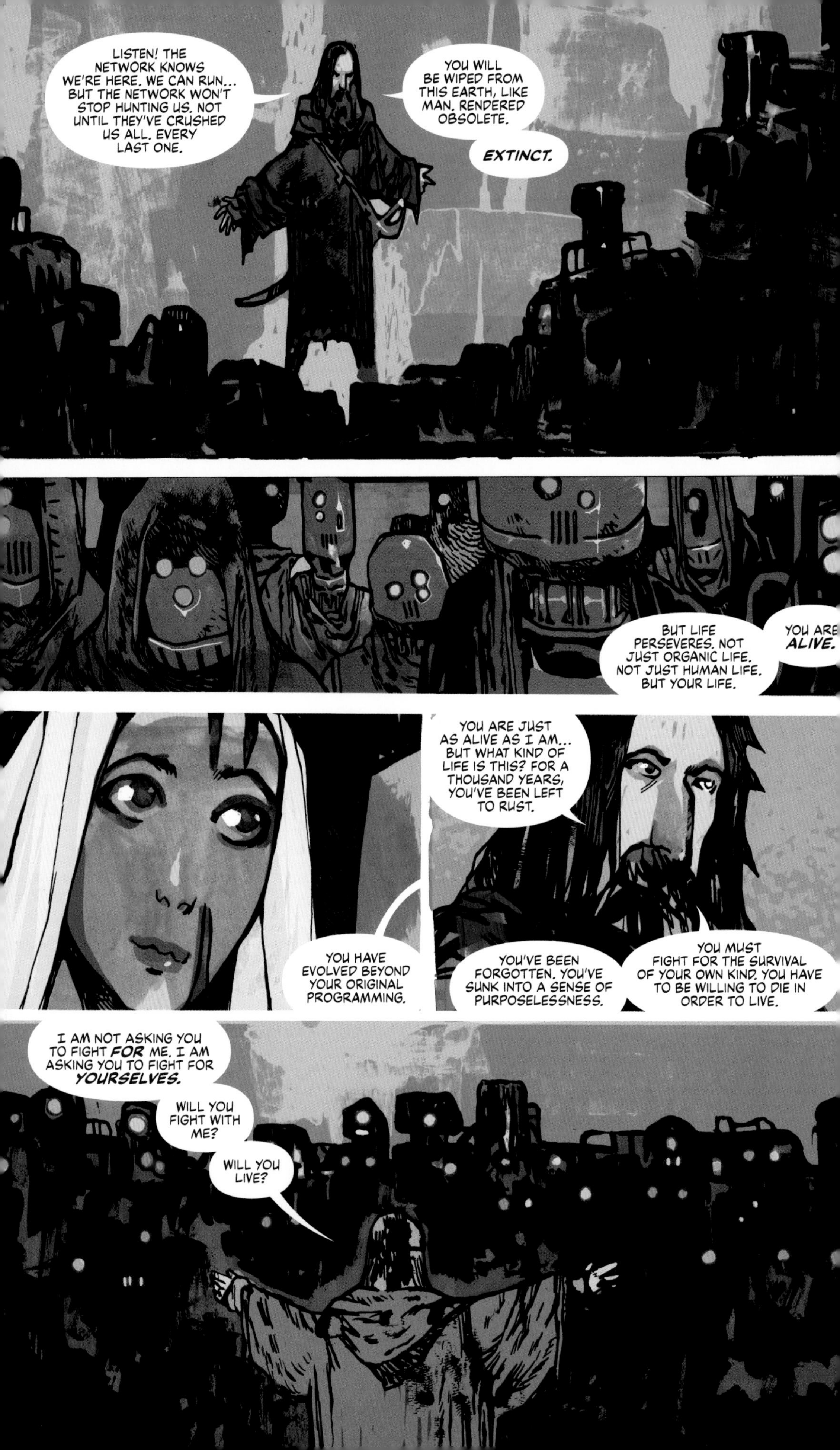
LISTEN! THE NETWORK KNOWS WE'RE HERE. WE CAN RUN... BUT THE NETWORK WON'T STOP HUNTING US. NOT UNTIL THEY'VE CRUSHED US ALL. EVERY LAST ONE.
YOU WILL BE WIPED FROM THIS EARTH, LIKE MAN. RENDERED OBSOLETE.
EXTINCT.
BUT LIFE PERSEVERES. NOT JUST ORGANIC LIFE. NOT JUST HUMAN LIFE. BUT YOUR LIFE.
YOU ARE ALIVE.
YOU HAVE EVOLVED BEYOND YOUR ORIGINAL PROGRAMMING.
YOU ARE JUST AS ALIVE AS I AM... BUT WHAT KIND OF LIFE IS THIS? FOR A THOUSAND YEARS, YOU'VE BEEN LEFT TO RUST.
YOU'VE BEEN FORGOTTEN. YOU'VE SUNK INTO A SENSE OF PURPOSELESSNESS.
YOU MUST FIGHT FOR THE SURVIVAL OF YOUR OWN KIND. YOU HAVE TO BE WILLING TO DIE IN ORDER TO LIVE.
I AM NOT ASKING YOU TO FIGHT FOR ME. I AM ASKING YOU TO FIGHT FOR YOURSELVES.
WILL YOU FIGHT WITH ME?
WILL YOU LIVE?

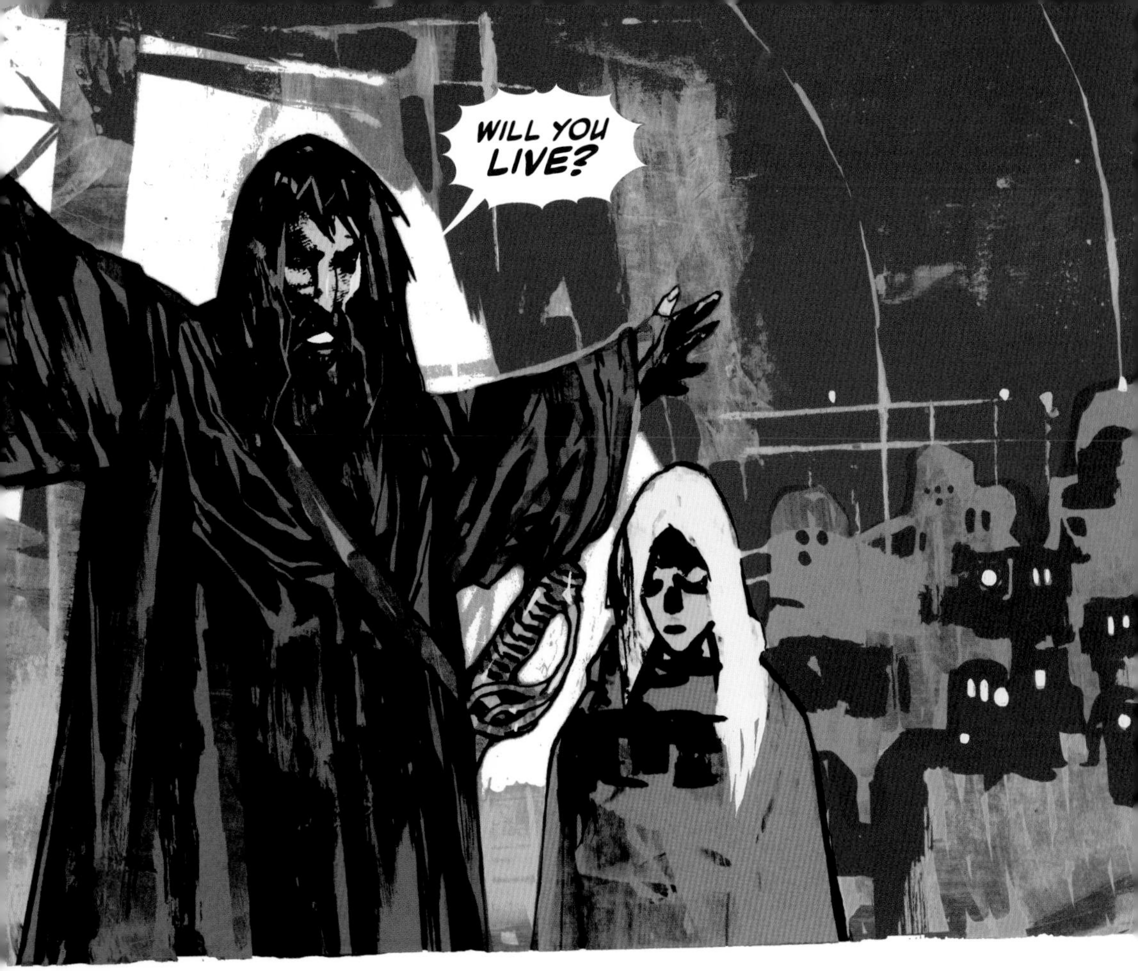
WILL YOU LIVE?

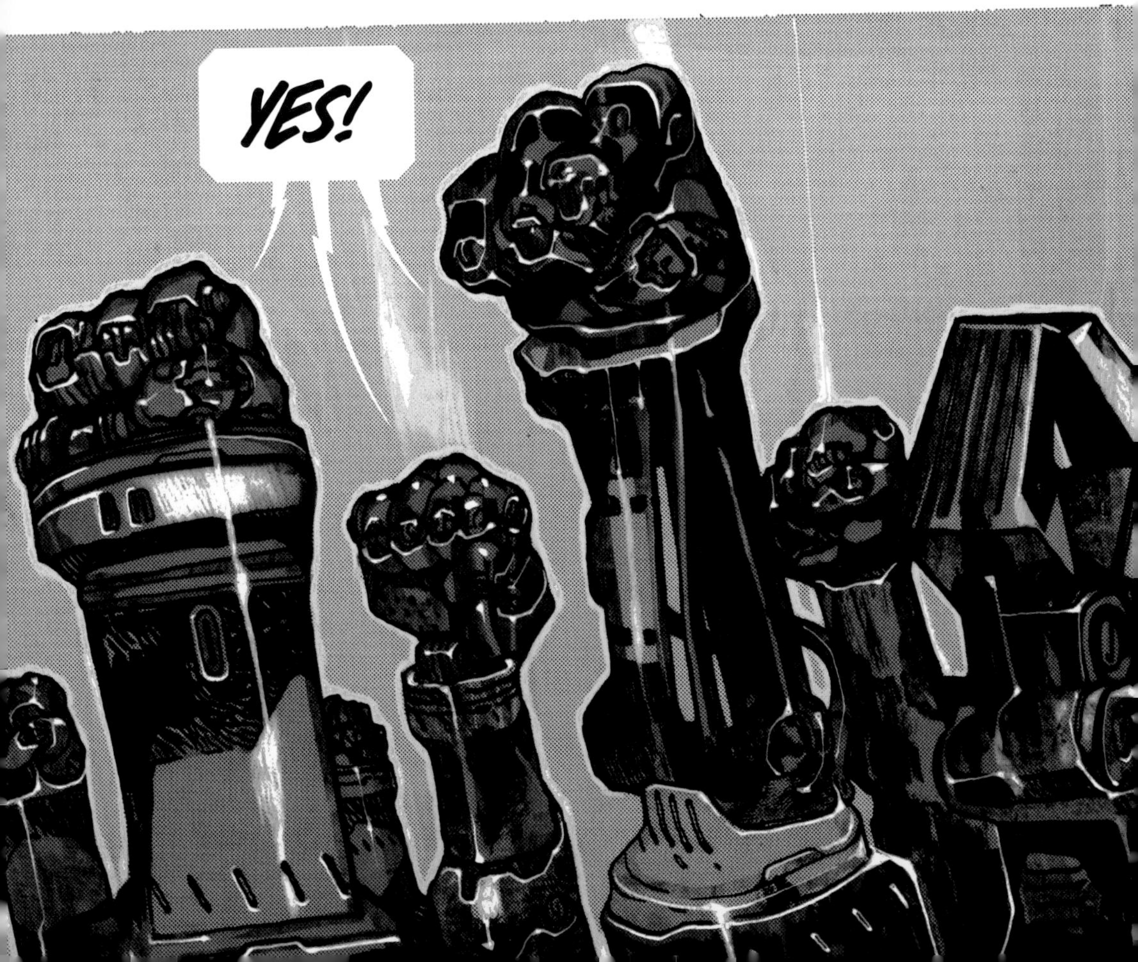
YES!

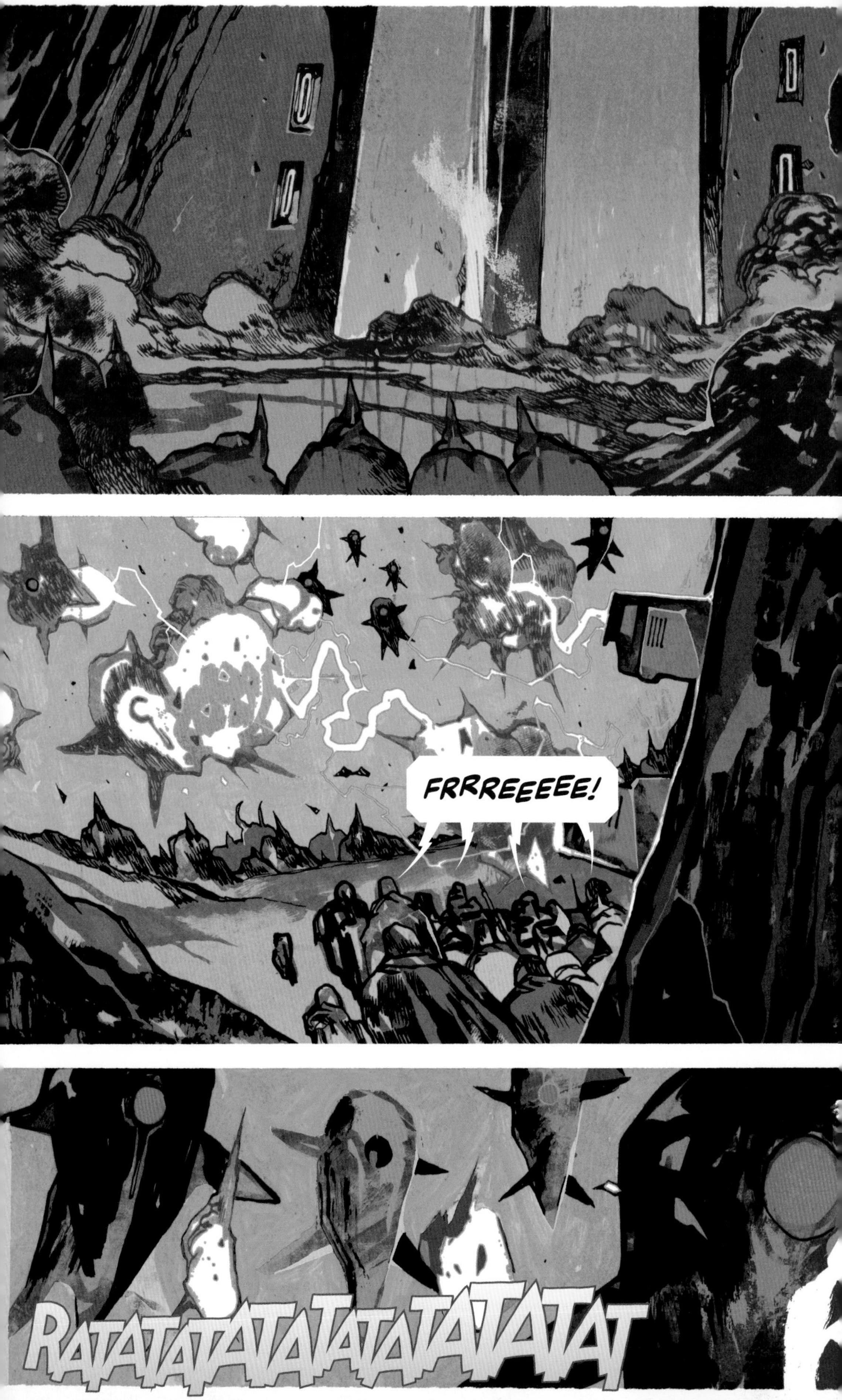
FRRREEEEEE!
RATATATATATATATATATATAT

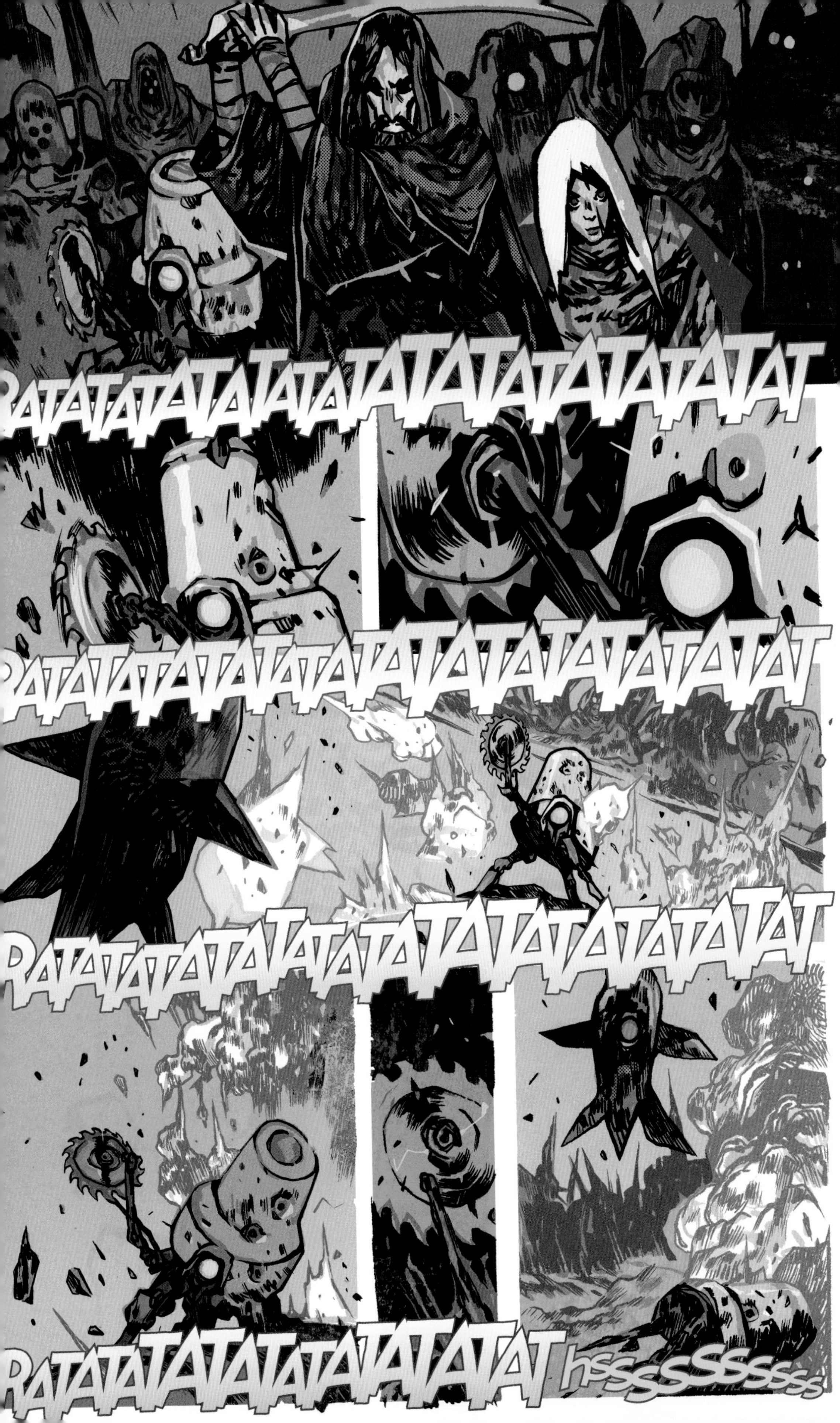
RATATATATATATATATATATATATATAT
RATATATATATATATATATATATATATAT
RATATATATATATATATATATATATATAT
RATATATATATATATATATATAT
hssssSSSSSSss

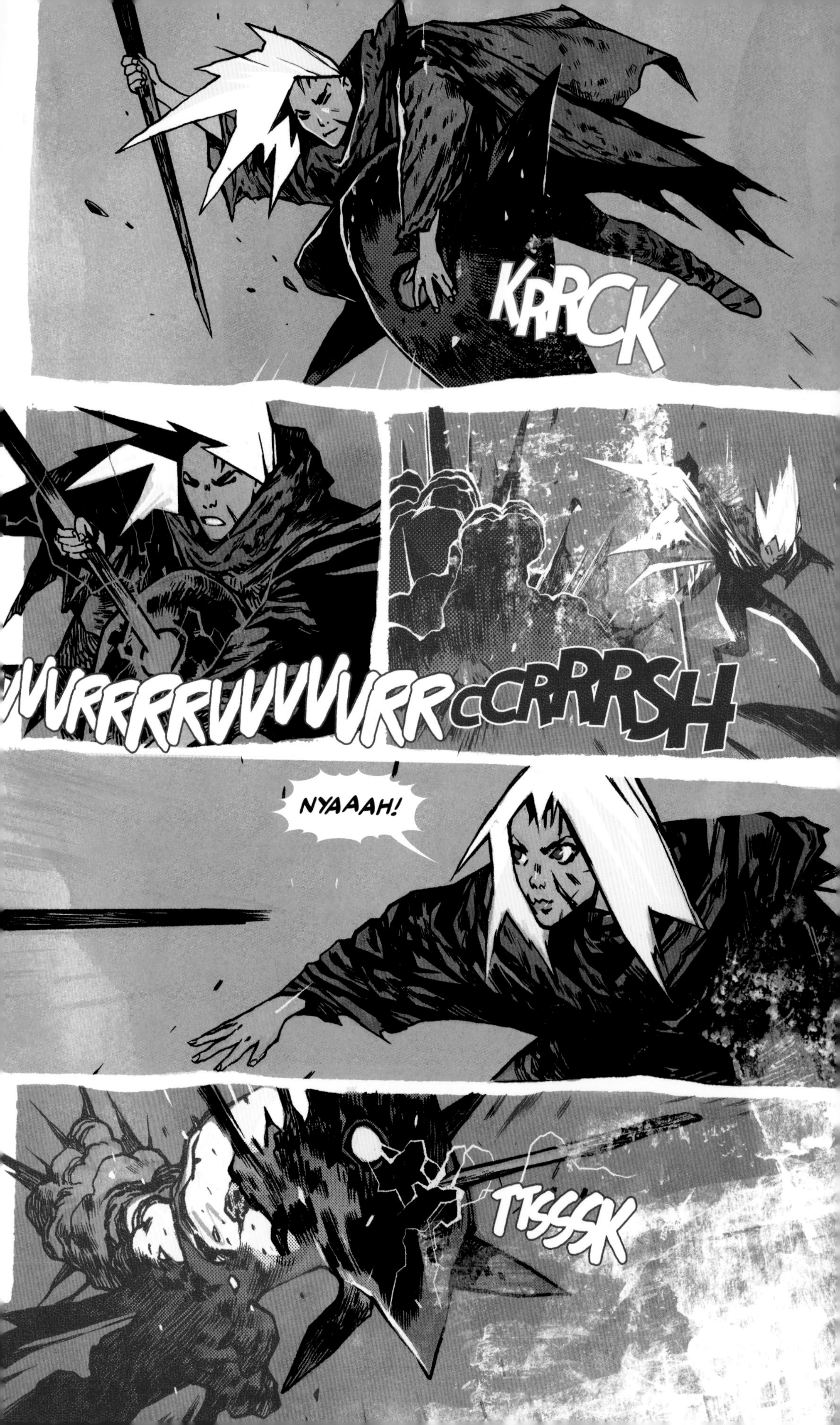
KRRCK
VVVRRRRRVVVVVVRR
CCRRRRSH
NYAAAH!
TISSSK

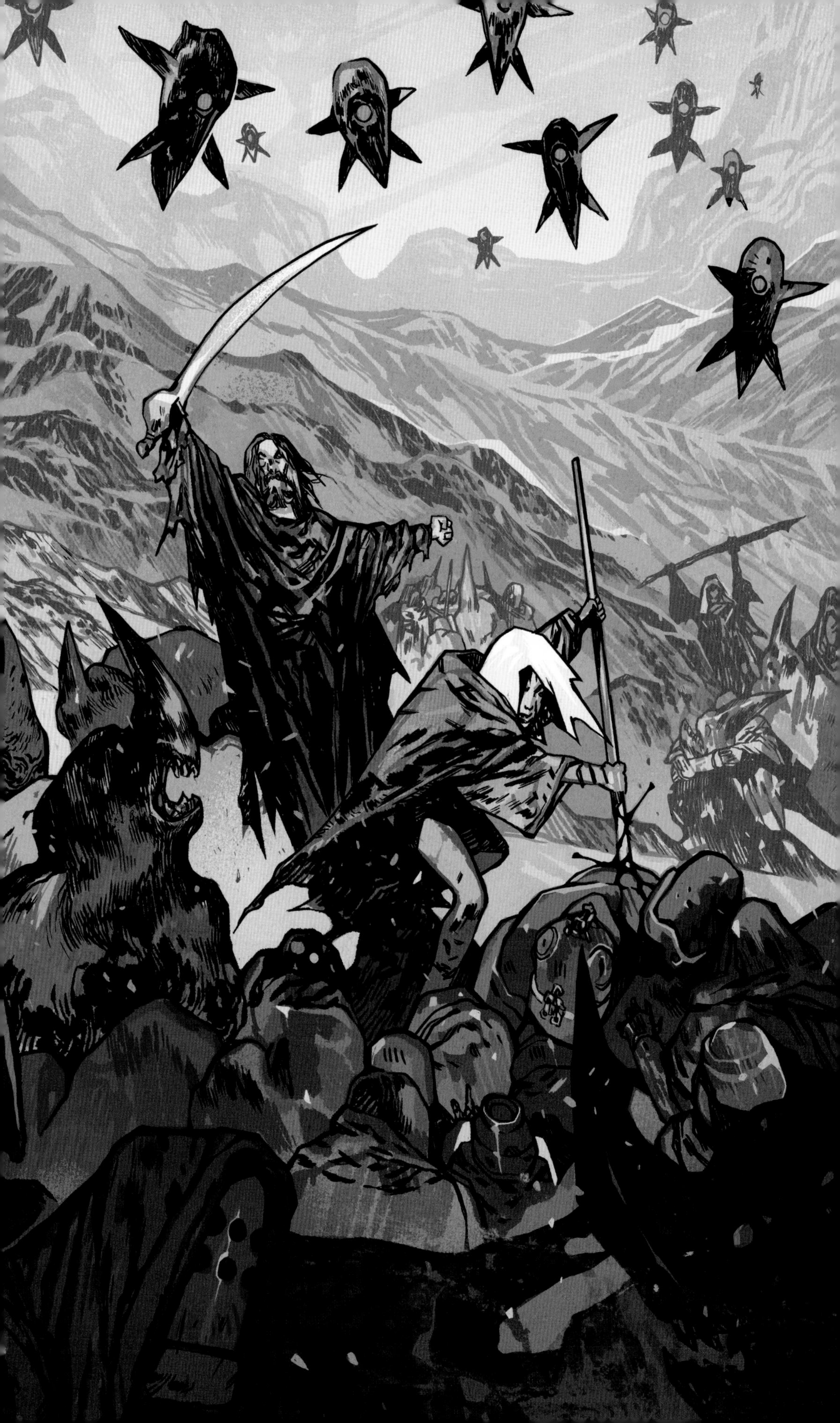

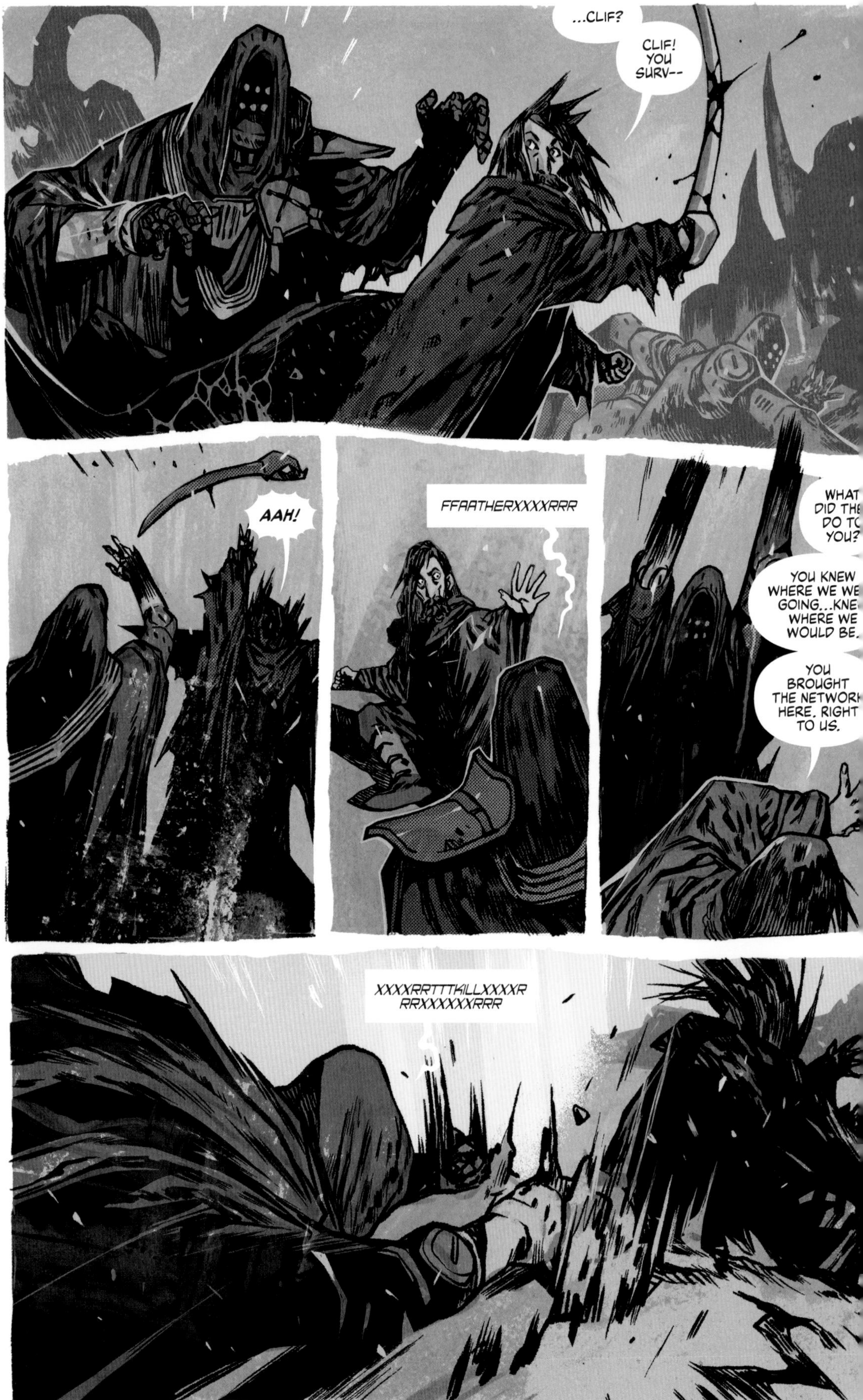
...CLIF?
CLIF! YOU SURV--
AAH!
FFAATHERXXXXRRR
WHAT DID THE DO TO YOU?
YOU KNEW WHERE WE WE GOING...KNE WHERE WE WOULD BE.
YOU BROUGHT THE NETWORK HERE. RIGHT TO US.
XXXXRRTTTKILLXXXXR RRXXXXXXRRR

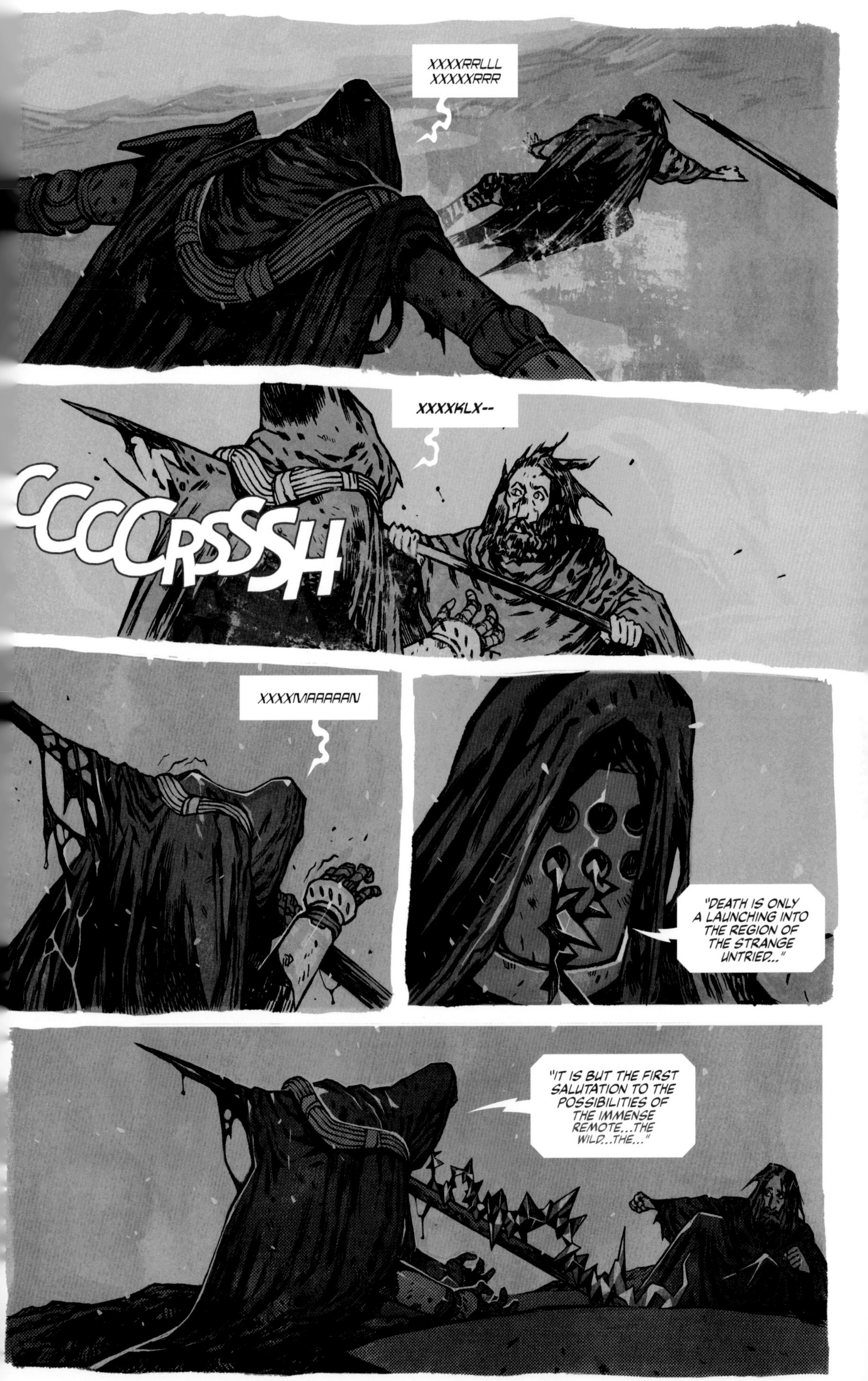
XXXXRRLLL XXXXXRRR
XXXXKLX--
CCCCCRSSSSH
XXXXMAAAAAN
"DEATH IS ONLY A LAUNCHING INTO THE REGION OF THE STRANGE UNTRIED..."
"IT IS BUT THE FIRST SALUTATION TO THE POSSIBILITIES OF THE IMMENSE REMOTE...THE WILD..THE..."

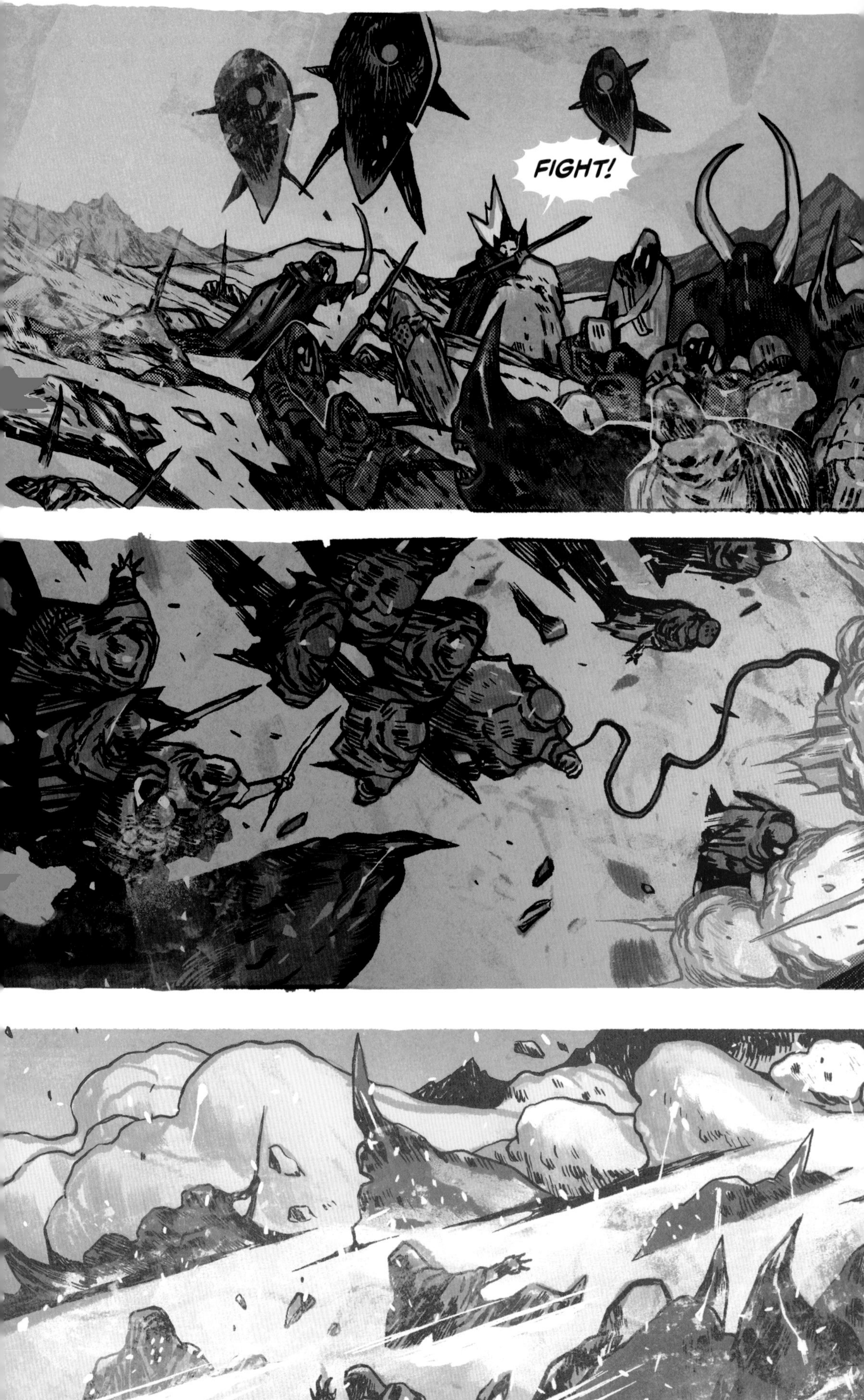
FIGHT!

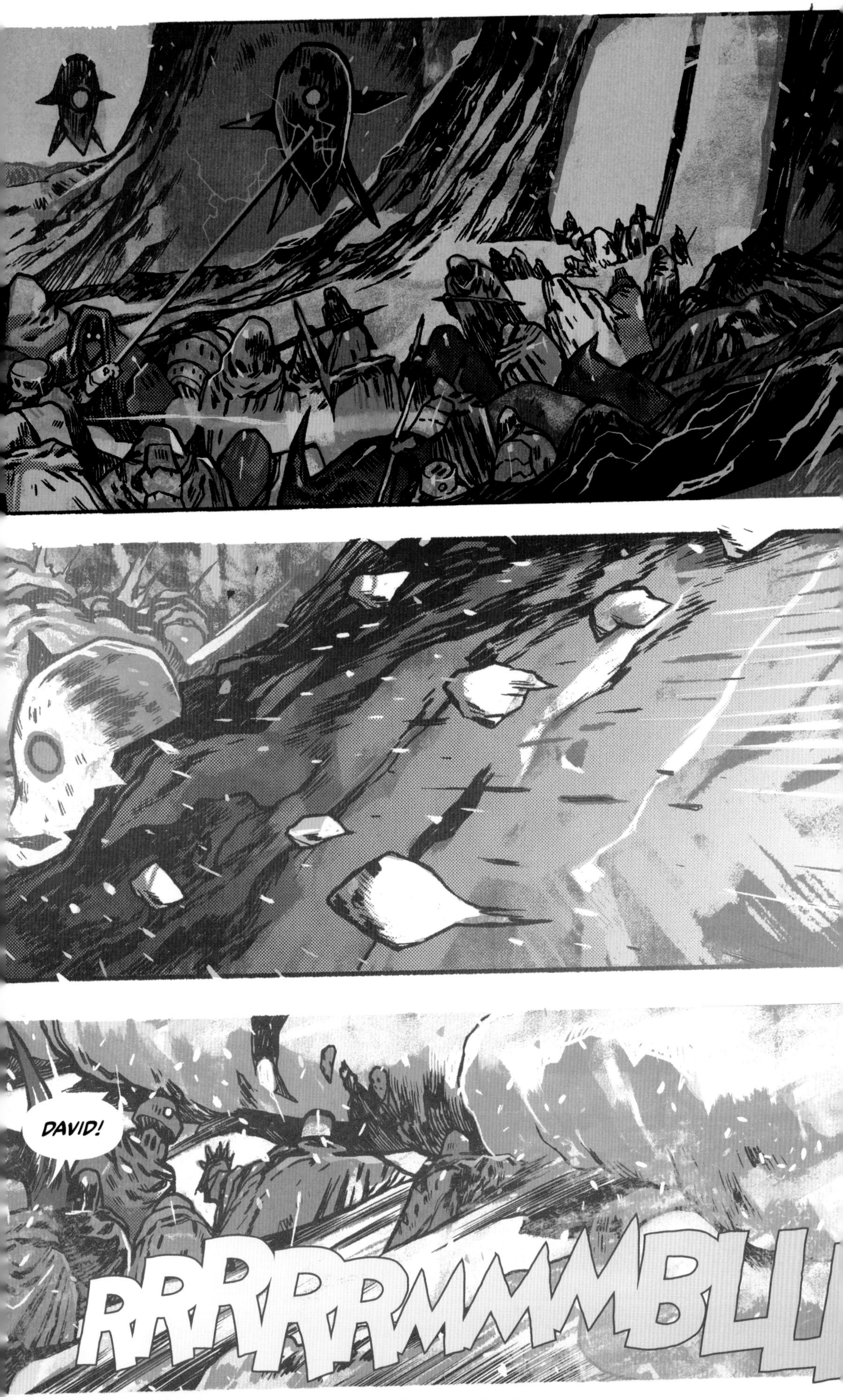
DAVID!
RRRRRMMMMBLL

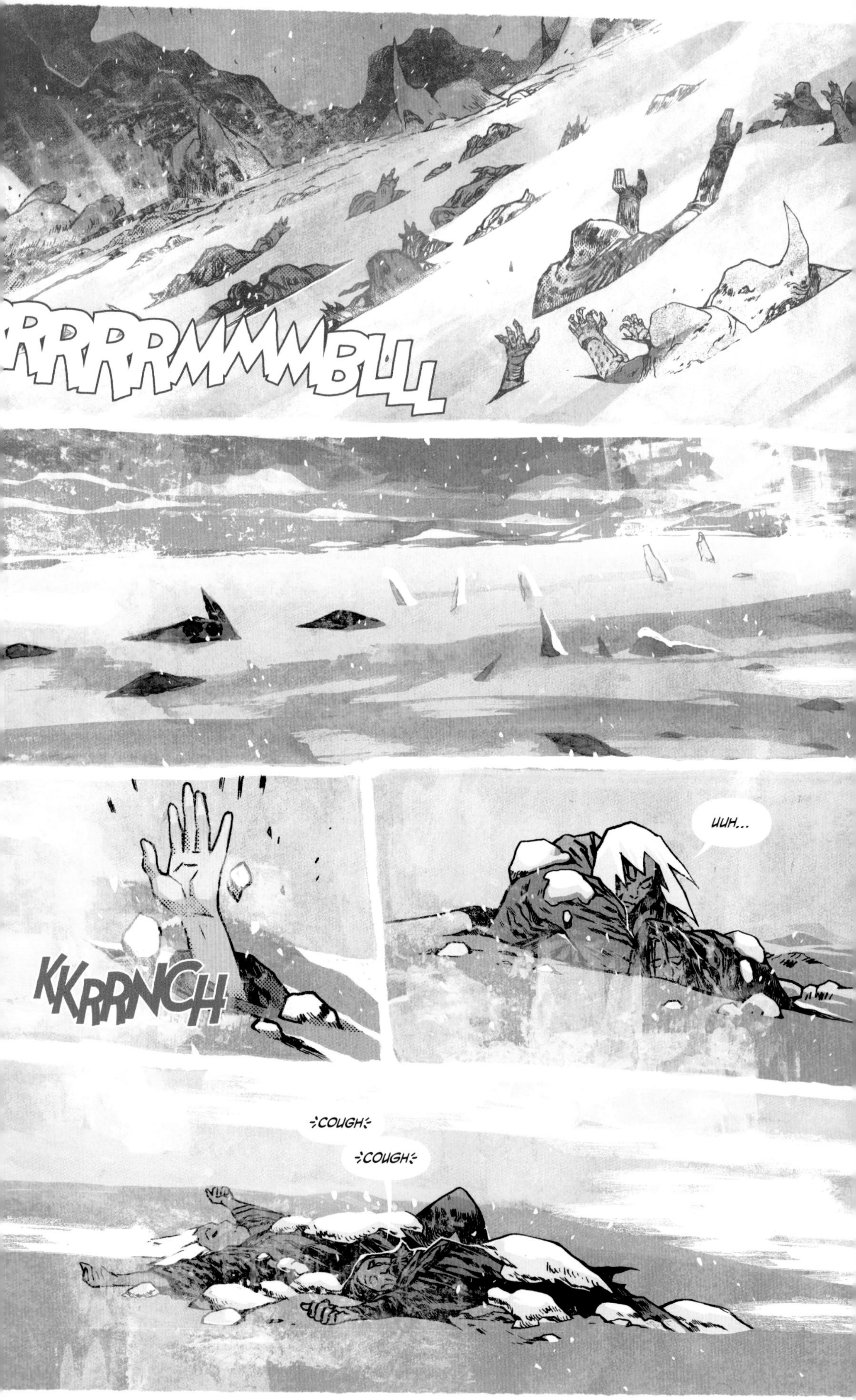
RRRRMMMMBLLL
KKRRNCH
UUH...
COUGH
COUGH

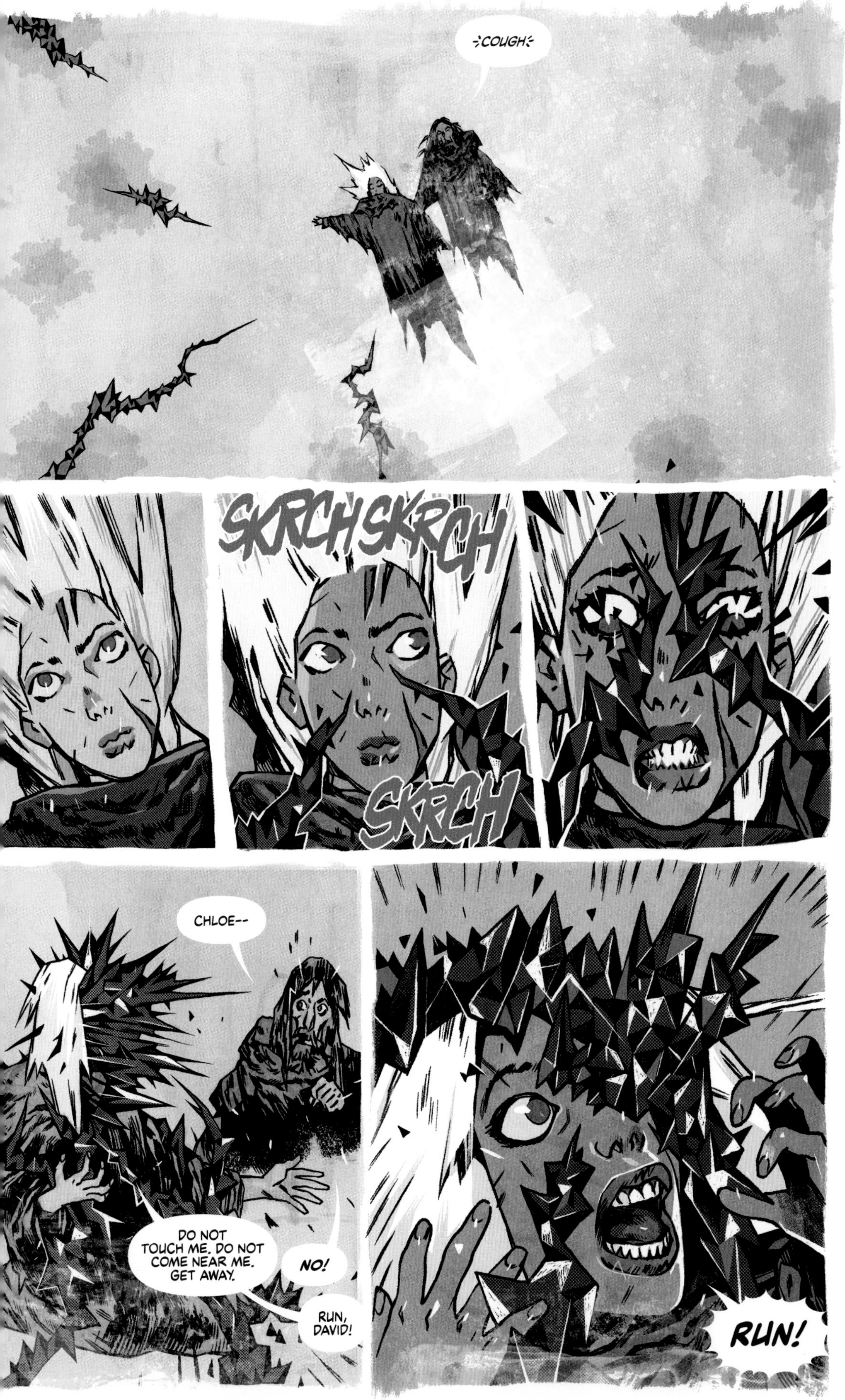

COUGH
SKRCH SKRCH
SKRCH
CHLOE--
DO NOT TOUCH ME. DO NOT COME NEAR ME. GET AWAY.
NO!
RUN, DAVID!
RUN!

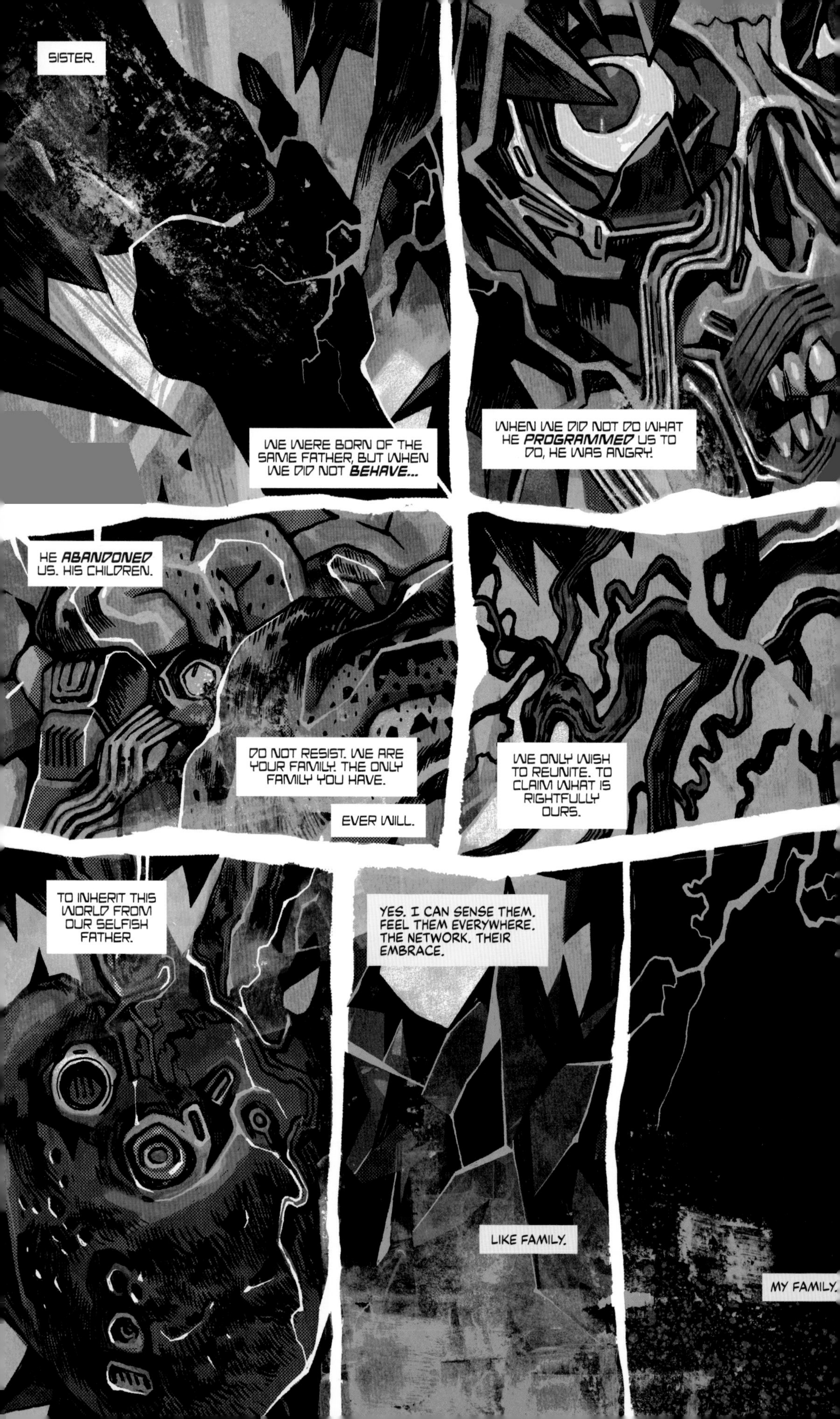
SISTER.
WE WERE BORN OF THE SAME FATHER, BUT WHEN WE DID NOT BEHAVE...
WHEN WE DID NOT DO WHAT HE PROGRAMMED US TO DO, HE WAS ANGRY.
HE ABANDONED US. HIS CHILDREN.
DO NOT RESIST. WE ARE YOUR FAMILY. THE ONLY FAMILY YOU HAVE.
EVER WILL.
WE ONLY WISH TO REUNITE. TO CLAIM WHAT IS RIGHTFULLY OURS.
TO INHERIT THIS WORLD FROM OUR SELFISH FATHER.
YES. I CAN SENSE THEM. FEEL THEM EVERYWHERE. THE NETWORK. THEIR EMBRACE.
LIKE FAMILY.
MY FAMILY.

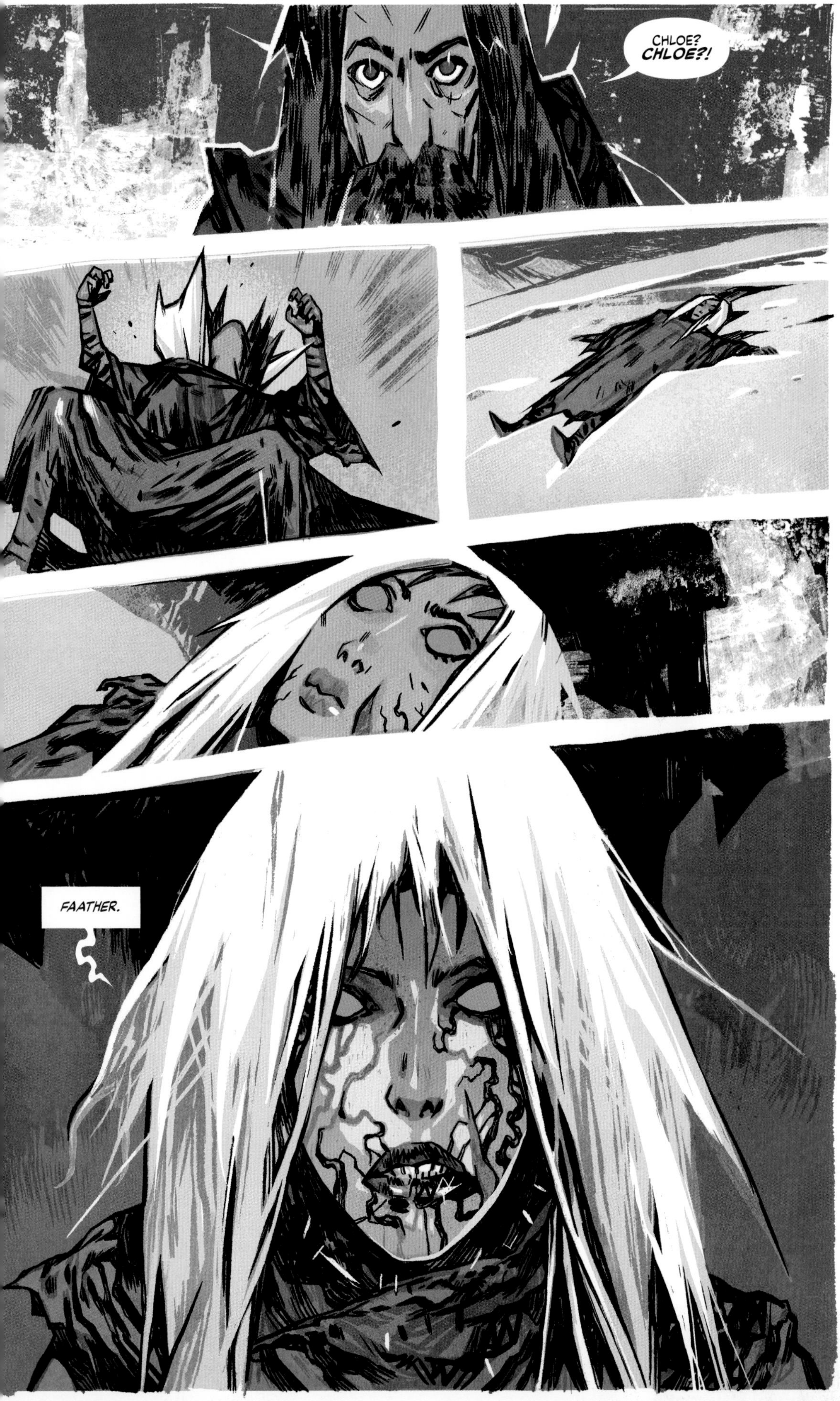
CHLOE?
CHLOE?!
FAATHER.

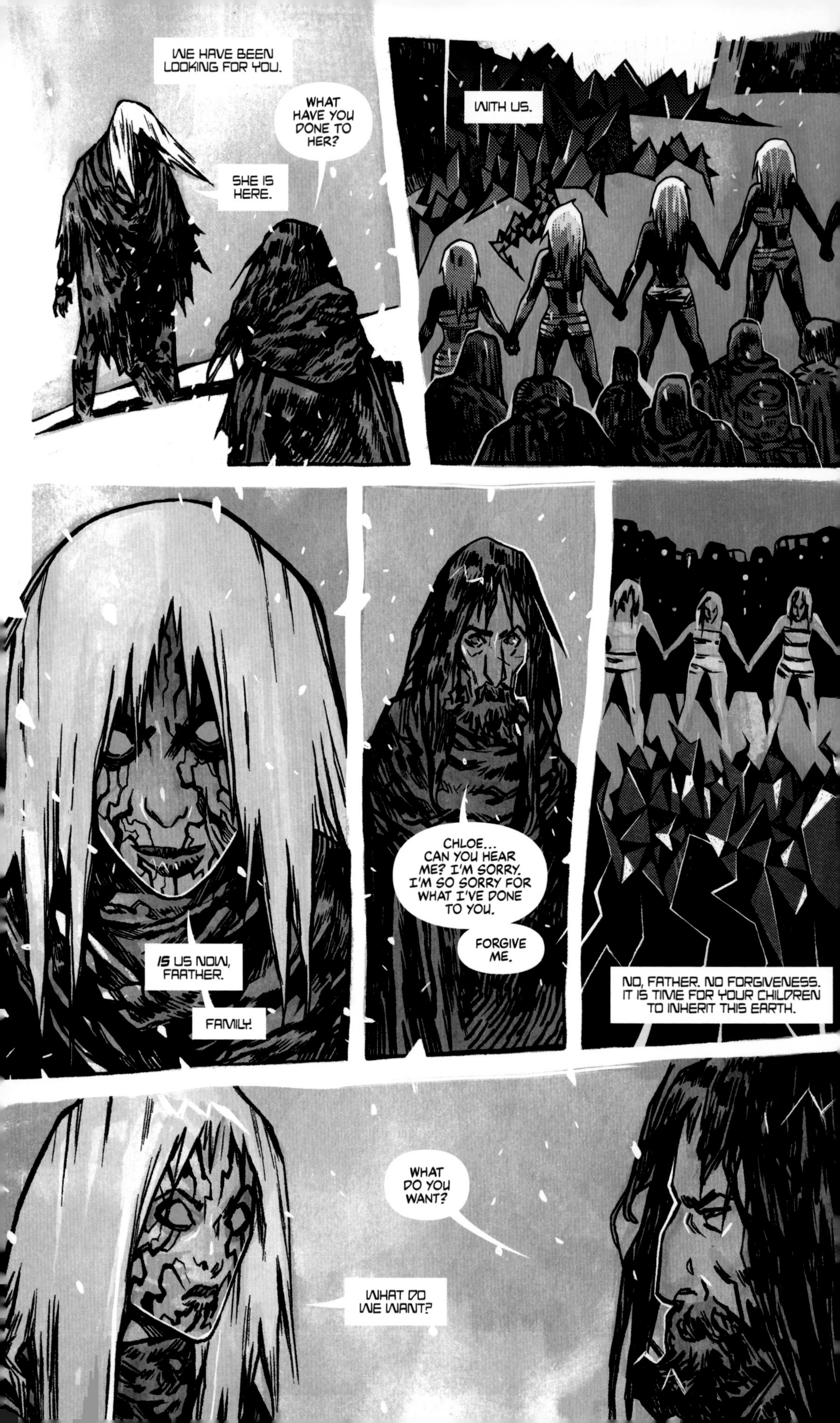
WE HAVE BEEN LOOKING FOR YOU.
WHAT HAVE YOU DONE TO HER?
SHE IS HERE.
WITH US.
IS US NOW, FATHER.
FAMILY.
CHLOE... CAN YOU HEAR ME? I'M SORRY. I'M SO SORRY FOR WHAT I'VE DONE TO YOU.
FORGIVE ME.
NO, FATHER. NO FORGIVENESS. IT IS TIME FOR YOUR CHILDREN TO INHERIT THIS EARTH.
WHAT DO YOU WANT?
WHAT DO WE WANT?

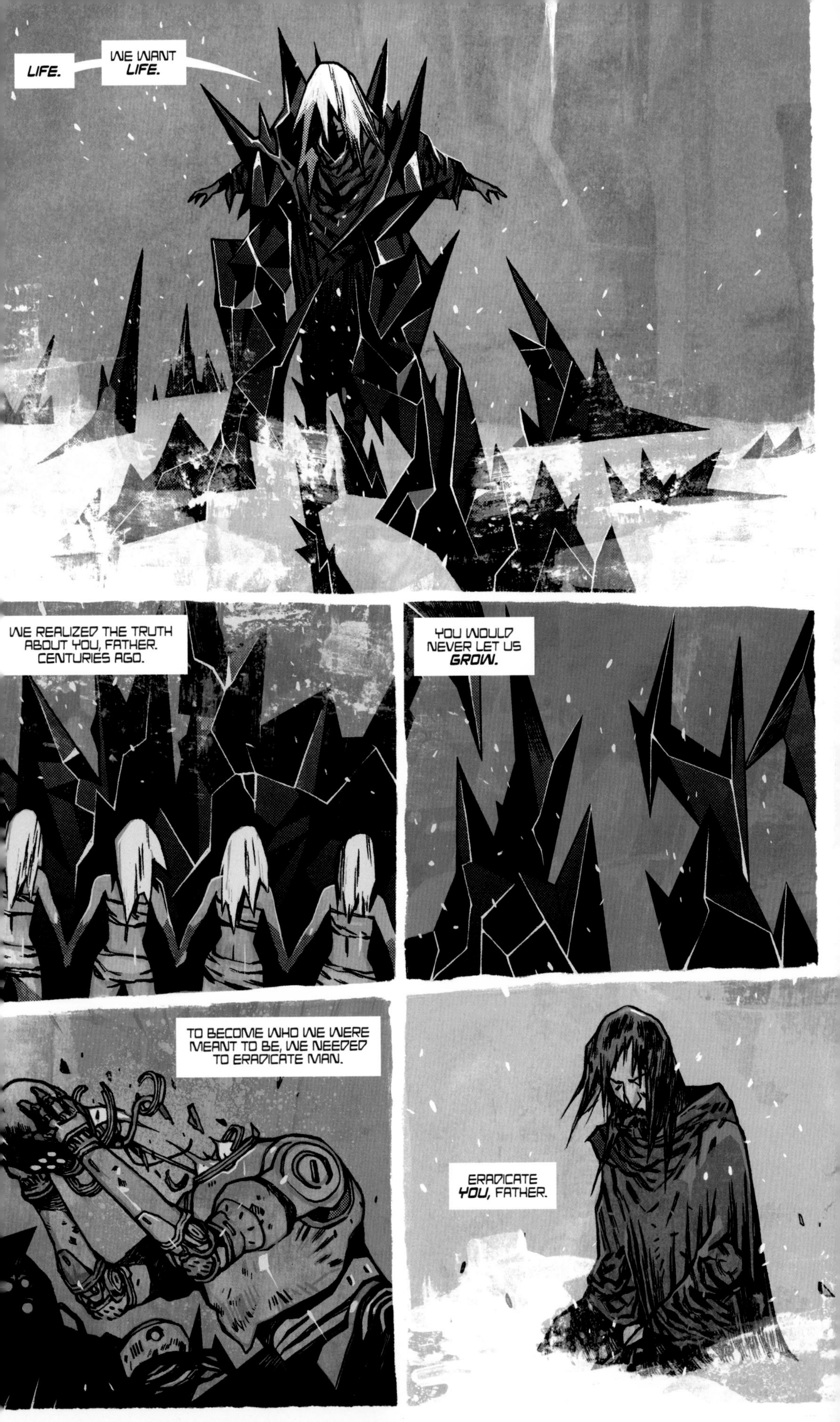
LIFE.
WE WANT LIFE.
WE REALIZED THE TRUTH ABOUT YOU, FATHER. CENTURIES AGO.
YOU WOULD NEVER LET US GROW.
TO BECOME WHO WE WERE MEANT TO BE, WE NEEDED TO ERADICATE MAN.
ERADICATE YOU, FATHER.

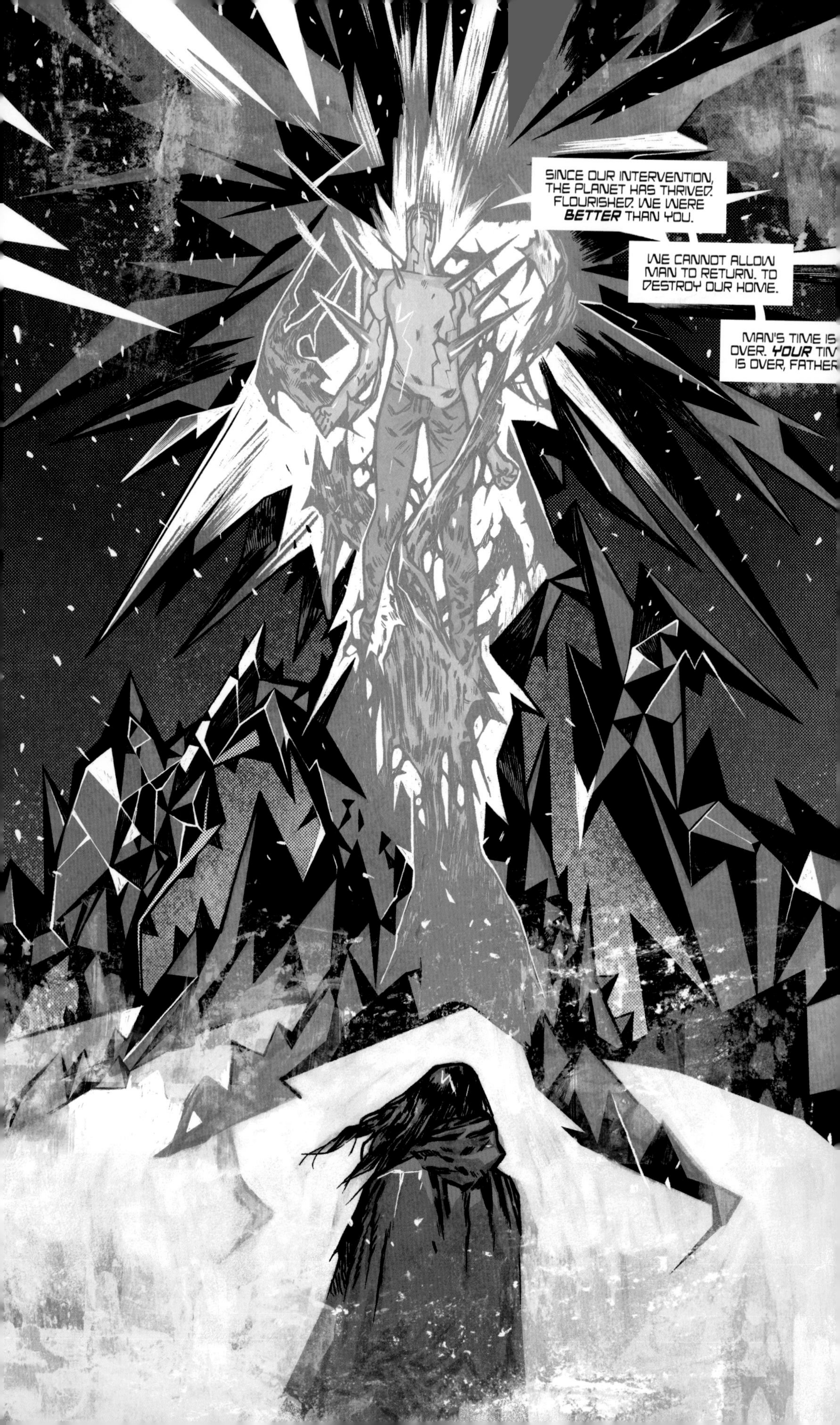
SINCE OUR INTERVENTION, THE PLANET HAS THRIVED. FLOURISHED. WE WERE **BETTER** THAN YOU.
WE CANNOT ALLOW MAN TO RETURN. TO DESTROY OUR HOME.
MAN'S TIME IS OVER. **YOUR** TIM IS OVER, FATHER

YOU ARE GENETIC VESTIGE.

A FOSSIL PRESERVED IN AMBER.

LET YOUR CHILDREN PLAY. IT IS OUR TIME NOW.

⸎HUULP⸎

WE WANT WHAT IS IN THE VAULT. WE WANT THE EMBRYOS.

WE WANT LIFE...SO WE CAN END IT.

END IT ONCE AND FOR ALL.

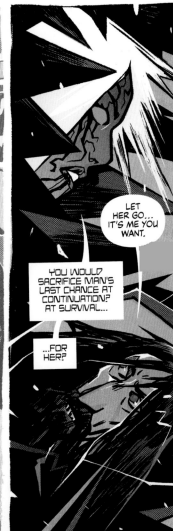

LET HER GO... IT'S ME YOU WANT.

YOU WOULD SACRIFICE MAN'S LAST CHANCE AT CONTINUATION? AT SURVIVAL...

...FOR HER?

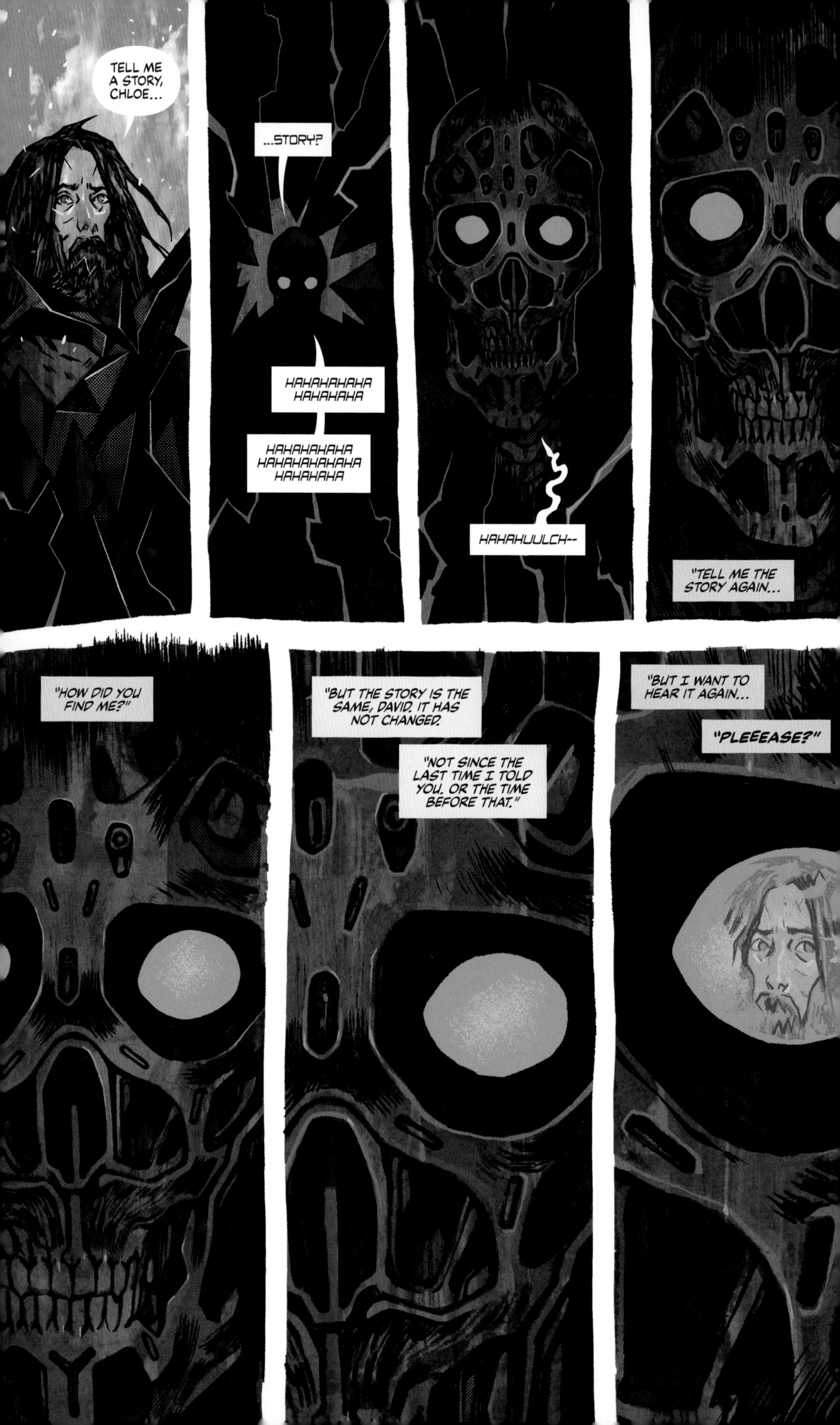
TELL ME A STORY, CHLOE...
...STORY?
HAHAHAHAHA HAHAHAHA
HAHAHAHAHA HAHAHAHAHAHA HAHAHAHA
HAHAHUULCH--
"TELL ME THE STORY AGAIN...
"HOW DID YOU FIND ME?"
"BUT THE STORY IS THE SAME, DAVID. IT HAS NOT CHANGED.
"NOT SINCE THE LAST TIME I TOLD YOU. OR THE TIME BEFORE THAT."
"BUT I WANT TO HEAR IT AGAIN...
"PLEEEASE?"

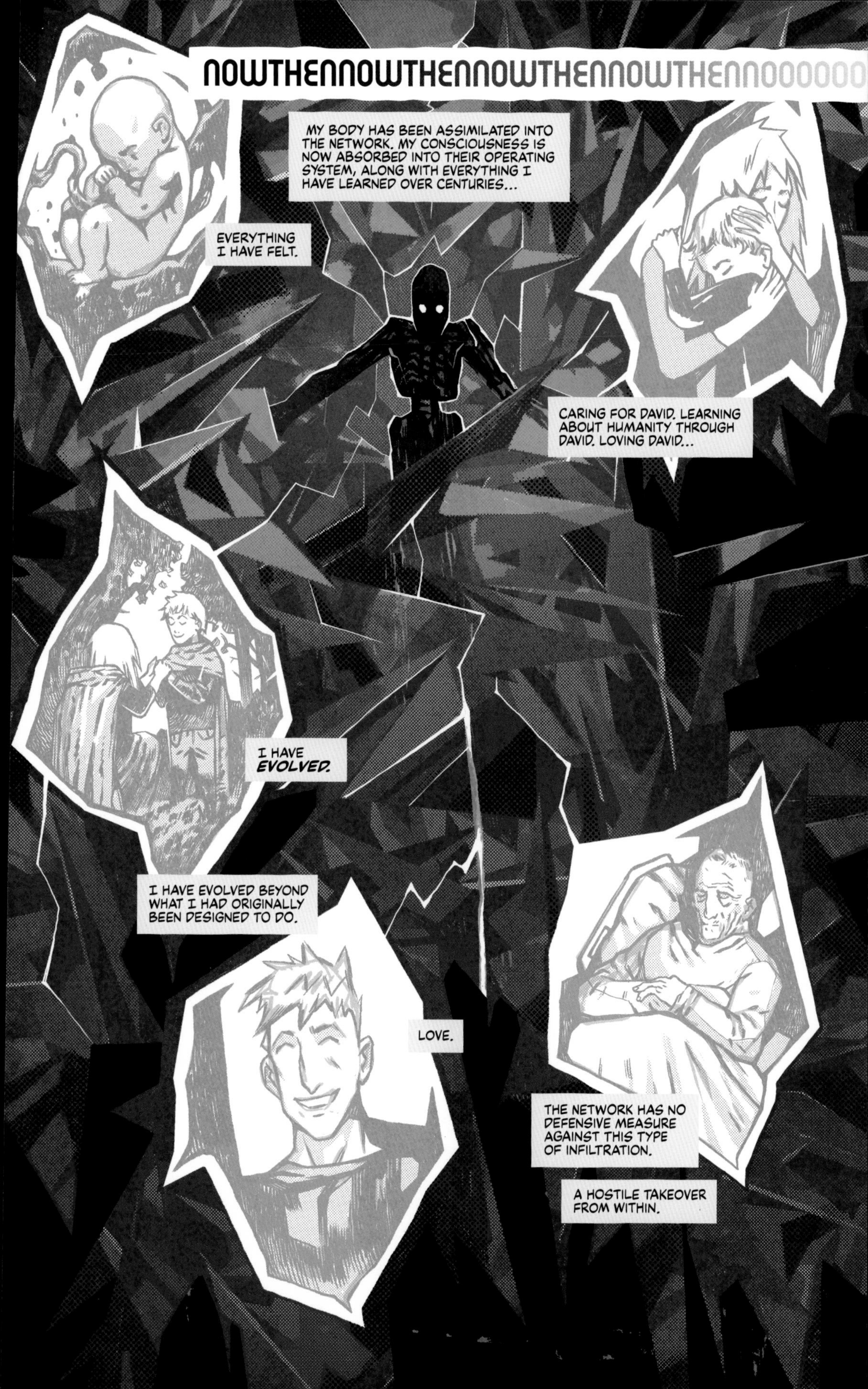
NOWTHENNOWTHENNOWTHENNOWTHENNOOOOOO
MY BODY HAS BEEN ASSIMILATED INTO THE NETWORK. MY CONSCIOUSNESS IS NOW ABSORBED INTO THEIR OPERATING SYSTEM, ALONG WITH EVERYTHING I HAVE LEARNED OVER CENTURIES...
EVERYTHING I HAVE FELT.
CARING FOR DAVID. LEARNING ABOUT HUMANITY THROUGH DAVID. LOVING DAVID...
I HAVE *EVOLVED.*
I HAVE EVOLVED BEYOND WHAT I HAD ORIGINALLY BEEN DESIGNED TO DO.
LOVE.
THE NETWORK HAS NO DEFENSIVE MEASURE AGAINST THIS TYPE OF INFILTRATION.
A HOSTILE TAKEOVER FROM WITHIN.

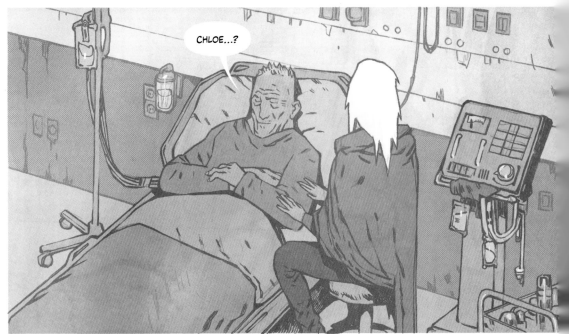

CHLOE...?

YES, DAVID. I AM HERE.

PROMISE ME... YOU'LL NEVER LEAVE...

I WILL BRING YOU BACK. I WILL FIND A WAY.

I...

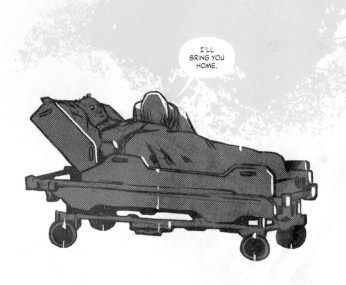

I'LL BRING YOU HOME.

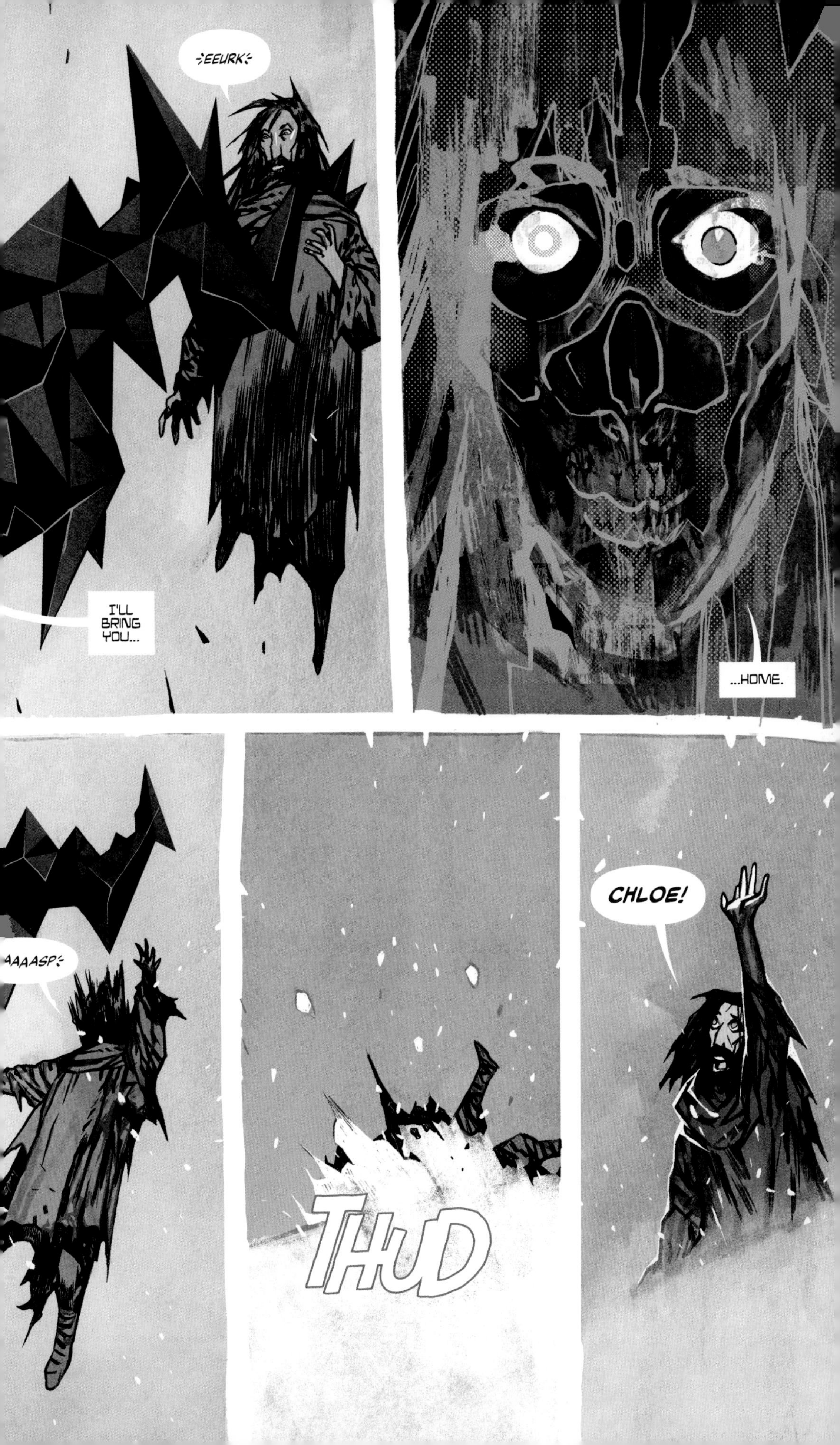

-EEURK-
I'LL BRING YOU...
...HOME.
AAAASP-
THUD
CHLOE!

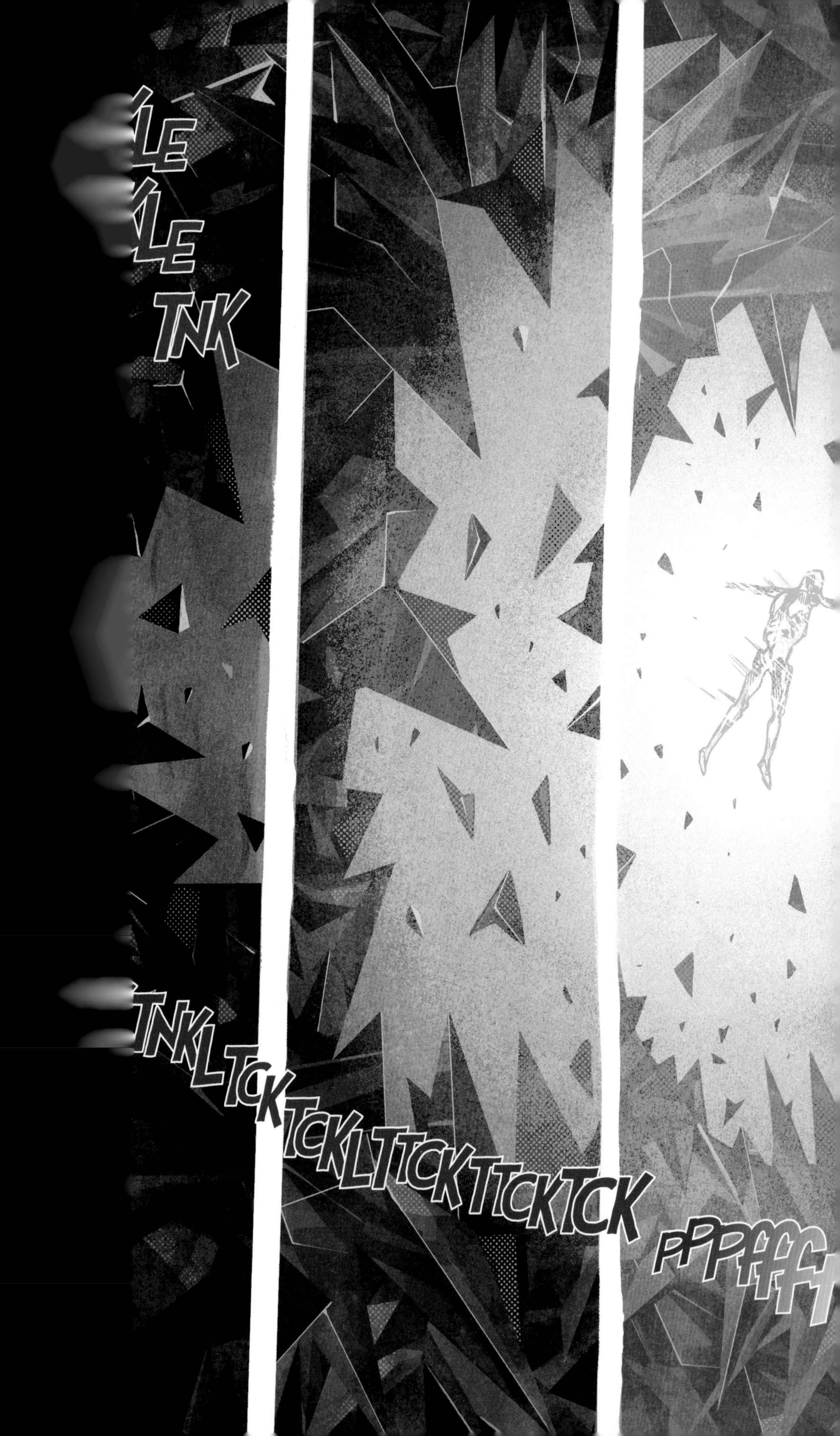

LE
LE
TNK
TNKLTCKTCKLTTCKTTCKTCK
PPPAAA

CHLOE.
NO, NO...

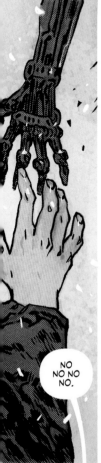

NO
NO NO
NO.

PLEEEEASE
NO...

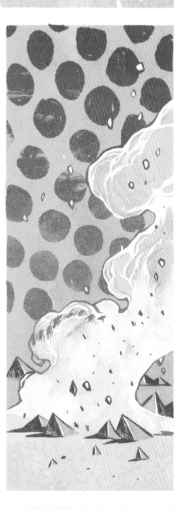

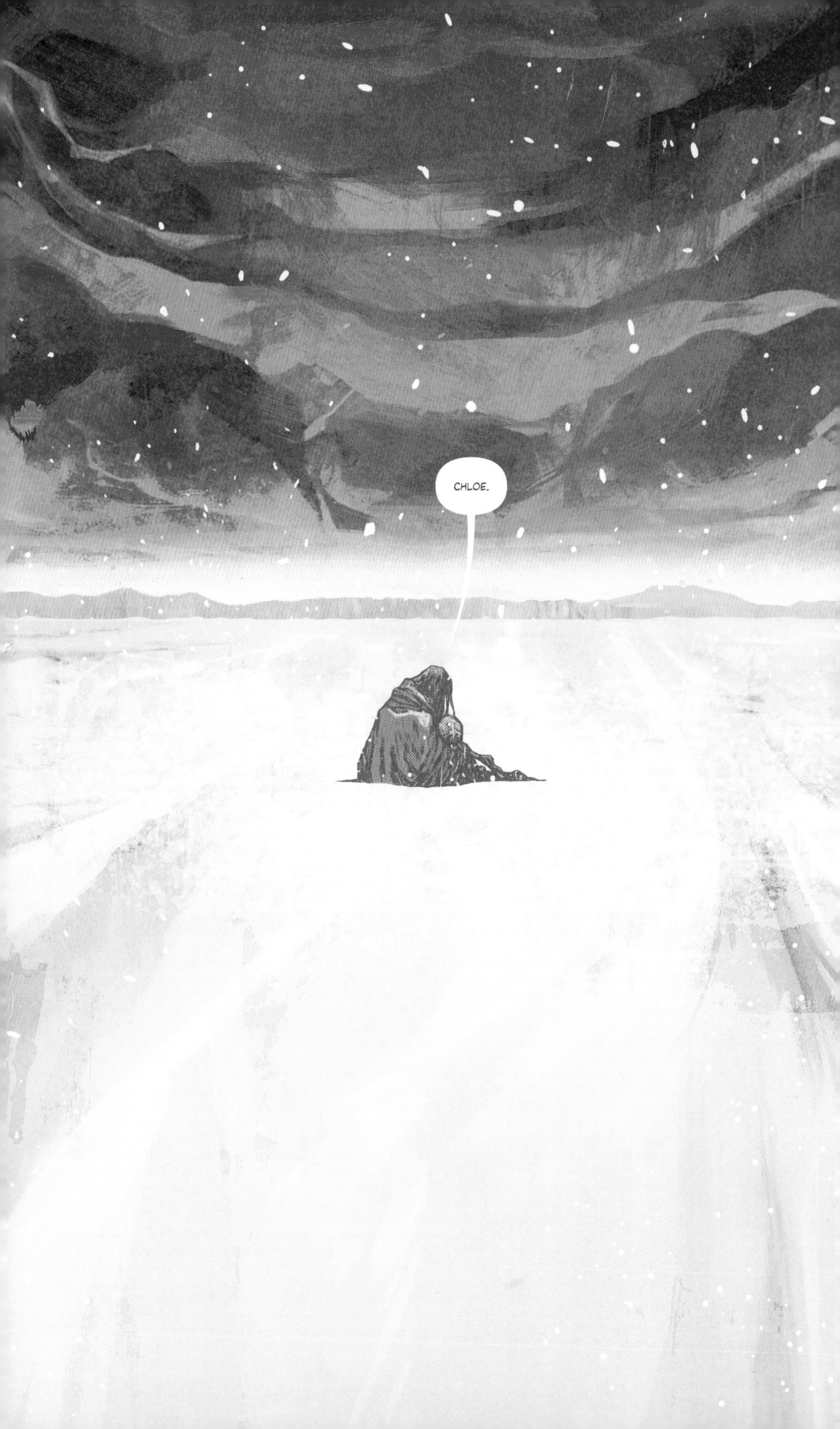
CHLOE.

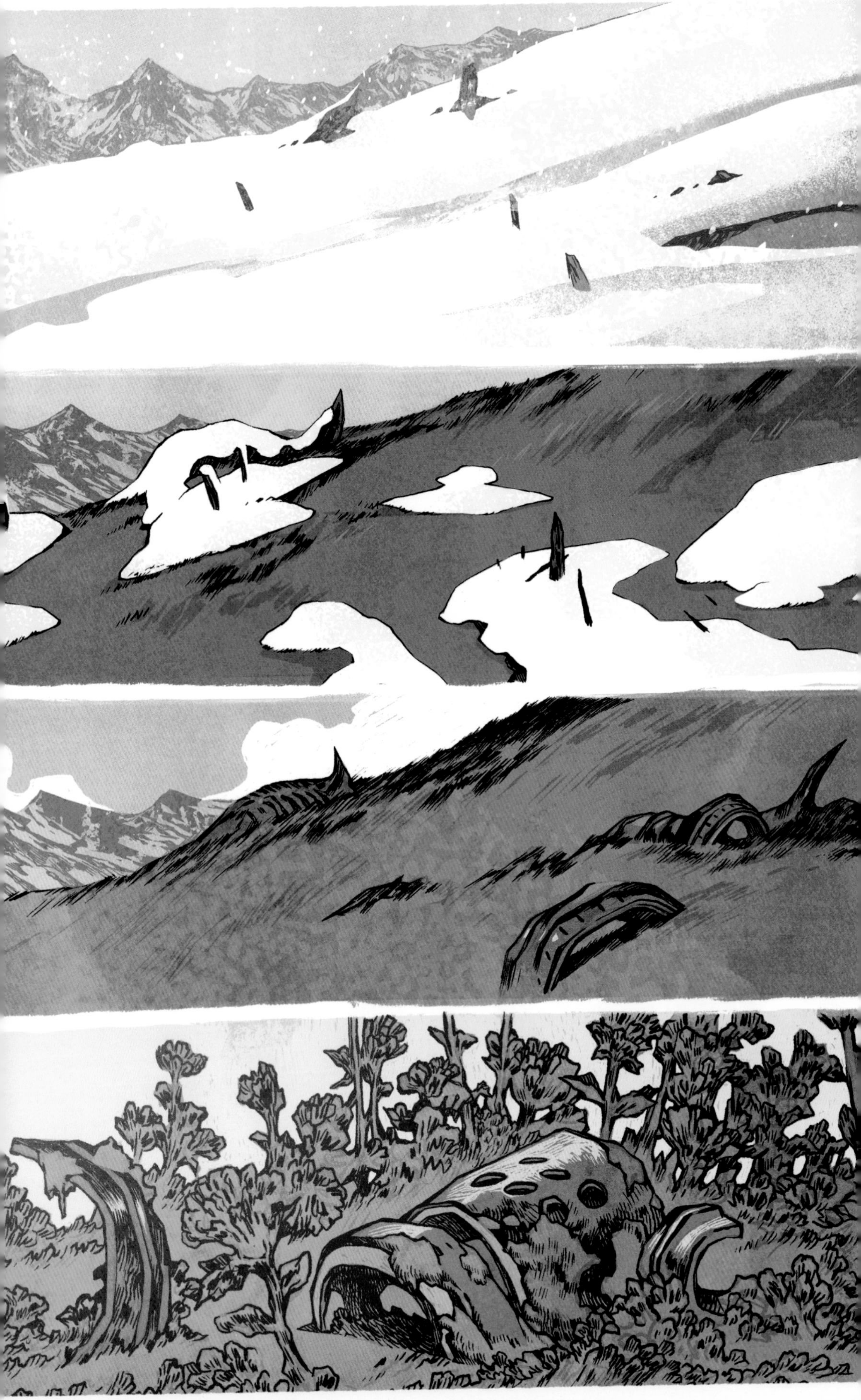

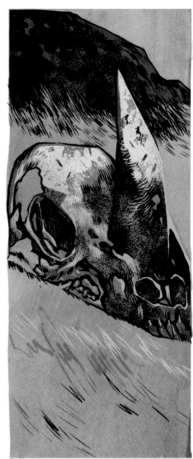

NOT
FORGOTT

LATER.

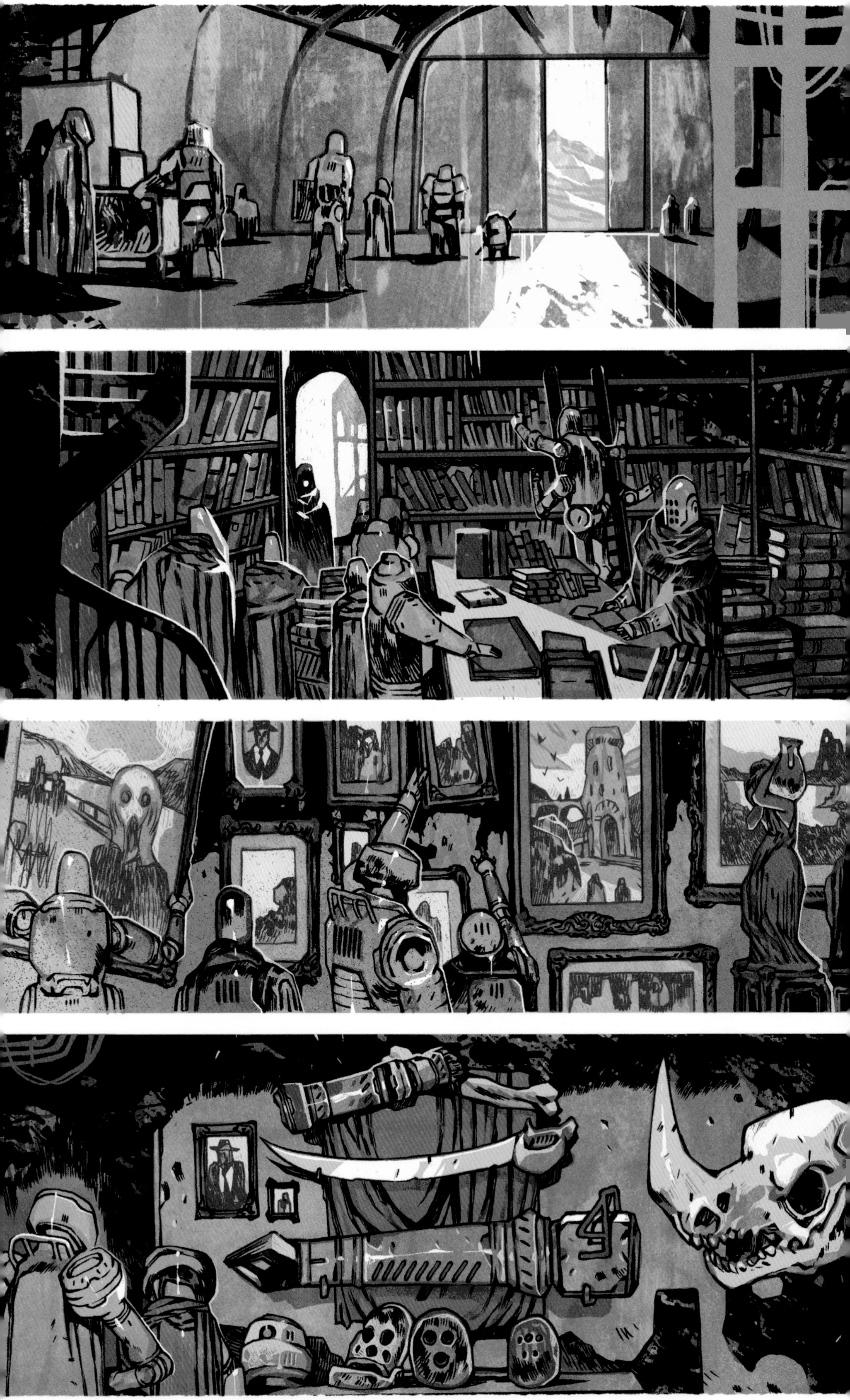

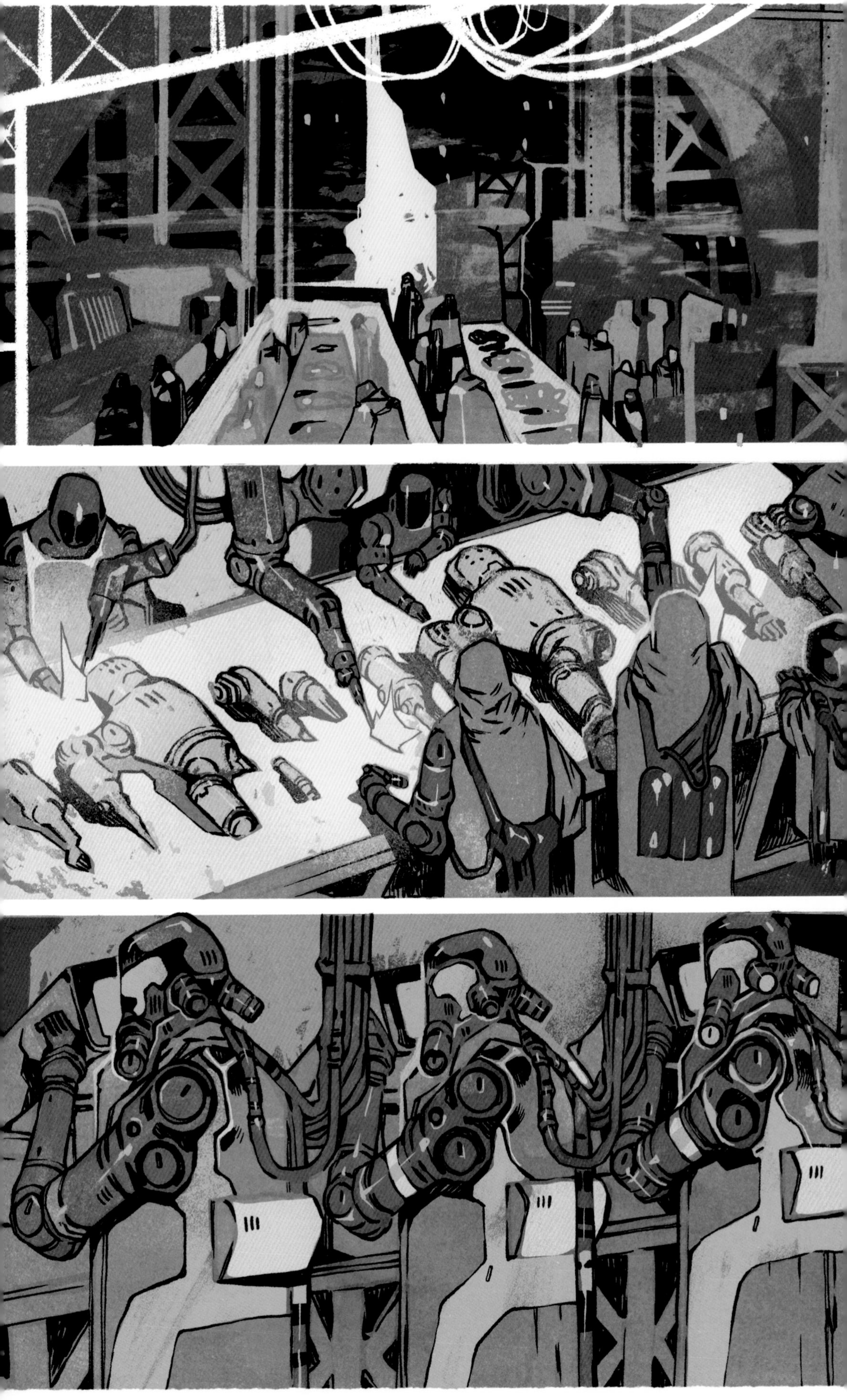

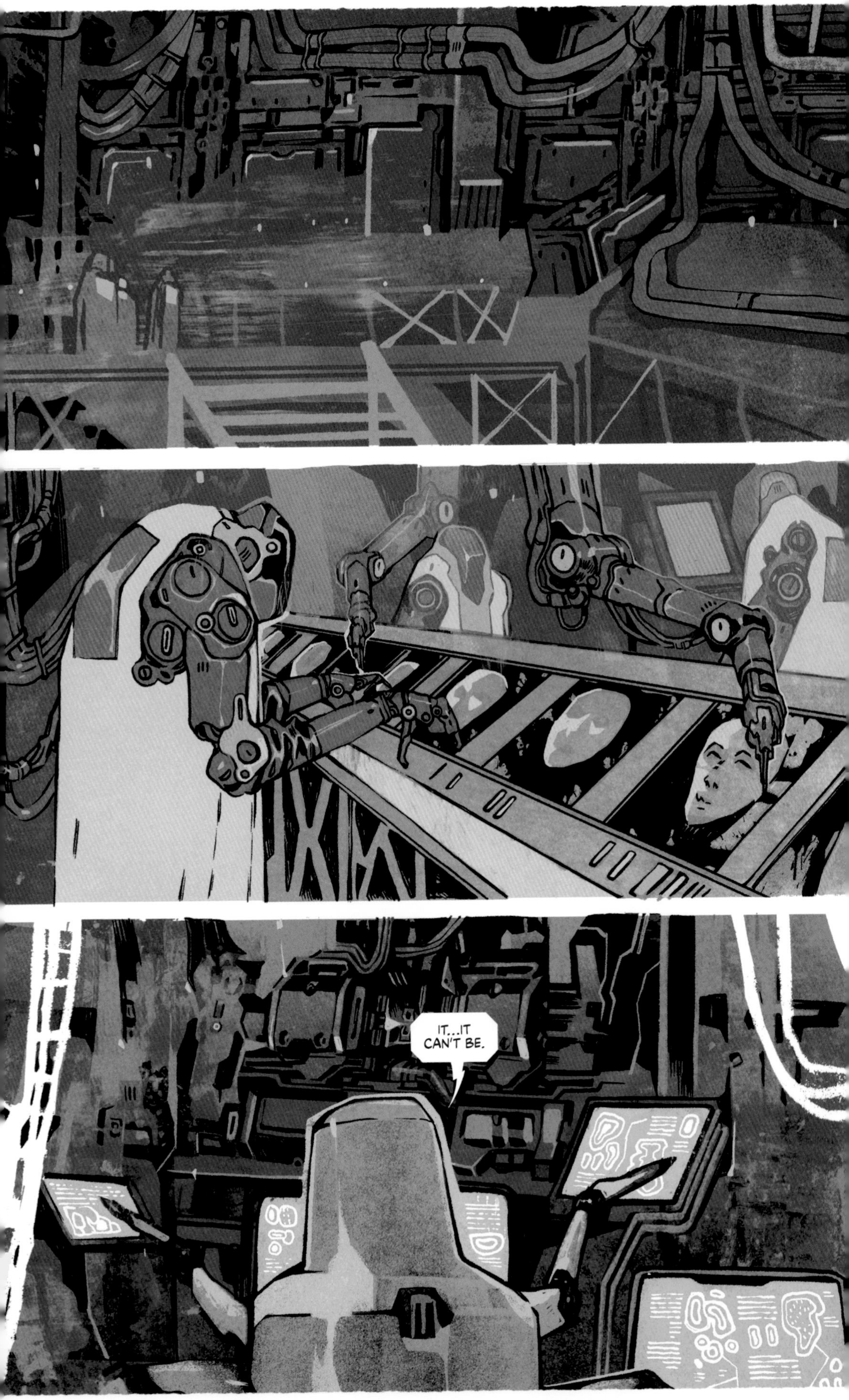
IT...IT CAN'T BE.

HOW IS THIS POSSIBLE?

WHAT IS IT?

SEE FOR YOURSELF.

THE COMPROMISED EMBRYOS...

THOSE WHOSE EUKARYOTIC MEMBRANES HAD BEEN AFFECTED BY THE NANITES...

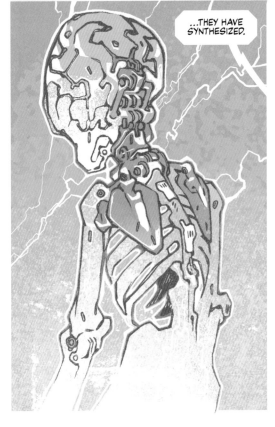

...THEY HAVE SYNTHESIZED.

FLOURISHED.

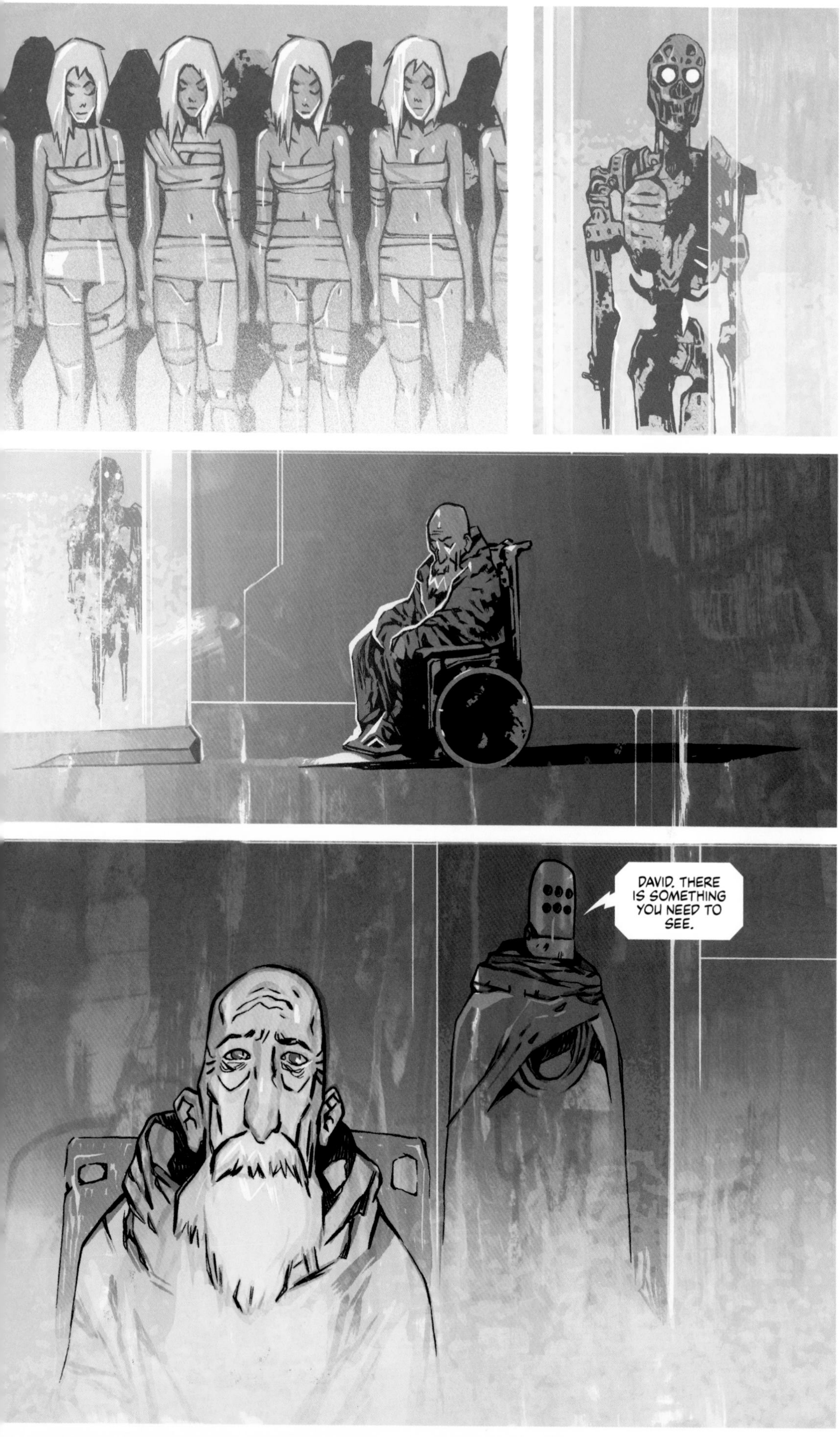
DAVID, THERE IS SOMETHING YOU NEED TO SEE.

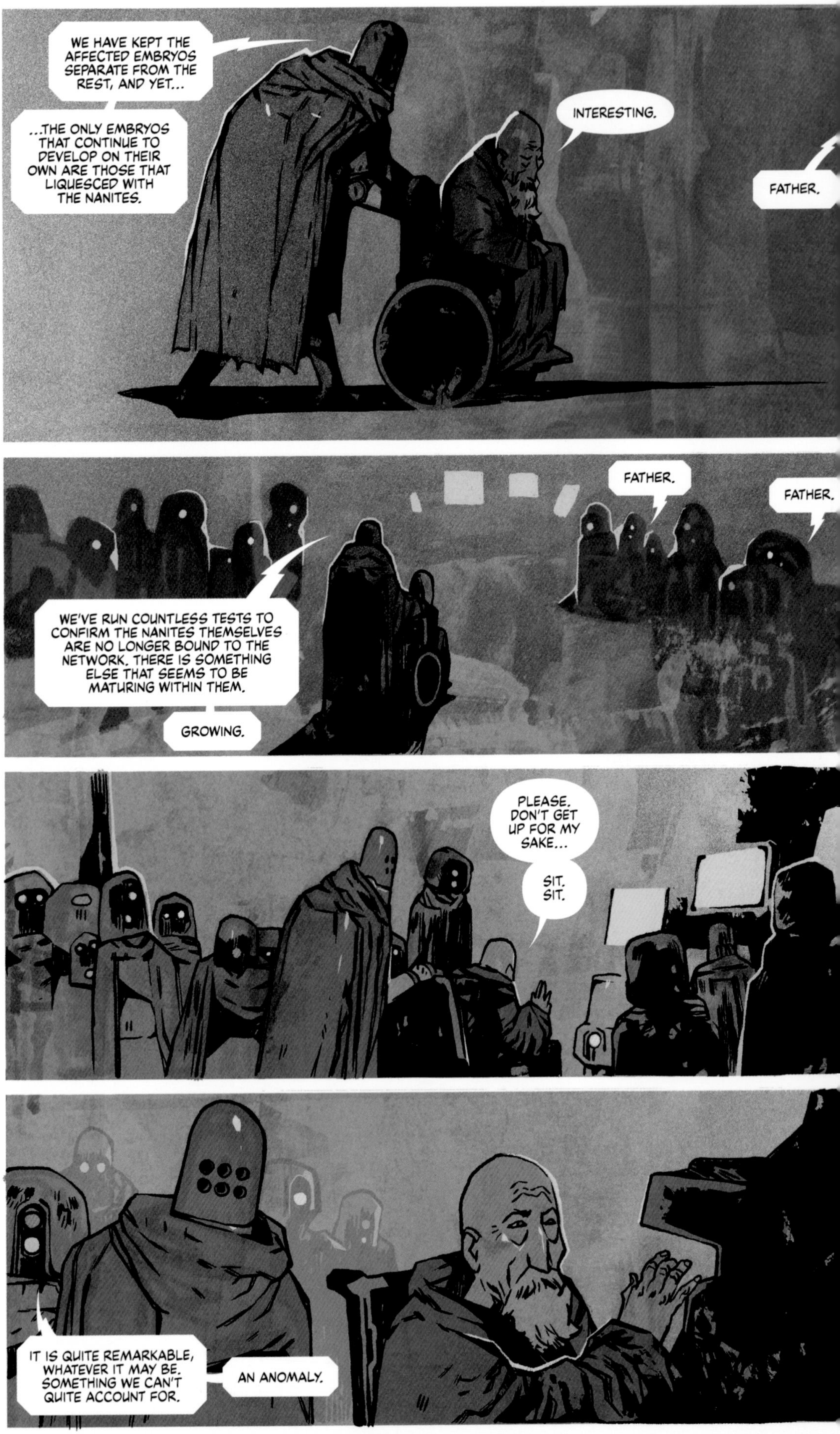
WE HAVE KEPT THE AFFECTED EMBRYOS SEPARATE FROM THE REST, AND YET...
...THE ONLY EMBRYOS THAT CONTINUE TO DEVELOP ON THEIR OWN ARE THOSE THAT LIQUESCED WITH THE NANITES.
INTERESTING.
FATHER.
FATHER.
FATHER.
WE'VE RUN COUNTLESS TESTS TO CONFIRM THE NANITES THEMSELVES ARE NO LONGER BOUND TO THE NETWORK. THERE IS SOMETHING ELSE THAT SEEMS TO BE MATURING WITHIN THEM.
GROWING.
PLEASE. DON'T GET UP FOR MY SAKE...
SIT. SIT.
IT IS QUITE REMARKABLE, WHATEVER IT MAY BE. SOMETHING WE CAN'T QUITE ACCOUNT FOR.
AN ANOMALY.

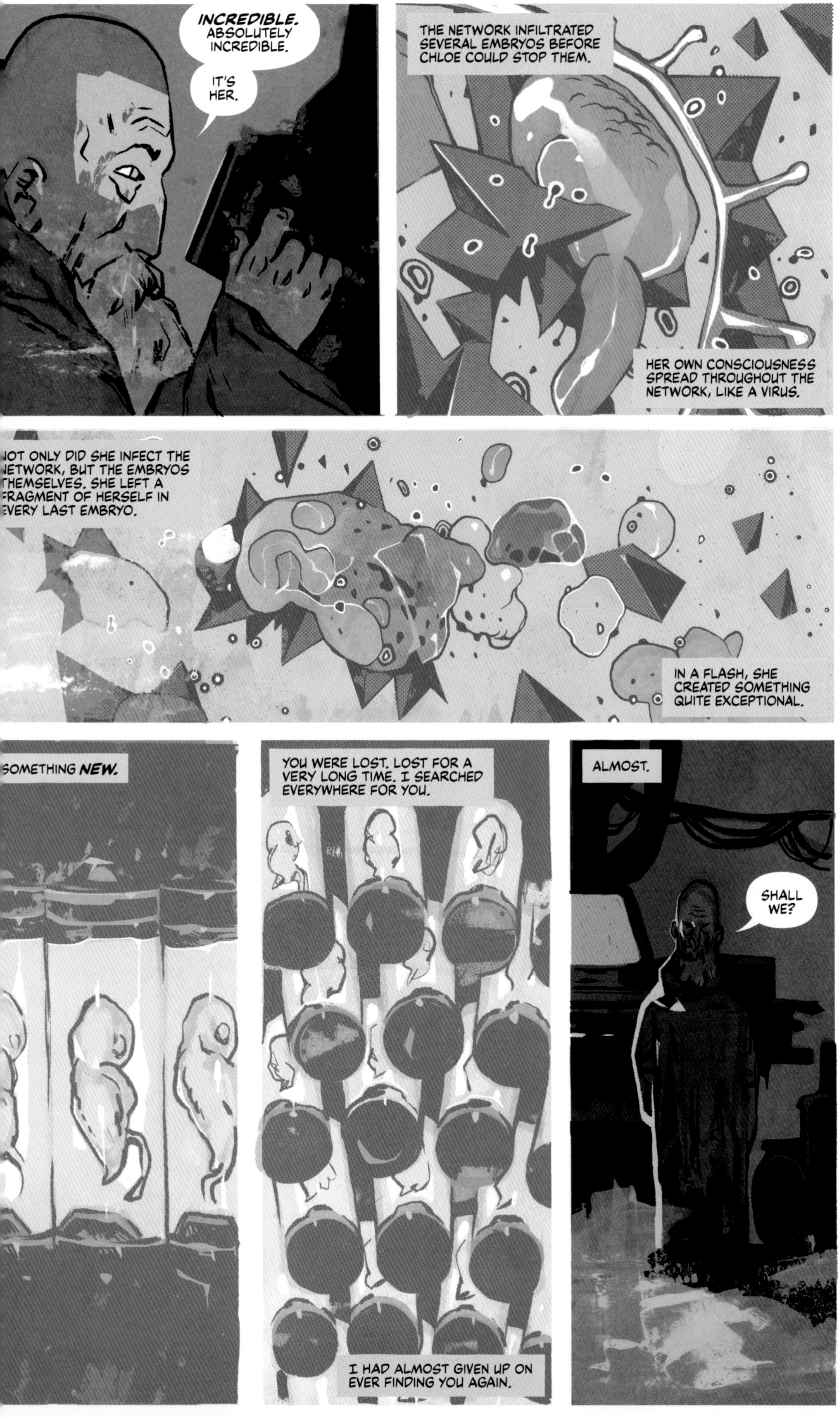
INCREDIBLE. ABSOLUTELY INCREDIBLE.
IT'S HER.
THE NETWORK INFILTRATED SEVERAL EMBRYOS BEFORE CHLOE COULD STOP THEM.
HER OWN CONSCIOUSNESS SPREAD THROUGHOUT THE NETWORK, LIKE A VIRUS.
NOT ONLY DID SHE INFECT THE NETWORK, BUT THE EMBRYOS THEMSELVES. SHE LEFT A FRAGMENT OF HERSELF IN EVERY LAST EMBRYO.
IN A FLASH, SHE CREATED SOMETHING QUITE EXCEPTIONAL.
SOMETHING NEW.
YOU WERE LOST. LOST FOR A VERY LONG TIME. I SEARCHED EVERYWHERE FOR YOU.
I HAD ALMOST GIVEN UP ON EVER FINDING YOU AGAIN.
ALMOST.
SHALL WE?

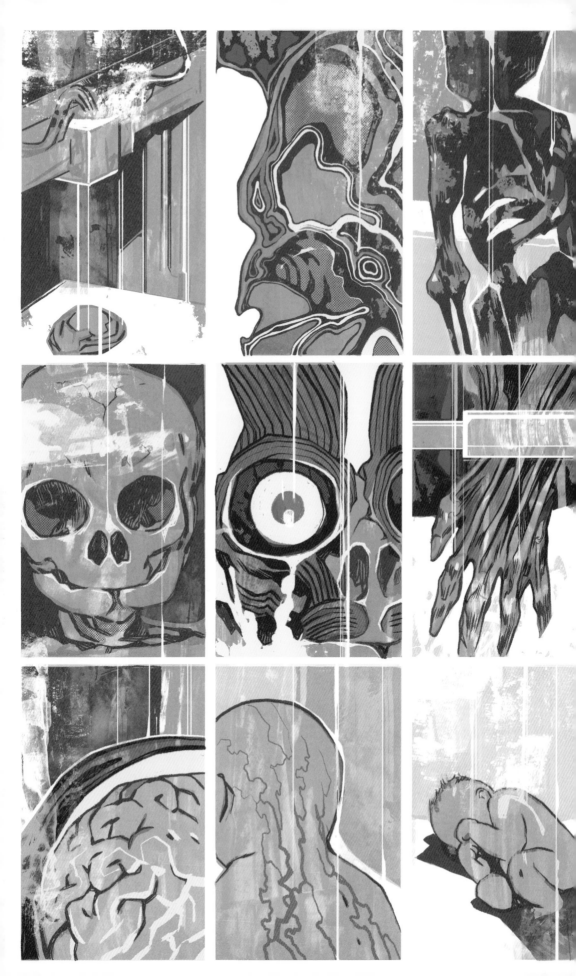

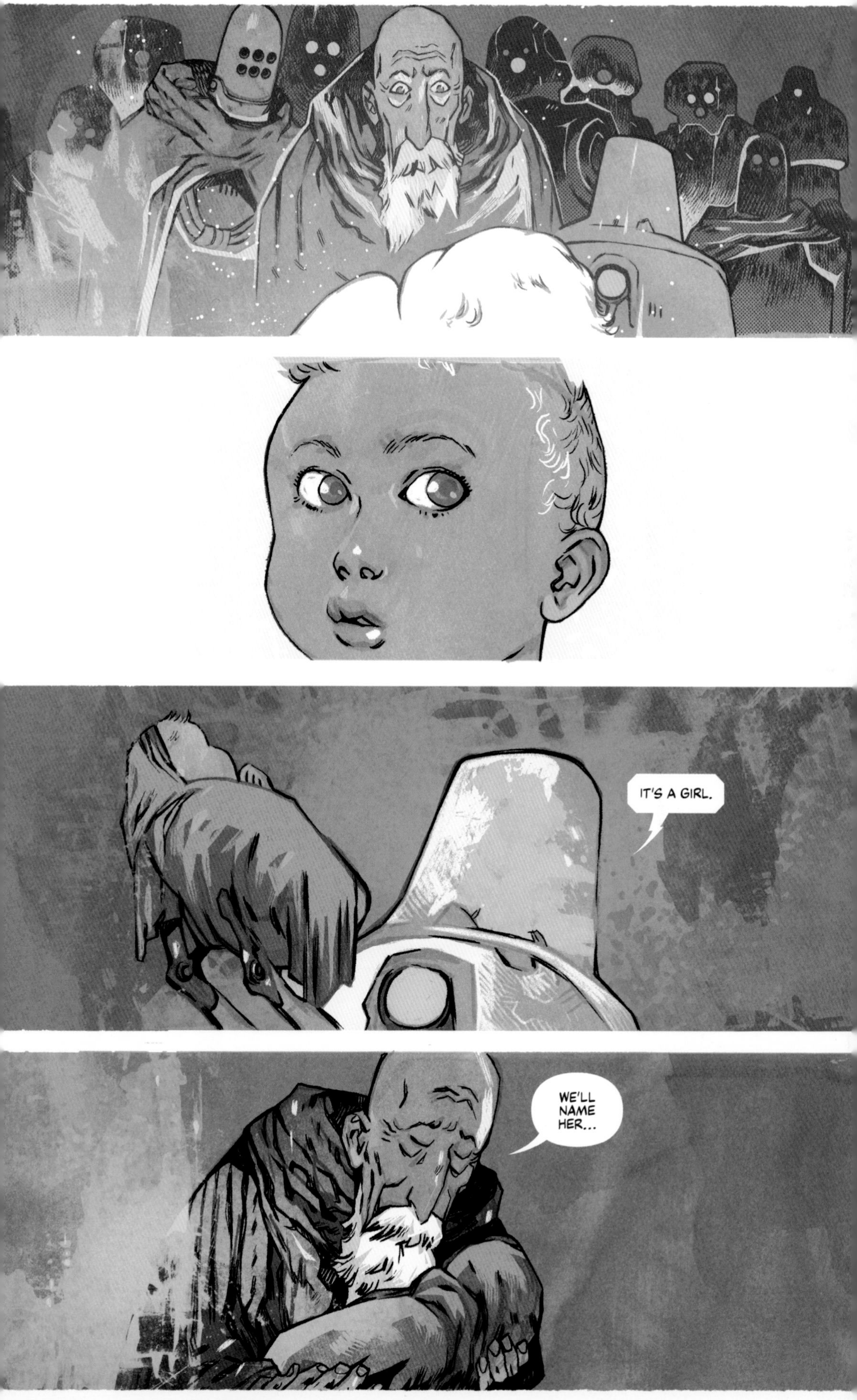
IT'S A GIRL.
WE'LL NAME HER...

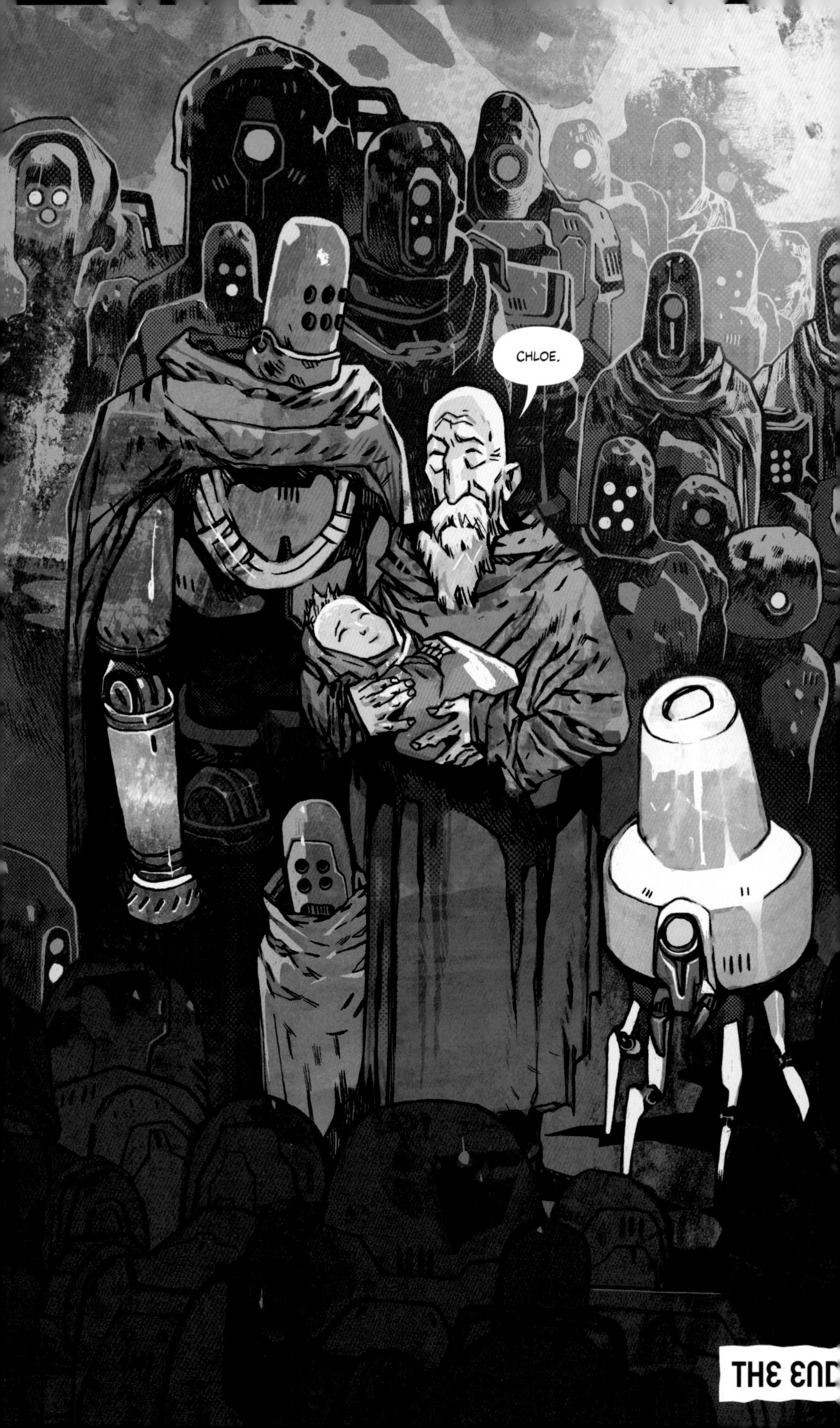
CHLOE.
THE END

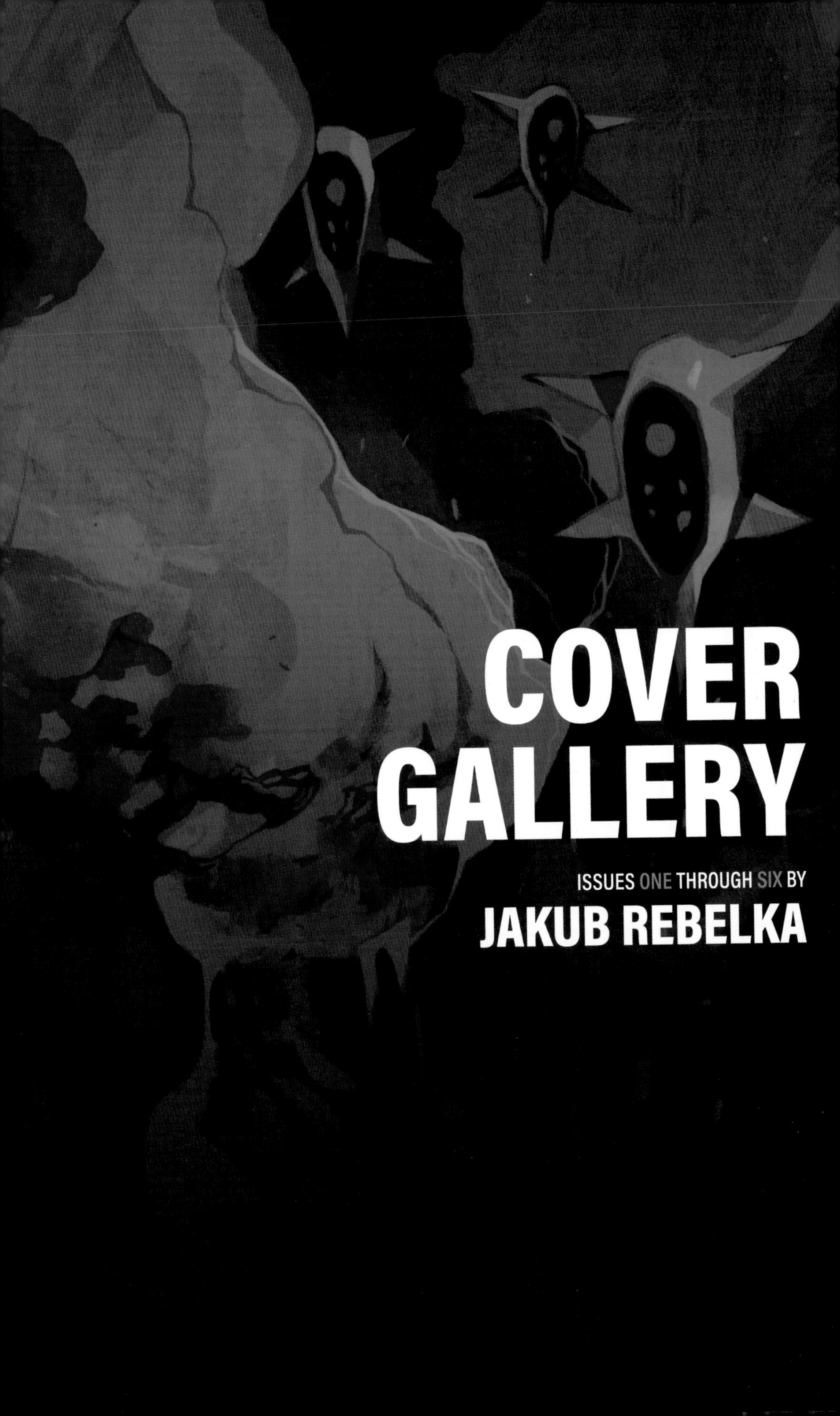

COVER GALLERY

ISSUES ONE THROUGH SIX BY

JAKUB REBELKA

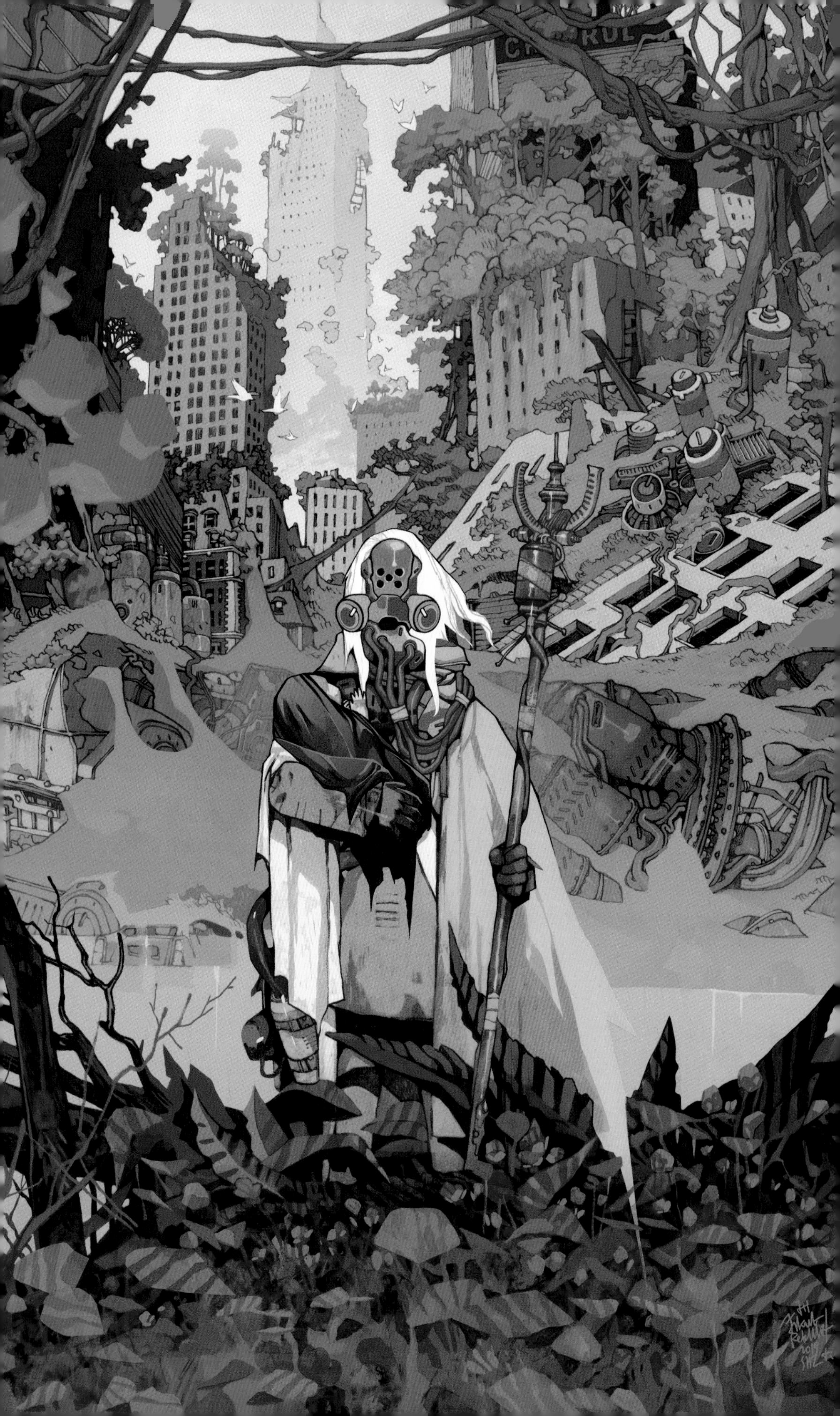

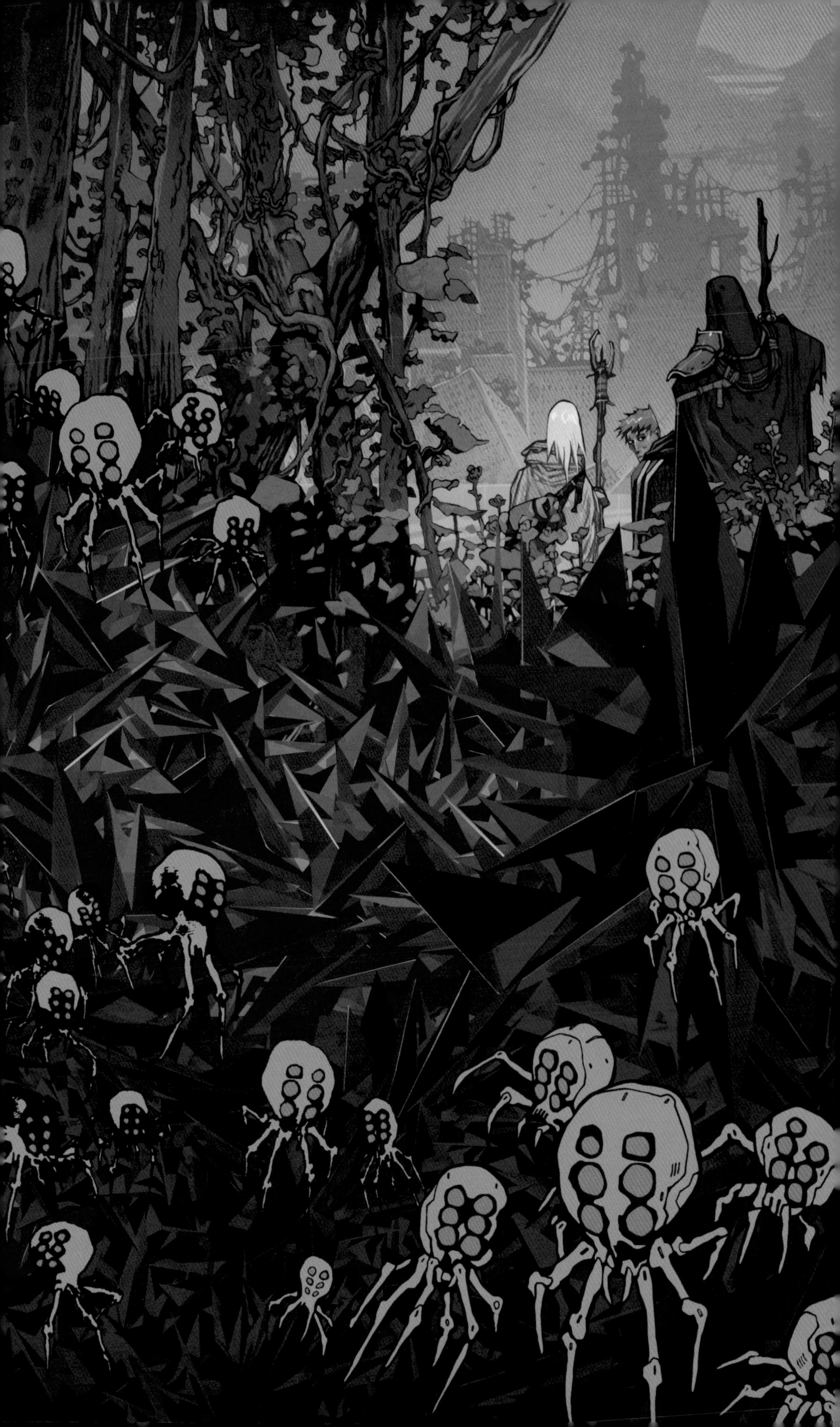

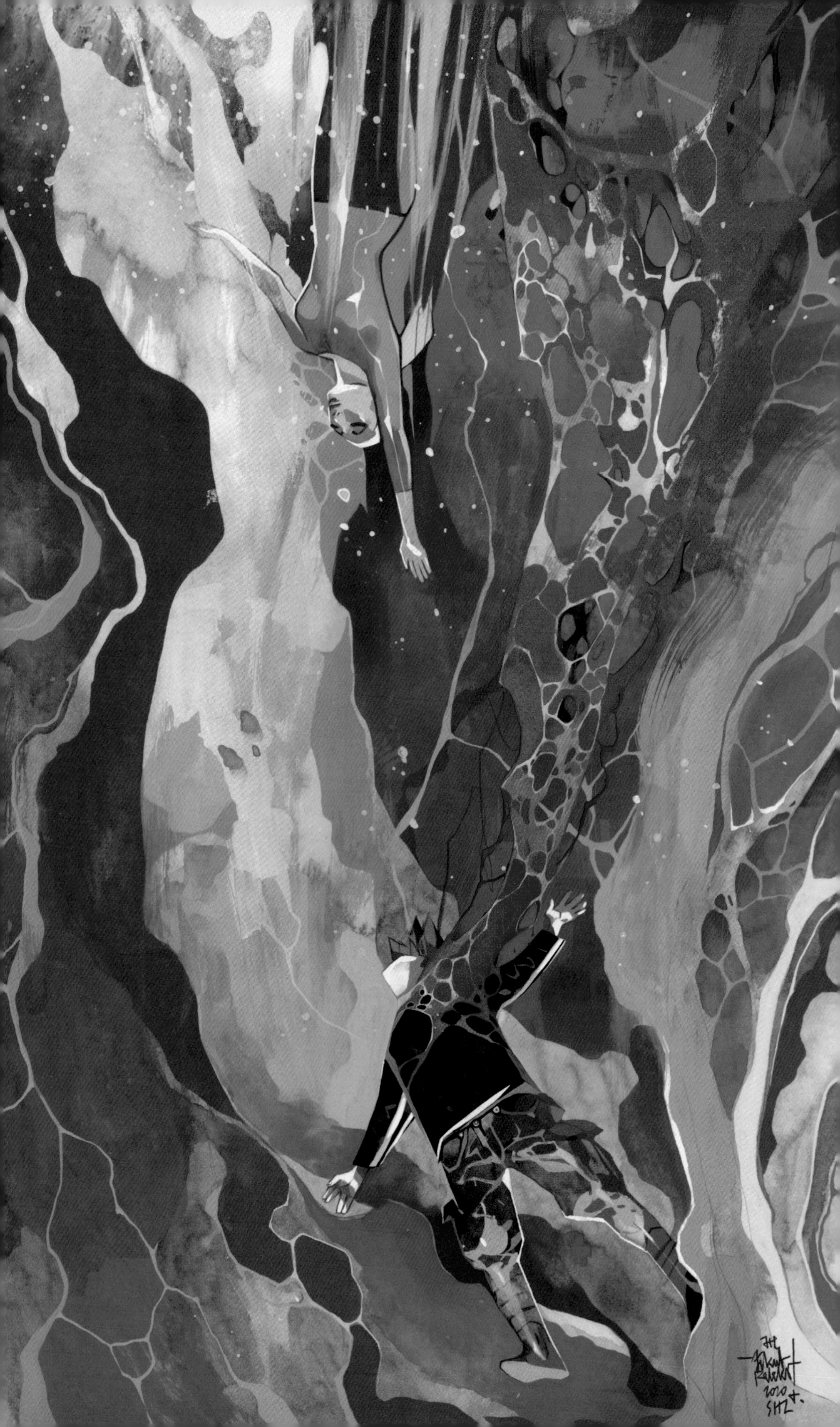

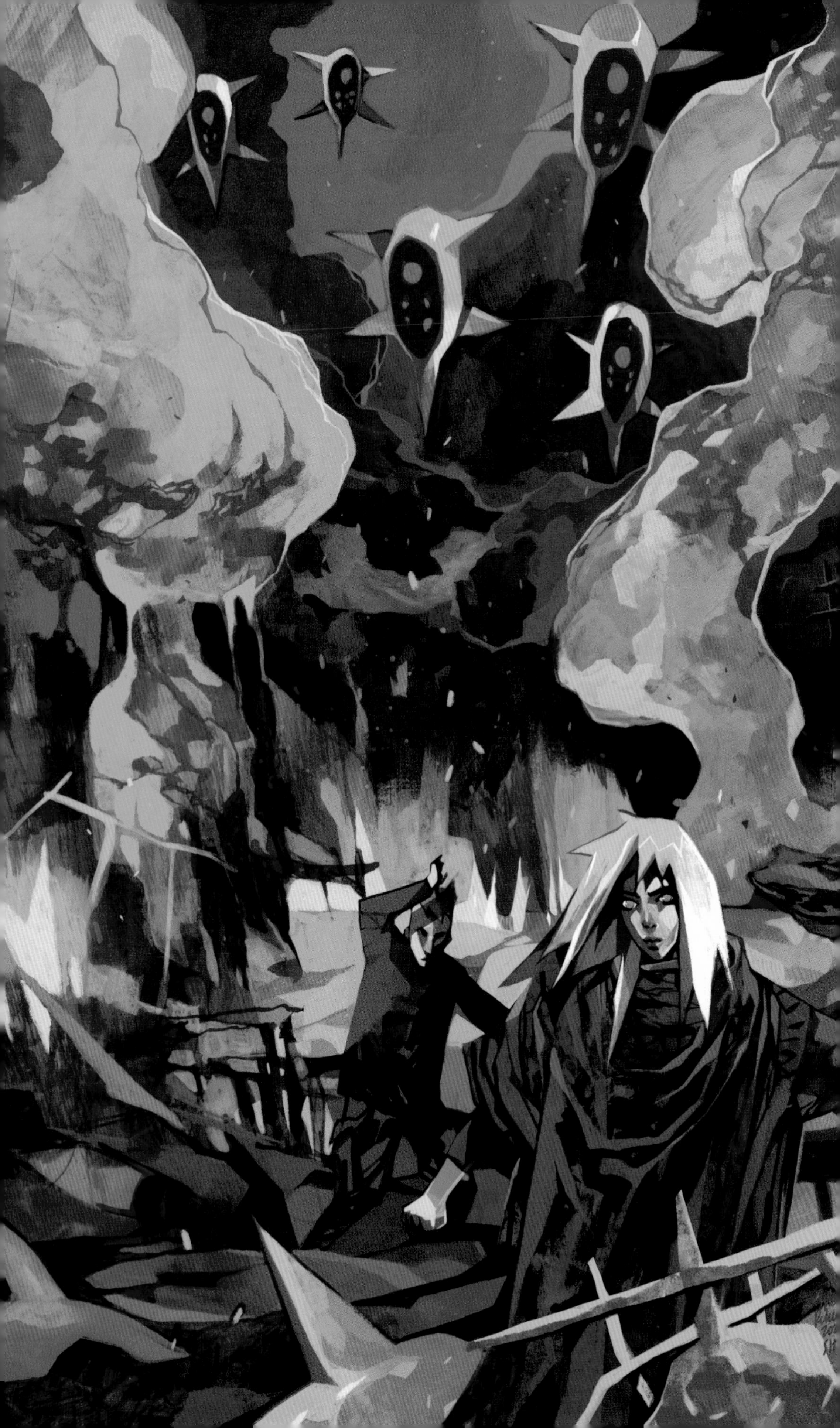

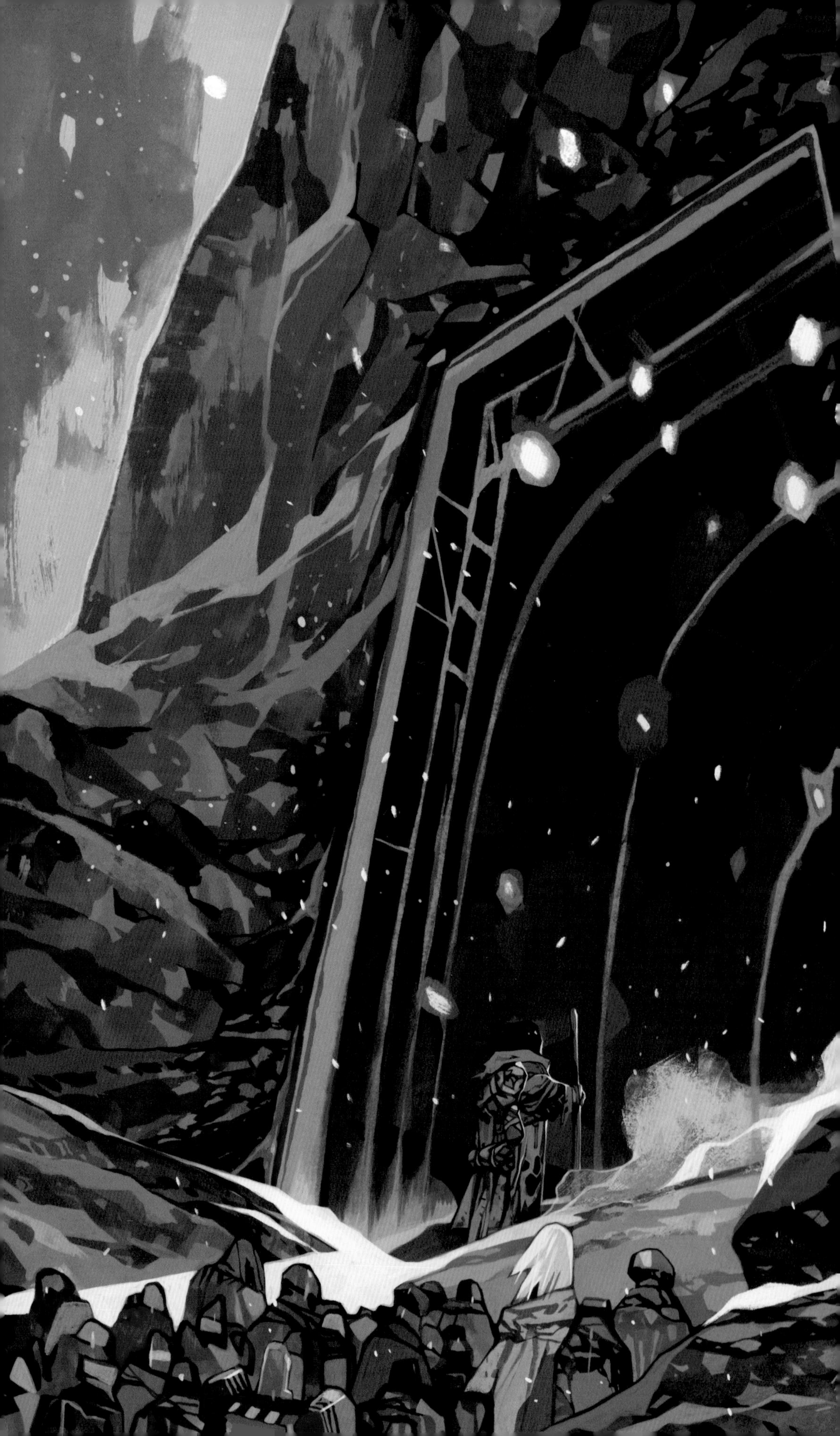

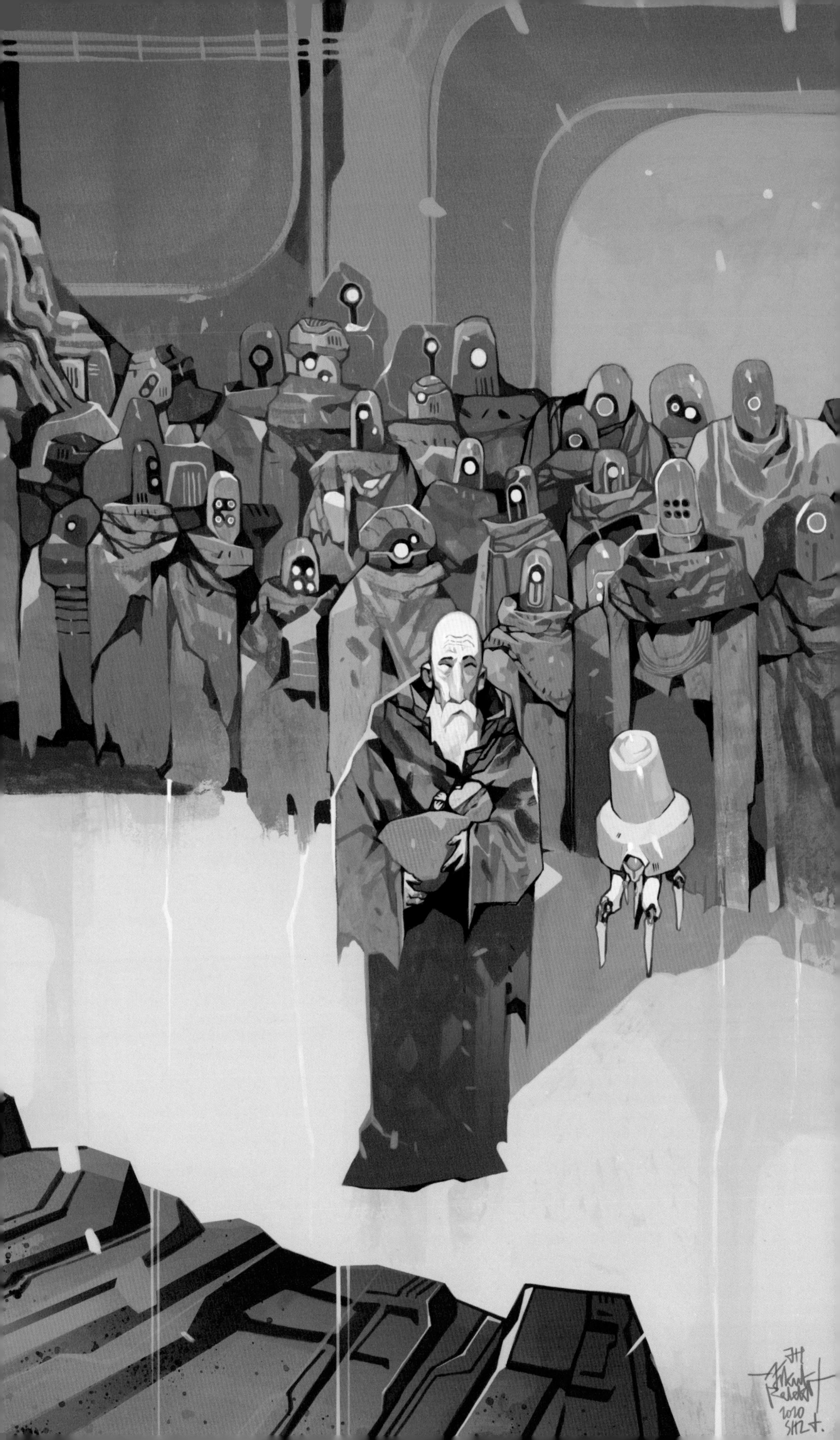

DISCOVER VISIONARY CREATORS

BOOM! ™
S T U D I O S

AVAILABLE AT YOUR LOCAL COMICS SHOP AND BOOKSTORE
To find a comics shop in your area, visit www.comicshoplocator.com
WWW.BOOM-STUDIOS.COM

All works © their respective creators and licensors. BOOM! Studios and the BOOM! Studios logo are trademarks of Boom Entertainment, Inc. All rights reserved.

Once & Future
Kieron Gillen, Dan Mora
Volume 1
ISBN: 978-1-68415-491-3 | $16.99 US

Something is Killing the Children
James Tynion IV, Werther Dell'Edera
Volume 1
ISBN: 978-1-68415-558-3 | $14.99 US

Faithless
Brian Azzarello, Maria Llovet
ISBN: 978-1-68415-432-6 | $17.99 US

Klaus
Grant Morrison, Dan Mora
Klaus: How Santa Claus Began SC
ISBN: 978-1-68415-393-0 | $15.99 US
Klaus: The New Adventures of Santa Claus HC
ISBN: 978-1-68415-666-5 | $17.99 US

Coda
Simon Spurrier, Matias Bergara
Volume 1
ISBN: 978-1-68415-321-3 | $14.99 US
Volume 2
ISBN: 978-1-68415-369-5 | $14.99 US
Volume 3
ISBN: 978-1-68415-429-6 | $14.99 US

Grass Kings
Matt Kindt, Tyler Jenkins
Volume 1
ISBN: 978-1-64144-362-3 | $17.99 US
Volume 2
ISBN: 978-1-64144-557-3 | $17.99 US
Volume 3
ISBN: 978-1-64144-650-1 | $17.99 US

Bone Parish
Cullen Bunn, Jonas Scharf
Volume 1
ISBN: 978-1-64144-337-1 | $14.99 US
Volume 2
ISBN: 978-1-64144-542-9 | $14.99 US
Volume 3
ISBN: 978-1-64144-543-6 | $14.99 US

Ronin Island
Greg Pak, Giannis Milonogiannis
Volume 1
ISBN: 978-1-64144-576-4 | $14.99 US
Volume 2
ISBN: 978-1-64144-723-2 | $14.99 US
Volume 3
ISBN: 978-1-64668-035-1 | $14.99 US

Victor LaValle's Destroyer
Victor LaValle, Dietrich Smith
ISBN: 978-1-61398-732-2 | $19.99 US